# FOUR SEASONS *of* TRAVEL

Come fall, the trees lining Michigan's Lower Au Sable River glow brightly.

# FOUR SEASONS *of* TRAVEL

## 400 OF THE WORLD'S BEST DESTINATIONS IN WINTER, SPRING, SUMMER, AND FALL

Foreword by Andrew Evans, *National Geographic Traveler* magazine
contributing editor and "Digital Nomad"

NATIONAL GEOGRAPHIC
WASHINGTON, D.C.

In Provence, the lavender and sunflowers of Plateau de Valensole—derived from the Latin for "valley of the sun"—luxuriate beneath the summer sun.

# CONTENTS

True to its name, the Seventh Heaven Express slope near Whistler, Canada, offers spectacular winter skiing.

# FOREWORD

By Andrew Evans, *National Geographic Traveler* magazine contributing editor and "Digital Nomad"

N OWHERE FEELS COLDER than St. Petersburg in late December. Ice cuts my lungs at every breath, and my chest aches from the severe subzero air. The pastel mansions look like petit fours that line the frozen Moyka, now a slab of solid white ice that frames the original noble city of Peter the Great.

Two minutes on the street is all I can handle. Seeking warmth, I dip into a tea shop where people keep their coats on and sip cups of strong black chai that flows from the bubbling copper samovar. "Come back in June," says the red-faced waitress, "for White Nights." She describes the long summer sun, but for now, I am happy to know these short white days of winter, when Russia turns clean and quiet.

Winter is my favorite season—until spring arrives and Holland explodes into the colored stripes of endless tulip fields. Now is the time to relive my Boy Scout thrills of shooting heavy rapids in West Virginia or return to my youth in France and the vivid spectacle of wailing Romanies as they parade a painted effigy of St. Sara into the milky blue Mediterranean of Saintes-Maries-de-la-Mer.

Summer brings a new celebration of life, with state fairs and street carnivals, warm nights for stargazing, and rambling bears in the woods. And yet just when I am convinced that these warmer months are my favorite, fall arrives with its red glow and ready vineyards.

Travel offers us an eclectic calendar of changing moods, when time and place converge into the perfect moment. Those of us who wander are destined to discover the splendor of each season, whether it's a stampede of zebras kicking up clouds of dust or the glistening blue ice of the Antarctic summer.

This book explores the beauty of the right place at the right time: Kenya's mass gathering of pink flamingos, Polynesia when the air turns sweet with vanilla flowers, Norway's northern lights, India's elaborate monsoon weddings, and Venice dressed in mysterious masquerade. These pages celebrate the span of seasons across the globe and offer up the simple reminder that it's not just where you go—but when.

*Travel offers us an eclectic calendar of changing moods, when time and place converge into the perfect moment.*

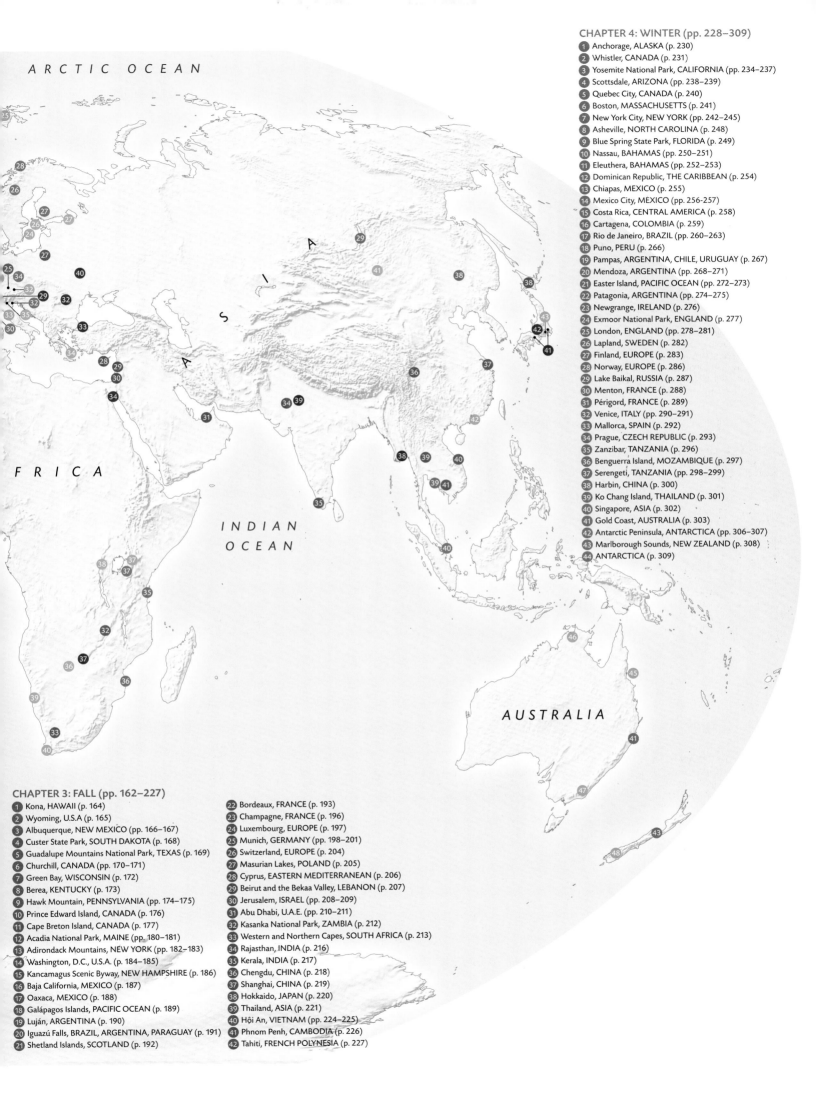

ARCTIC OCEAN

ASIA

AFRICA

INDIAN OCEAN

AUSTRALIA

# SPR

BUDDING BLOSSOMS, ANIMALS
ON THE MARCH, CARIBBEAN
REEFS, AND WORLD MUSIC

ING

Nagoya Castle, a 17th-century fortress, now stands watch over the (short-lived) invasion of cherry blossoms each spring.

# SAN JUAN CAPISTRANO

**Join the swallows that migrate to this ancient mission each spring.**

The swallows don't really come to Mission San Juan Capistrano on the same day every year. Legend says the magic day is March 19, St. Joseph's Day, but like any party, some show up early, some show up late, and, let's face it, birds aren't that big on watching the calendar anyway. Which is a good thing: It gives admirers more time to see them as they fill the old mission.

For a century or more, people have described the city's sky around St. Joseph's Day as black with swallows, and the adobe walls of San Juan Capistrano seemed like they'd been built by ancients just as a place for the birds to perch. Today, as you hear the mission bells, you can imagine the sounds of the swallows singing along. In the tiny, narrow Serra Chapel in front of the gold-decked altar, visitors leave candles that flicker like flitting wings.

Fewer and fewer swallows have been showing up over the past years. The mission is doing everything to bring them back so that the springtime music of thousands of them singing into the chapel's open windows never stops.

**PLANNING  San Juan Capistrano** www.sanjuancapistrano.org. **Mission** www.missionsjc.com. About an hour's drive south of Los Angeles, the mission is in the city center.

## IN THE KNOW
### The Mission Trail

San Juan Capistrano is the seventh of 21 missions making up California's mission trail, which traces the old El Camino Real. Stretching from San Diego to north of San Francisco, the missions were built by the Spanish between the late 1700s and early 1800s, each roughly a day's journey apart and designed to be almost an independent city, with farms, smithies, and workshops. The churches themselves run from quiet chapels to huge, busy buildings with daily services, all lit by tiny windows and spring light. A trip along the trail, mostly following U.S. Highway 101, opens up the heart of the state. www.parks.ca.gov

The San Juan de Capistrano mission bells silently wait for the legendary swallows to come back to roost.

One of the sure signs of spring's arrival in southern Idaho: pronghorn blazing trails through the remaining snow

IDAHO

# CRATERS OF THE MOON

**Catch the pronghorn migration across the lunar landscape of a western national monument.**

You'll always find an otherworldly vista at Idaho's Craters of the Moon National Monument and Preserve. But visit the vast lava field park during a brief window in March and April and the scene becomes alive with pronghorn. The deerlike animals amble along a narrow corridor, making their way from their winter feeding grounds to their summer range in the Pioneer Mountains. (In October, the migration reverses.)

While the several hundred pronghorn don't sprint through the park, they don't dilly-dally either. Luckily they're creatures of habit, and their route paralleling U.S. Highways 20/26/93 doesn't vary. "The path they take is so precise and ingrained, you can see it on Google Earth," says monument wildlife biologist Todd Stefanic. A distinct species closely related to the giraffe, pronghorn indeed look out of Africa, with discrete white striping on their necks.

The challenge for pronghorn-watchers is timing. The creatures move in groups over a period of a month or so. They can be spotted from a car or after a short hike across the windswept sagebrush plain. But don't expect to get closer than 100 yards (90 m)—pronghorn are easily spooked and are among the fastest creatures on Earth, reaching speeds of more than 50 miles an hour (80 kph).

**PLANNING Craters of the Moon National Monument and Preserve** www.nps.gov/crmo/nature science. The migration period is quite short. For updates, call the park at (208) 527-1335.

## IN THE KNOW
### *Hemingway's Idaho*

Ernest Hemingway may have drunk in Havana and caroused in Paris, but he retreated to Idaho. The novelist bought his house in the late 1950s and lived his last years in Ketchum, about 90 minutes from Craters of the Moon. It's easy to see the appeal. Hemingway enjoyed the glamour of nearby Sun Valley Resort, where he spent time with movie stars like Gary Cooper and Ingrid Bergman. But he also cherished the small-town anonymity of Ketchum. He was happiest hunting and fishing in nearby mountains and valleys, including spring-fed Silver Creek, a pinnacle of trout fishing. Hemingway's son Jack helped create a nature preserve there. The author's grave is in Ketchum, encircled by three towering evergreens. www.nature.org

Along with Roosevelt's popular bison and prairie dogs, upward of 100 feral horses roam the park's lands—and, at times, roads.

NORTH DAKOTA

# THEODORE ROOSEVELT NATIONAL PARK

**Hike through prairie and past stunning geologic formations to a petrified forest.**

Though it's in North Dakota, the least visited of all U.S. states (an honor it certainly doesn't deserve), Theodore Roosevelt National Park isn't immune to the crowds that hit the road during the summer travel season. And winters get—and stay—chilly. Late spring is the time to see the park's lesser known badlands and its abundance of wildlife (bison, wild horses, prairie dogs). "The North Dakota badlands is where Theodore Roosevelt turned from 'a skinny scrawny New York dude' into a 'cowboy,' " says Eileen Andes, the park's chief of interpretation and public affairs. It's also, she adds, where Roosevelt's "ideas about conservation began to solidify."

Drive through the South Unit entrance—the preseason quiet allows time for a nice chat with the ranger—and take a quick left into the Medora visitor center. There, gather intel (a trail map, directions to the Peaceful Valley Ranch trailhead) and fill your water bottles. A short drive and moderately challenging hike to one of the country's largest concentrations of petrified wood is ahead. It's doubtful you'll see anybody else as you walk through tall prairie grass and pass by otherworldly geologic formations—"It's in the wilderness area," Andes notes—then, on to the Petrified Forest, with its massive pieces of no-longer-wood, including plenty of standing stumps. Adds Andes: "It's a really special collection."

**PLANNING** **Theodore Roosevelt National Park** www.nps.gov/thro. Consider staying at the Rough Riders Hotel (*www.medora.com/rough-riders*), named for Roosevelt's Spanish-American War regiment.

TENNESSEE

# NASHVILLE

**Listen up as big music stars and their hit songwriters play their tunes on stages all over town.**

Between attention for its eponymous hit TV show and its better-than-ever food scene, few U.S. cities have been hotter than Nashville during the last few years. Some of its best rewards come from a springtime visit, when the temps are walk-around perfect and, thanks to the Tin Pan South Songwriters Festival, the city's best crop—songwriters—is in full bloom.

Stretching over five nights, Tin Pan South hits music venues around town. Stages are loaded with everybody from big-name singer-songwriters to songwriters whose work turned singers into big names (from country to rock and beyond). And after hearing them play their tunes, you'll remember their names.

Though songwriting is a competitive industry, it's also one of Nashville's strongest communities. "Any [Tin Pan South] audience is 50 percent people who want to be songwriters, 40 percent fans, and 10 percent other songwriters going in and supporting their friends," says Grammy-winning songwriter Tia Sillers.

Tin Pan South energizes even industry vets. "I went to Nashville many years after I had my greatest success," says Paul Williams, Academy Award–winning songwriter and president of the American Society of Composers, Authors, and Publishers. "But I feel my real love affair with music—the birthplace of that—is Tin Pan South."

**PLANNING  Nashville** www.visitmusiccity.com. **Tin Pan South Songwriters Festival** www.tinpansouth.com.

**FOR FOODIES**
*Nashville Farmers' Market*

From the collards at Jamaic-away to the day's specials at Nashville star chef Arnold Myint's AM@FM, there are fields' upon fields' worth of springtime, locally sourced strawberries, turnip greens, and more on the menus of the food stalls and restaurants of Nashville Farmers' Market. After grazing your way around, cross into the farm-stand building where the growers offer up more goodies so you can cook your own Southern spring masterpieces. Or, at least, photograph them. Drove into town? Make sure you leave plenty of room in the trunk for your market haul: Fresh greens take up some serious space. nashvillefarmersmarket.org

Musicians muscle their instruments across Nashville's Broadway, likely bound for one of the world-famous honky-tonks that line "Lower Broad."

# INDIANAPOLIS 500

"When the drivers round Turn 4, the green flag snaps and what sounds like the drone of a muscular swarm of 1,600-pound [726 kg] metal hornets screams past the stands, releasing a most hellacious noise. It is very loud and very scary—and extremely exciting."

—GARY MCKECHNIE, AUTHOR OF NATIONAL GEOGRAPHIC'S *USA 101*

First held in 1911, the Indianapolis 500 takes place on the last weekend in May at the Indianapolis Motor Speedway (the largest sporting spectator facility in the world). *Pictured:* Sam Hornish, Jr., tears around a turn.

# MEMPHIS

**Devour some of the blues capital's best local 'cue during the barbecue world championships in May.**

The South doesn't feel quite right when the heat isn't on. But *too* hot, and the day is cooked. So, May, with highs in the low 80s°F (high 20s°C) and, better, a barbecue festival, promises some serious sweet heat.

When it comes to Memphis's dedication to barbecue, there's no contest. "Two things Memphis is known for: churches and barbecue restaurants on every corner," says Ron Childers, a certified barbecue contest judge and meteorologist for WMC-TV. So it's fitting that the city hosts the World Championship Barbecue Cooking Contest every May. One of the premier events on the BBQ cooking contest circuit, the championship welcomes smokers of all shapes and sizes—BBQ smokers, that is—ready to put their recipes to the test and, tongs crossed, bag some bragging rights. Contestants can't feed the public (health laws won't have it). But competitors do right by your eyes by dressing up their tents and smokers; Childers remembers a group of pilots who built a smoker shaped like a miniature airplane.

To actually feast on some 'cue, head to one of Memphis's many great barbecue restaurants. You can get excellent chicken or beef, but Childers recommends the classic cuts. "Memphis-style barbecue is pork ribs, pork shoulder, or whole hog. Pork and a sweet rub."

Sounds like a winner.

**PLANNING** **Memphis** www.memphistravel.com. **World Championship Barbecue Cooking Contest** www.memphisinmay.org.

Beale Street was calling them. During the first half of the 1900s, the Memphis street that stretches nearly 2 miles (3 km) from the Mississippi River became the go-to locale for musicians who wanted to make names for themselves. Early on, an upbeat blues style emerged. After World War II, things took a harder edge and musicians, including Howlin' Wolf and B. B. King, went from being Beale Street players to internationally famed household names. The street's appeal still holds true—though it has more of a touristy vibe than it did in decades past. Go anyway. Venues offer everything from Memphis blues to its offspring, rock and roll. www.bealestreetonline.com, www.bealestreet.com

Look for hot barbecue turkey drumsticks or baby back ribs on Memphis menus.

The New Orleans Jazz and Heritage Festival in 2012 featured guitarist Vasti Jackson among its many talented performers.

LOUISIANA

# NEW ORLEANS

**Overwhelm your senses at the Jazz Fest, where legendary sounds mix with the city's rich cultural gumbo.**

Jazz is one of many musical styles that bursts the sound barrier of the New Orleans Fair Grounds Race Course, where thousands gather for the annual Jazz Fest. Its official title—the New Orleans Jazz and Heritage Festival—is more apt. Indigenous genres like Cajun and zydeco are performed alongside contemporary international styles equally alive in the city—all at a festival that pays tribute to the larger culinary, linguistic, artistic, and cultural traditions with which music is always entwined. The late April festival—perched on the brink of summer, just before the swampy Louisiana heat sets it—has been held since 1970, drawing A-listers like Bruce Springsteen and Jimmy Buffett, as well as big-name New Orleans legends like Fats Domino and the Preservation Hall Jazz Band.

The best way to experience it is to meander, exposing your ear to the festival's 12 stages and countless impromptu musical shows that erupt next to, behind, and in between them. "You'll experience a little bit of everything: gospel, rock, blues, zydeco, funk, African, Latin, brass, R&B," says annual festivalgoer Monica Corcoran, plus "the traveling brass bands, second-liners, and Mardi Gras Indians that weave their way among the crowds, carrying people along with their music."

**PLANNING New Orleans Jazz and Heritage Festival** www.nojazzfest.com. Tickets may be purchased at most Ticketmaster outlets, online, or at the New Orleans Arena.

---

### IN THE KNOW
*The George Wein Legacy*

The New Orleans Jazz and Heritage Festival was the brainchild of George Wein, founder of the legendary Newport Jazz Festival in Rhode Island. When Wein presented his first Newport festival in 1954, it was a groundbreaking platform for jazz musicians to reach wider audiences at a time when they were largely relegated to dusty nightclubs. By the time he was hired to produce the New Orleans Jazz Fest in 1970, the genre had gained widespread popularity. Recognizing the reach of jazz in New Orleans, Wein conceived of an event to celebrate the music within the larger context of the city's vibrant culture that nourished—and continues to nourish—it today.

# Lisa Ling
## Austin's South by Southwest

As soon as my husband Paul and I boarded our flight from Los Angeles to Austin, Texas, and looked around at all the artist types traveling to the Longhorn City, we knew we were going to be doing something cool. Every year in the early spring, Brooklynites, Angelinos, and young hipsters from all over the country and world flee their hometowns and head to Austin for the South by Southwest music, film, and interactive technology festival. Regulars refer to the trifecta of events as "Southby."

Southby takes place over the course of a week and a half, usually starting in early March. The festival is undeniably a colossal party scene. But the days are filled with speakers, workshops, and an exhibit hall for those who want to learn more about any or all of the three different genres. Music starts midway through and ends the festival.

I was blown away by the throngs of young, aspiring Internet and gaming entrepreneurs who show up with hopes of debuting their ideas and becoming the next Mark Zuckerberg—who has been a speaker at Southby. After all, it was here in 2007 that one of the biggest social networks on Earth, Twitter, was introduced to the world. It was so interesting to see thousands of college kids, college dropouts, and ambitious young people working the rooms trying to make it big in an industry that barely existed 20 years ago.

After the tech festival came to a close, we readied ourselves for some long nights of shots and amazing music. With huge mainstream acts like Jay-Z, the Foo Fighters, Metallica, and the White Stripes, as well as legendary and indie rockers, Austin's stages and bars come alive. Every bar in Central Austin hosts a series of bands, and we came across sounds that we'd never heard before. Though I'd seen probably 15 bands over the course of several days, as someone who came of age in the '80s, the highlight for me was seeing my first crushes, Duran Duran. It was hot, sweaty, and way overcrowded, but the wild boys—or slightly old men by now—didn't disappoint.

Big note for those wanting to experience Southby: Wear comfortable shoes!

*Lisa Ling is the executive producer and host of* Our America *on the Oprah Winfrey Network. She also hosts CBS TV's* The Job.

*"I was blown away by the throngs of young, aspiring … entrepreneurs who show up with hopes of … becoming the next Mark Zuckerberg."*

From start-up companies to bands on the cusp, Austin's "Southby" showcases the next big new. Here, the Pipettes blow it up in their trademark polka dots.

In an age-old tradition, farmers near West Brattleboro, Vermont, collect sap with the help of a horse-drawn gathering tank.

# VERMONT

**Indulge in the sticky, naturally sweet tastes and aromas of fresh maple syrup during its spring coming out party.**

At the time when most farmers are just beginning to think about spring planting, maple syrup producers across Vermont are already enjoying their harvests. Vermont leads the country in syrup production with an ideal combination of climate, soil, and aged trees. Syrup season climaxes with the Vermont Maple Festival, a nearly half-century-old tradition in the northern town of St. Albans, where visitors gather to taste all four grades of Vermont's legendary syrup, each with a distinct bouquet, body, taste, and finish. "Everyone tries the syrups in little cups, starting with the lighter grades and moving to the darker," says festival cochair Carolyn Perley. Like the other planners of the volunteer-run festival, the Perleys are sugarmakers.

To best see syrupmaking in action, arrive before the April festival. Syrup season begins when spring's first breath warms the thaw just enough to awaken the dormant trees and start sap pumping. Snow still conceals the forest floors when sugarmakers trek into the woods to tap the trees. Sap is collected and boiled in sugarhouses, creating clouds of steam laced with sweet aromas. In order to bear the label "Vermont Maple Syrup," all syrup must be 100 percent natural with nothing added.

**PLANNING  Vermont Maple Festival** www.vtmaplefestival.org. **Vermont's maple syrup season** www .vermontmaple.org. Many of Vermont's sugarhouses are open to the public, some seasonally and others throughout the year.

## GREAT STAYS
*Eat, Sleep, Learn, and Play on a Vermont Farm*

• **FOUR SPRINGS FARM:**  A single-owner farm with a cabin and campground. Immerse yourself in farm life by helping out with the morning chores or picking your own vegetables. www.four springsfarm.com

• **HOLLISTER HILL FARM:**  A small, family-run farm with four dairy cows that supply raw milk to farm customers. Stay in an early 19th-century farmhouse and spend your mornings in the barn feeding and watering the animals. www.hollisterhillfarm.com

• **TREVIN FARMS:**  A working farm with chickens, horses, goats, and chemical-free vegetable gardens. Spend the morning gathering eggs from the henhouse for breakfast and milking the goats to gather the milk you'll use later at cheesemaking class. www.trevinfarms.com

# WEST VIRGINIA

**Raft the currents of West Virginia's rivers, renowned for both their beauty and brute force.**

Water is a powerful force in the mountains of southern West Virginia, a region threaded with rivers that have been harnessed for industry and recreation alike. At times the rivers twist lackadaisically around soft curves and bends. But know that flows can shift with bipolar rapidity, transforming into roiling hydraulic pools and violent rapids that churn over steep drops.

Spring is the best time to challenge the New River, one of the most popular runs for white-water rafting, as melting snow increases the level and force of the flow. Likewise, the Gauley River holds its own springtime powers, notorious for muscular rapids and steep gradients that draw large crowds in the fall when the dam is opened. "Spring is an open book for us," says river manager Rick Miller. "Fall is predictable, but some of our best trips are in the spring."

Despite their reputations, certain sections of the rivers are better known for their calmer personalities. The upper New River, which cascades through picturesque canyons, is best for beginners. "That's the beauty of the river," says Turner Sharp of the West Virginia Rivers Coalition. "It's flowing all the time. But when you go slower, you get to enjoy the scenery."

Though enjoyed by thousands of enthusiasts and beginners alike each season, white-water rafting is risky. If you've never rafted before, start easy and get a taste of the experience. As you must always be prepared to swim a rapid if the raft capsizes, assess your health and physical limitations before making a decision about which run to take. Beyond personal safety, increased tourism from the rafting industry carries environmental risks as well. Carpool to rafting sites in order to reduce your carbon footprint, and consider camping away from the river to reduce degradation of the riverbanks.

**PLANNING  West Virginia white-water rafting** wvcommerce.org. Wildwater Expeditions *(www.wvaraft .com)* is the oldest rafting outfitter in West Virginia and the force that jump-started the industry.

Adventurists paddle their way through the mist kicked up by West Virginia's powerful Gauley River.

# VIRGINIA

**Taste your way through the Old Dominion's pastoral wine country, rooted in American history and celebrated with spring festivals.**

Resting in the foothills of the Blue Ridge, the mansion of James Madison, the United States' fourth President, provides a majestic backdrop for one of the oldest celebrations of Virginia wine. One of many festivals held each spring to kick off Virginia's wine season, the Montpelier Wine Festival draws local winemakers who present their variations on the theme of Virginia grapes. On the periphery of the 2,700-acre (1,100 ha) estate, families spread picnic blankets accompanied by their bottles of choice.

Virginia's foray into the art of grape cultivation began with U.S. Founding Fathers like Madison, many of whom were well-read agriculturists. With visions of a New World wine industry, Thomas Jefferson planted vineyards at his Monticello estate. Though his grapes failed, Jefferson established a tradition that contemporary winemakers continue to reference.

Events at historic estates convey a sense of past while allowing visitors to sample the varied fruits of local labor and passion. "Dry, fruity, spicy—there's a whole gamut of wines to taste," observes Montpelier's Barbara Bannar. Bannar suggests talking to the outgoing winemakers themselves, who, like their enterprising forefathers, are craftspeople.

**PLANNING Virginia wine festivals** Montpelier, www.montpelierwinefestival.com; Monticello, monticello winetrailfestival.com; Ash Lawn–Highland, www.ashlawnhighland.org.

A lesser known achievement on Thomas Jefferson's impressive résumé is his status as a Founding Father of American wine. The third U.S. President put his heart into his vineyards, but the effort never yielded wine. Jefferson's vines were revived in the mid-1980s by Italian-born viticulturist Gabriele Rausse, who grafted and replanted the original varieties at Monticello. "Jefferson planted tobacco first," Rausse recounts, but soon realized that tobacco ruined the soil and advocated grapes as an alternative. "But nobody listened, and the future of Virginia was tobacco." Two centuries and 200 wineries later, Virginia is now listening to Jefferson.

Quench your thirst with vino that owes its existence to a winemaking tradition inspired by Thomas Jefferson's agricultural aspirations.

The crowd goes quiet waiting to see if the seventh green at Augusta National Golf Club will be kind to the next competitor.

## GEORGIA

# AUGUSTA

**Watch golf's superstars play the famed greens of Augusta in a gracious, historic Southern city.**

Every April, just as the azaleas begin to bud, the storied Masters Tournament brings the world's top golfers to east Georgia. While the private Augusta National Golf Club closely guards the coveted badges for admittance to the four-day contest, the unwashed have a chance to step onto the fabled grounds during three days of practice rounds. Tickets are distributed by lottery, and the lucky winners get a chance to watch the sport's top players chip, drive, and putt around golf's most famous—and some say most beautiful—course. Highlights include Magnolia Lane, the club entryway, lined by trees that create a stunning springtime allée; Rae's Creek, the course's lowest point, into which many a rueful player has watched his ball roll; and Butler Cabin, from where TV broadcasts the tournament each year.

Take advantage of one beautiful spring day to explore the city itself, when Augusta is "almost Caribbean," claims Brad Usry, a lifetime resident and owner of the popular soul food joint Fat Man's Mill Café. "Dogwoods in bloom, mild mornings, flowers shining in warm sunlight. The climate is blissful, and folks are happy." Take a quiet stroll along the Savannah River on the Riverwalk, visit the city's magnificent antebellum mansions, and check out the boyhood home of President Woodrow Wilson.

**PLANNING Augusta** www.augustaga.gov. **Masters Tournament** masters.com. Online lottery registration for practice-day entry begins shortly after the previous year's tournament ends, but winners are few; try eBay and Craigslist. Note that state law prohibits ticket sales near the course.

# GREAT SMOKY MOUNTAINS NATIONAL PARK

"In the North the spring holds back, then comes with a rush, tumbles its treasures in a heap at your feet, and is gone. Here, the spirit of the South prevails, and the spring gradually unfolds for three months, rising in a strong, slow tide that finally breaks over the land in a tremendous flood of color and fragrance and song."

—MARGARET W. MORLEY, *THE CAROLINA MOUNTAINS* (1913)

**Great Smoky Mountains National Park spans more than 800 square miles (2,100 sq km) along the Tennessee–North Carolina border. Initially created in 1934 to protect the land from excessive logging, the park remains home to a biologically diverse 17,000 species of flora and fauna. *Pictured:* Sunrise over the park's Oconaluftee Valley**

Even Hawaii's flowers would be jealous of the underwater color blast served up by the Caribbean's fish, coral, and bright orange sea stars.

THE CARIBBEAN

# PUERTO RICO

**Try snuba to explore the underwater tropical splendor of the Caribbean's great coral reefs.**

Just off Puerto Rico's sultry, palm-shaded southern coast, 15 feet (4.5 m) beneath the water's surface, flirt with royal blue sergeant majors, tunnel through staghorn and elkhorn coral, and float across waving sea grass dotted with enormous conch shells. The experience may feel like scuba diving—but it's not. It's snuba.

Developed in 1989, snuba is popular in tropical paradises worldwide. But Puerto Rico—where the U.S. dollar is currency, passports are unnecessary, and English is widely spoken—is a top choice in spring.

The trip begins on a short boat ride from Copamarina Beach Resort in Guánica, during which the bronzed guide tells you the basics. A cross between snorkeling and scuba diving, snuba involves placing in your mouth a breathing device that's attached to an air tank above on a pontoon raft. You have swim fins and a diving mask, but no heavy tanks to carry on your back, and no certificate or prior experience is required. A weight around your waist makes sure you sink to the seafloor.

As you glide through the pellucid waters, the swim becomes a meditation on amazing beauty, on the wonder of sweet rainbow fish darting to and fro, and on the vast blue world all around you.

**PLANNING Aqua Adventure at Copamarina Beach Resort** www.copamarina.com, www.aquaadventurepr.com.

---

## IN THE KNOW
*Hidden Puerto Rico*

Puerto Rico's southwest corner remains happily undiscovered. Hike through the cactus-sprinkled Guánica Dry Forest Reserve (with only 30 inches/ 76 cm of rain a year, the opposite of a rain forest); paddle to seashell-speckled Gilligan's Island, part of the Biosphere Reserve of Guánica; watch the sun set atop cliffs at the Cabo Rojo lighthouse; or explore the sun-drenched village of Guánica, invaded by American forces in 1898 in the first step of Puerto Rico becoming a U.S. territory. In February, the weeklong Carnaval de Ponce descends on Ponce's colonial core with costumed parades and *bomba y plena* music.

# ST. LUCIA

**Hike among this tropical island's wild orchids and lush rain forests as spring clears the way.**

A tropical paradise of overpowering beauty, the mountainous island of St. Lucia is blessed with some of the Caribbean's most dramatic scenery. Its majestic peaks of Petit and Gros Piton jut from the coast like sugarloaves, while in the interior lie miles and miles of verdant rain forest. The best time to come is April and May, before the summer rainy season begins and between waves of visitors. On hikes, you may have the place to yourself.

The rain forest is a veritable Garden of Eden, laced with 29 miles (47 km) of hiking trails, each one more breathtaking than the last. Fragrant wild orchids, jasmine, and frangipani carpet St. Lucia's fertile soil. Hummingbirds flit among exotic flowering lobster claws beneath a swaying canopy of palms and colorful *dédéfouden* trees. A fitting introduction is the Parrot Trail, a four-hour jaunt near the town of Micoud. "Since Hurricane Tomás hit the opposite coast in 2010, more gorgeous birds have settled here than ever before," says tour guide Fabian Philip. Many come to spot the elusive Amazona versicolor, St. Lucia's indigenous parrot, with its bright blue face, red throat, green wings, and tail dipped in yellow. You can usually hear it shrieking long before it streaks into view.

**PLANNING St. Lucia** www.visitstlucia.net, www.saintlucia-tourism.com. **Hiking** Fabian Tours, www.fabian toursstlucia.com; ATV Paradise Tours, www.atvstlucia.com.

## BEST OF THE BEST
### Night Zip-lining

Can't buy a thrill, you say? Try zipping through the rain forest canopy of St. Lucia at full moon. From the northern town of Chassin, guides lead three-hour night excursions to the root-encrusted Eagle's Claw, a volcanic boulder deep in this eco-adventure park. Here, you clamber up a set of "floating steps" to your launch point, hitch up to the cables, and race from tree to tree. Nocturnal creatures blink curiously into the beam of your headlamp. At the last of the platforms—invitingly named the Tarantula's Nest—you rappel back to the jungle floor. www.rainforestadventure.com

St. Lucia's most visible geographic formations, the Pitons are part of a volcanic complex. Their neighbors include fumaroles and hot springs.

# ANTIGUA

**Jump aboard or celebrate dockside during Sailing Week as hundreds of yachts compete in the season's grand, final regatta.**

You've sailed before, but nothing like this—a full-scale regatta around the island of Antigua in the eastern Caribbean. Three days of hard-core sailing punctuated by rowdy beach parties at Dickenson Bay and the aptly named Jolly Harbour. And now you're on the home stretch, speeding along the island's southern shore as you make for English Harbour and the finishing line.

Fun in the sun and dead-serious sailing make Antigua's annual Sailing Week at the end of April one of the globe's premier water-sport events. By day, skilled crews compete in 29 categories broken down by size, shape, and national origin of vessel. By night, everyone parties like the dickens on the island's beaches and dockside. Spring weather—after the rainy season and before the hurricanes blow in—provides ideal sailing conditions.

"Antigua Week is one of the most original Caribbean regattas," says Englishman Christian Reynolds, who's raced his 51-foot (16 m) *Northern Child* half a dozen times in the event. Even rookies can get into the action by signing up to crew aboard a yacht in one of the not-so-competitive categories. Nor do landlubbers need to miss out; they can get swept up in the maritime hoopla by attending the parties, concerts, and other special events at Nelson's Dockyard on the island's south coast.

**PLANNING Antigua** www.antigua-barbuda.org. **Antigua Sailing Week** www.sailingweek.com. A number of boats offer crew positions, including the *Northern Child (www.northernchild.com).*

## IN THE KNOW
*Lord Nelson in Antigua*

Horatio Nelson arrived in Antigua in 1784 as a 26-year-old Royal Navy officer commanding the frigate H.M.S. *Boreas*. He had the unpopular assignment of enforcing the British Navigation Acts and preventing trading with the recently independent United States. For one of the few times in his life, Nelson failed and was even sequestered aboard *Boreas* for eight months facing possible legal action. On the other hand, his social life blossomed. On nearby Nevis, the dashing Nelson met young widow Fanny Nisbet and the two soon married. In the summer of 1787, Nelson sailed back to England, destined for immortality 18 years later at Trafalgar.

In their quest to win the race or, at the very least, keep their boat's speed from flagging, the crew sets to trimming the jib.

With just hours to create a temporary street fresco on Calle de las Alfombras, artists turn sawdust into an eye-catching work of art.

## NICARAGUA
# LEÓN

**Celebrate Holy Week in a town where authentic Latin American ritual fuses with artistic passion.**

The hot, steamy intellectual capital of Nicaragua's northwest is something of an unpolished gem, its Spanish colonial churches rubbing shoulders with gritty student bars and peeling revolutionary Sandinista murals. León's earthy traditions are on display during Semana Santa, the authentic Easter rituals marked by slow-moving religious processions, dirges, and wailing among the devout.

On Good Friday, the main avenue erupts into vivid splashes of color called *alfombras de aserrin,* or "sawdust carpets." Working late into the night, and often poring over ragged photos for reference, residents create amazing versions of Jesus, the Virgin Mary, and other sacred motifs from pine needles, flower petals, sand, and dyed sawdust. The method originated in León more than a century ago and, unlike in other places celebrating Holy Week, the artists still work freehand rather than with molds.

"Anyone can claim a space on the street and do it," says Richard Leonardi, general manager at Tours Nicaragua. "Most of these people don't produce art the rest of the year, so it's very democratic." Family members, friends, and onlookers alike offer advice, perhaps on how to improve a halo or crown of thorns. The pieces have an ephemeral quality: Worshippers en route to Good Friday services at León's humongous cathedral trample the creations.

**PLANNING León** www.visit-nicaragua.com, www.nicaragua.com. **Cultural tours** www.toursnicaragua .com, www.vapues.com. Book hotels well in advance—and watch your valuables; thieves abound during Holy Week.

### FOR FOODIES
*Central Market*

For mouthwatering cuisine during Holy Week, look no farther than León's atmospheric Mercado Central, the central market. Vendors on and around the square will be selling traditional Easter sweets like *huevos chimbos* ("fake eggs" of cane sugar and almonds) and *almibar* (soft mango-chestnut drops) alongside more rustic offerings of *gaspar* (dried salted gar) and *pinol de iguana* (iguana soup). Year-round, sidewalk barbecues serve heaping portions of *gallo pinto* (rice and beans), *papas rellenas* (stuffed potatoes), and *comida corriente,* a fresh spread of whatever's on that day. Wash it all down with popular *chicha,* an unfermented corn drink.

# OUTDOOR FLOWER MARKETS

**Flood the senses with irresistible blooms by the bucket load, exotic and everyday.**

## CUENCA FLOWER MARKET

*Cuenca, Ecuador*

One of the world's great historic cities, Cuenca boasts more than 50 churches from the Spanish colonial era. But its major draw is the daily flower market, lurking in the shadow of the monumental Catedral de la Inmaculada Concepción. Vendors at dozens of stands offer quivering orchids, arum lilies, and giant roses.

*www.incuenca.com*

## MARCHÉ AUX FLEURS

*Île de la Cité, Paris, France*

Risk sensory overload at the 200-year-old *marché aux fleurs,* the sort of setting that brings to mind Madame Bovary. A delicious cloud of freesia, jasmine, and tuberose wafts across these Belle Époque halls—except on Sunday, when blossoms give way to beaks at the *marché aux oiseaux* (bird market).

*www.parisinfo.com*

## BLOEMENMARKT

*Amsterdam, The Netherlands*

Hugging an attractive stretch of the Singel canal, Amsterdam's "floating" Bloemenmarkt is an apparition of colors so crazy, it's no wonder the 19th-century merchants got tulip mania. The barge stalls overflow with popular varieties like Queen of the Night. Pick up a bag of bulbs or some clogs to take home.

*www.amsterdamtourist.com*

## CAMPO DEI FIORE

*Rome, Italy*

Founded in the 15th century, this little produce market occupies a special place in Romans' hearts. The romance begins at dawn, when farmers wheel in nature's bounty. The flower stalls are the last to close; stick around until 1 p.m., when the vendors really get the gab and throw in an extra rose or two.

*www.turismoroma.it*

## ADDERLEY STREET FLOWER MARKET

*Cape Town, South Africa*

The country's largest flower hall market is renowned for the barbed wit of its female vendors, some of whom have been snipping and grinning here for decades. Prepare to shake, haggle, and roll away with heaps of carnations, lilies, and a lovely pincushion proteas, a native of South Africa.

*tourismcapetown.co.za*

## PHOOL MANDI

*New Delhi, India*

Blooms plucked across the globe pop up at the *phool mandi,* one of Asia's most spectacular and bustling flower markets. It's wholesale, meaning the fragrant piles of *rajnigandha* (tuberoses), chrysanthemums, and lilies are bigger than usual. Bright orange marigolds, a favorite for traditional garlands, are sold from burlap bags the size of ottomans. Vendors start at dawn but vanish by 9 a.m.

*www.delhitourism.gov.in*

## PAK KHLONG TALAT

*Bangkok, Thailand*

The Pak Khlong flower market is one of Bangkok's most nimble and arresting sights. Open around the clock, the stands are best enjoyed in the cool air after midnight, when boats on the Chao Phraya River deliver lotus blossoms in electrifying pink and white.

*www.bangkoktourist.com*

## CAOJIADU

*Shanghai, China*

A vine-encrusted arch heralds the entrance to Caojiadu, the largest and busiest of Shanghai's flower markets. Spread over three floors, the sheer variety of plants and greenery can overwhelm anyone's Zen, although everyone agrees the prices are heavenly. There's enough here to equip a minibiosphere—birds, fish, turtles, and gurgling fountains.

*www.meet-in-shanghai.net*

## DANGWA FLOWER MARKET

*Manila, The Philippines*

If love is in the air, pick up a bouquet from Dangwa—round about midnight. On Valentine's Day, crowds of Manila residents will be doing the very same thing. Stuffed into four lanes in the student quarter of Sampaloc, the stalls never think about closing; the bouquets are freshest when the barflies wilt.

*www.manila.gov.ph*

## FLEMINGTON FLOWER MARKET

*Sydney, Australia*

Sydney's best kept secret is its cavernous flower market, achingly beautiful and buzzing from 5 a.m. with green energy. By about 9 a.m., the hustle fades as florists make off with their day's booty.

*www.sydney.com*

Two symbols of Amsterdam: A bicyclist stops to admire (and, perhaps, buy) some blooms at the city's flower market, Bloemenmarkt.

MEXICO

# TEOTIHUACAN

**Renew the spirit with the multitudes who gather each March to watch the sun rise over ancient ruins.**

T housands gather atop the Pyramid of the Sun on March 20, awaiting daybreak at Teotihuacan, the ancient ruins on the northern outskirts of Mexico City. Many are clad in white; some have brought crystals and amulets to capture the energy of the rising sun. When the orb finally appears over the Sierra Madre, people start to chant, sing, and pray, raising their arms to welcome the spring equinox.

Visitors will find the experience indelible. Explains Kenneth Fagan, who filmed the rites for Arizona State University, "It's very impressive to see nearly one million people in one location, mostly all in white, laughing, talking, singing, banging drums, dancing, playing flutes, and making animal sounds—people young and old, walking and climbing all over the ruins." For Mexicans, the celebration "connects them to their past, their history, and their family," Fagan says.

The "love-in" ambience invites everyone to participate. Join Aztec dancers and other troupes from all around Mexico. Munch freshly made tamales or bargain for trinkets with the many wandering vendors. Inhale the heady aroma of the copal incense burned by those who still believe in the ancient gods. Get your fortune told by a shaman. And have evil spirits exorcized by *brujos* (witches), on hand just in case the future doesn't look bright.

**PLANNING Teotihuacan** www.visitmexico.com. A good source of information on the ancient city is Arizona State University's Teotihuacan website, archaeology.asu.edu/teo.

---

### IN THE KNOW
*Pyramid of the Sun*

S oaring 20 stories above the ancient city of Teotihuacan, the Pyramid of the Sun is the world's third largest pyramid and an iconic Mesoamerican structure. Construction began roughly 2,000 years ago. The pyramid's footprint is thought to be determined by the position of the setting sun on the spring and fall equinoxes. The adobe, stone, and plaster pyramid contains about 2.5 million tons (2.26 million tonnes) of rubble. No chambers have been found inside, but underneath is a mysterious lava-tube cave that may have been a religious shrine or royal tomb. Reach the flat summit by climbing its 248 steps.

Musicians dressed in traditional Indian costume are among those who gather at the Teotihuacan ruins to celebrate spring's arrival.

A woman in Guayaquil, Ecuador, sorts cacao beans destined for chocolatemaking abroad.

# ECUADOR

**See—and savor—fine chocolate during cacao's spring harvest in the botanical birthplace of the ancient elixir.**

Cacao is harvested year-round all over Ecuador, but to indulge in the ultimate chocolate fantasy, head to the plantations in the tropical, Kichwa-speaking Amazon province of Napo. The region's chocolate recently made news when a special variety, Nacional, was found. The rare bean, once thought extinct, is considered the finest expression of cacao in the world.

Harvest in these parts begins in March, the first of two rainy seasons—but also the best time to experience the working side of the cacao production process when the drying, fermentation, and roasting occurs at the hands of small family farmers who've handed down harvest secrets over the generations. It's also the best time to witness the region's neon butterflies and intricately bejeweled hummingbirds for which this biodiverse hotspot—home to more than 4,000 plants, 1,000 birds, and 195 mammals—is known.

There are plenty of possibilities for exploring Ecuador's cacao farms, but the 850 family-run organic cocoa producers of the Kallari Association are especially worth seeking out. Each has earned kudos from Slow Food International for fair trade and sustainable agriculture practices, which help the local Kichwa people live without logging the rain forests.

**PLANNING Ecuador** www.ecuador.travel. Roast your own beans at the Chocolate Jungle plantation (*www.ecuadorjunglechocolate.com*), or ditch luxury for a chocolate volunteer vacation and Kichwa homestay at the Kallari Association (*kallari.com/internships.html*).

## IN THE KNOW
### *A Cacao Love Affair*

Though Venezuela claims the first cacao plants, Ecuador has played a starring role in the bean's rise. Today it is the world's largest producer of beans used to make fine chocolate. The country's Guayas Basin was home to the flavorful Arriba cacao bean, and new towns like Vinces in Los Ríos Province were founded on the wealth it brought to the region, where moneyed cacao barons settled. But a fungal outbreak in 1916–1919 ended the boom and decimated Ecuador's Arriba crops, and hardier, more disease-resistant varieties, like CCN-5, were planted instead.

# GUATEMALA HIGHLANDS

"Ancient and wild, Guatemala stands out as an exciting destination for nature lovers. During spring's migration season, more than 720 kinds of birds can be found, each bursting with its own mix of colors. Twenty-two of these species, though rarely seen, are entirely endemic to the Guatemala Highlands, a land of bubbling volcanoes and ancient Quechan villages along ruin-lined Lake Atitlán."

—ADAM GRAHAM, NATIONAL GEOGRAPHIC WRITER

Commonly referred to as Los Altos by the locals, the Guatemalan Highlands is an upland region in the southern part of the country. The diverse physical landscape of volcanoes, canyons, and mountains is also home to rich Maya culture. *Pictured:* Hiking Volcán Pacaya, an active volcano

Dubliners happily shed some of their modern-day ways (and dress) for the annual Bloomsday celebration. Here, a Joyce-inspired walk along Sandycove.

IRELAND

# DUBLIN

**Get wild and wacky with a dose of literary lunacy for James Joyce's Bloomsday.**

Where else but in Ireland—land of saints and scholars, sinners and storytellers—could you celebrate the secular feast day of a fictional character? On Bloomsday, Dublin toasts the genius of James Joyce, as his beguiling, bewildering novel *Ulysses* comes alive. June 16 is the day to dive into Dublin life at its most irreverent and surreal. The rain holds off—usually—and Dubliners wander the streets and bars, enjoying their short summer.

The original Bloomsday of 1904 follows Leopold Bloom and a host of other characters—real and fictional—from early morning onward. Today, Joyceans dress in Edwardian costume and gather at locations where episodes of *Ulysses* unfold. Among the citywide events, the James Joyce Centre hosts Bloomsday breakfasts (including fried kidneys, which Bloom eats for breakfast).

Entering into the spirit of Joyce's wandering Everyman is easy; all you need is a copy of the book, a map of the city, and a little imagination. Be (re)creative: Attend a funeral, lounge in a midday bath, stay out late. Enjoy, in the words of Irish-American author Frank McCourt, "a journey through Dublin and Ireland and family and Catholicism and eroticism and love." All the while declaring, like Molly Bloom, "yes I will Yes."

**PLANNING  Bloomsday in Dublin** jamesjoyce.ie. **Dublin walking tours** www.walkingtours.ie.

---

## IN THE KNOW
### *Bloomsday Fun*

You can always have a Guinness and an Irish cheddar sandwich. Joyce would approve of the subversion. But here are more "authentic" Bloomsday options:

● **DAVY BYRNES PUB:** Duke Street, where Bloom lunches on a Gorgonzola sandwich and a glass of Burgundy (Episode 8, "Lestrygonians"). www.davybyrnes.com

● **JAMES JOYCE MUSEUM:** Sandycove, where Bloom's day begins (Episode 1, "Telemachus"). www.visitdublin.com

● **SWENY'S PHARMACY:** Lincoln Place, "the worst Pharmacy in the city," where Bloom buys a bar of lemon soap (*Ulysses* Episode 5, "Lotus-Eaters"). The pharmacy is dedicated to preserving itself as it was in Joyce's time and hosts daily readings of the author's work. sweny.ie/site

# LOCH LOMOND

**Revel in the endless daylight and brilliant sunsets of Great Britain's largest lake.**

Loch Lomond, Great Britain's largest lake and the "gateway to the Highlands," lies just half an hour from Glasgow. But it's far more than a trailer for what's to come up north. Loch Lomond and the Trossachs National Park encompasses 720 square miles (1,865 sq km) of ancient forests, inviting villages, walking trails, tranquil lochs, and dramatic mountains to get up high and drink in the views.

Loch Lomond changes in color, weather, and mood by the hour as well as the season. But there's something special about the month of May, when Scotland's long days never seem to end. Soft, slow-burning sunsets last for hours; it can still be light at midnight.

"In May, the skies are decorated by puffy cumulus clouds, forming a dramatic backdrop for photographers, painters, or anyone who wants to enjoy the view," says Stevie Christie of Wilderness Scotland. "After rain showers, the light takes on a magical, translucent quality. Your nose is also in for a treat as spring flowers open up to receive the rain, filling the air with lovely scents."

There are fewer crowds in May, too, before the school vacations—and fewer midges, the tiny, itchy insects that can be a pest during the summer months.

**PLANNING  Scotland** www.visitscotland.com. **Loch Lomond** www.lochlomondtrossachs.org.uk, www.lovelochlomond.com. **Hiking and other activities** www.wildernessscotland.com. Bring a rain jacket and warm clothes.

## FOR FOODIES
### The Oak Tree Inn

This is Scotland, and it's just possible, while out on the hills or cruising the loch, that there could be rain. Muddy hiking boots are welcome at the Oak Tree Inn in Balmaha on the quieter eastern side of the loch. When needed, there's a roaring log fire. The menu has plenty of local produce, including smoked salmon, haggis, and creamy cullen skink (thick soup with smoked haddock, potatoes, and onions). Many of the ales are Scottish brews, and the bar has more than 50 malt whiskies, including the locally distilled Glengoyne. www.oak-tree-inn.co.uk

There's more to Loch Lomond than its sunsets—the lake's also a favorite destination for kayakers, windsurfers, water-skiers, and fishermen.

# GRAND ST. PATRICK'S DAY CELEBRATIONS

**Get your high-steppin' Irish on from Southie to the Costa Blanca.**

### NEW YORK CITY, NEW YORK

The granddaddy of all St. Patrick's Day parades (the first was staged in 1762 by homesick Irishmen serving in the British army) is also the world's largest, attracting more than two million spectators annually. Led by a military unit, the foot-powered procession (no cars or floats allowed) begins at 44th Street and marches on up Fifth Avenue for nearly six hours.

www.saintpatricksdayparade.com/nyc/newyorkcity.htm

### BOSTON, MASSACHUSETTS

In the nation's most Irish state (nearly a quarter of Massachusetts' residents claim Irish ancestry), South Boston is St. Patrick's Day central. Since 1901, "Southie" has hosted the city's colossal parade (held on the Sunday closest to March 17) as thousands of marchers and revelers celebrate all things Emerald. Listen for the mournful wail of bagpipes calling marchers to the Broadway T station starting point.

www.southbostonparade.org

### CHICAGO, ILLINOIS

Parade day (always a Saturday) begins with a wee bit of Irish magic (and 40 lb/18 kg of EPA-approved dye) to color the downtown Chicago River the perfect Kelly green. The St. Patrick's procession begins at noon, with bagpipers, horses, and high-stepping colleens leading the way north on Columbus Drive through Grant Park.

www.chicagostpatsparade.com

### SAVANNAH, GEORGIA

Georgia's first city has been hosting a St. Patrick's Day parade since 1813. It's a three-hour rolling street party held on March 17 (a day earlier if the 17th falls on a Sunday). Book several months in advance to score a Historic District hotel room facing the parade route.

www.savannahsaintpatricksday.com

### MONTSERRAT, WEST INDIES

The first Irish on this "Emerald Isle of the Caribbean" were former indentured servants fleeing religious persecution from neighboring islands in the 1600s. Shamrock passport stamps pay tribute to Montserrat's Hibernian roots, celebrated to a calypso beat during a weeklong St. Patrick's Festival. The Afro-Irish event also commemorates an attempted slave revolt on March 17, 1768.

www.visitmontserrat.com/St_Patricks_Festival

### MONTREAL, QUEBEC, CANADA

Neither rain nor snow has ever canceled the Montreal St. Patrick's Parade. Run consecutively since 1824, the three-hour cavalcade of floats, bands, and costumed characters is traditionally held on the Sunday closest to March 17. Post-parade, the party continues at McKibbin's, Hurley's, the Sir Winston Churchill Complexe, and other downtown pubs.

www.montrealirishparade.com

### DUBLIN, IRELAND

Dublin's St. Patrick's Festival is a four-day celebration of Irish culture and *craic* (good fun). The signature March 17 parade kicks off at noon from Parnell Square, continuing past Trinity College to the end point near St. Patrick's Cathedral. A half million revelers line the 1.6-mile (2.7 km) route, so for a view other than the back of someone's head, splurge for reserved grandstand seating.

www.stpatricksfestival.ie

### BIRMINGHAM, ENGLAND

On the Sunday closest to St. Patrick's Day, the United Kingdom's largest St. Patrick's parade hums and high-steps through Digbeth, Birmingham's postindustrial Irish Quarter. Packed pubs line the route and the dress code trends emerald green, but the passing floats, dancers, and drum corps increasingly reflect the city's cultural diversity.

stpatricksbirmingham.com

### CABO ROIG, SPAIN

Irish holidaymaker hot spot Cabo Roig hosts Spain's biggest St. Patrick's Day parade. Spend the morning at one of the town's white-sand Mediterranean beaches, and then snag a café table along the strip to cheer on the passing marching bands, motorbikes, and Irish dignitaries. A Guinness-fueled fiesta continues under the stars with karaoke, contests, fireworks, flamenco dancers, and more.

www.spain-holiday.com/Cabo-Roig

### AUCKLAND, NEW ZEALAND

New Zealand's largest city hosts the world's first St. Patrick's Day party each year. Since Ireland-to-Auckland emigration began in the 1840s and continues today, there's palpable pride in the city's Irish heritage. Celebrations include a parade, a *fleadh* (dance and music fest), and lighting the 1,076-foot (328 m) Sky Tower green.

www.stpatrick.co.nz

Bagpipers turn their art into a marathon event as they keep pace for the long walk up Fifth Avenue during New York City's St. Patrick's Day parade.

# AMSTERDAM

**Paint the town orange for King's Day, when the whole city turns out to toast the lord of the land.**

Stepping into the living Vermeer that is Amsterdam, with its tableau of canals and tidy homes, is the ultimate Dutch treat. Each spring, that poetic image turns on its head when thousands of merrymakers descend for King's Day, the apex of the Dutch annual calendar, on April 27.

The holiday is a kooky and unlikely show of national pride. Otherwise staid citizens dye their hair orange, don silly costumes, and slurp orange drinks to honor the official birthday of young King Willem-Alexander, known as Queen's Day until his mother Beatrix stepped down in 2013. The frenzy clogs streets in the central canal districts, forcing trams to grind to a halt.

"It's absolute mayhem," says Kimberley Lewis, who runs Randy Roy's walking tours of the red-light district. "The old center turns into one gigantic party." Meanwhile, every square inch of available sidewalk becomes a *vrijmarkt,* an open-air market where any Tom, Dirk, and Antje can hawk a few attic treasures.

Once the party's over, experience Dutch riches of a natural kind at the kaleidoscopic spring flower show at Keukenhof Gardens, 40 minutes southwest of Amsterdam. Wander onto these onetime royal hunting grounds and marvel at the choreographed blazes of blossoms—including, of course, Holland's world-famous tulips—blanketing 80 jaw-dropping acres (32 ha).

**PLANNING  King's Day Festival** www.koninginnedagamsterdam.nl/queensday.html. **Keukenhof Gardens** www.keukenhof.nl. Keukenhof Gardens is open from late March to May.

---

## IN THE KNOW
### *Tulip Mania*

In Amsterdam's flower markets, 20 euros (about $28) will get you a bag of premium bulbs with change left over. But in the 17th century, a speculative fever for exotic tulips pushed values to insane heights. The most precious varieties had frilly edges and streaked petals caused by a louse-borne viral infection. In early 1637, a single Semper Augustus bulb cost more than ten years' wages of a skilled craftsman. Within a matter of weeks, the market collapsed, sparking a wave of bankruptcies. And what of the Semper Augustus? The line died out, its vigor sapped by the very virus the merchants had nurtured.

All the world's an orange blaze—both from hair dye and, on the Amsterdam waterfront, life jackets—during the annual King's Day (formerly Queen's Day).

Dutch politicians and celebrities demonstrate proper herring-eating form at an alfresco seaside festival celebrating the return of their favorite catch.

THE NETHERLANDS

# SCHEVENINGEN

**Join a timeless Dutch bash celebrating fresh "silver from the sea" at this seaside resort.**

Back in the 18th century, Dutch fishermen would raise their festive *vlaggetjes* (pennants) when setting out to catch the first herring of the season. While that tradition has faded, every June a huge crowd gathers in Scheveningen, a beach town near The Hague, to fete Vlaggetjesdag (Flag Day). The harbor district quakes with marching bands, demonstrations of old crafts, and other traditional events. Fishing boats don their finest regalia, while ships of the Dutch Royal Navy lower their gangplanks to visitors.

On the Thursday before Flag Day, the first barrel of Hollandse Nieuwe, fresh young herring, is auctioned off for charity. Fat content is key: The minimum is 16 percent, and a really fine specimen has around 20 percent. The season lasts just six weeks, with the remaining catch frozen to be enjoyed at a later date. "Some fishmongers call it *nieuwe* the entire year," observes Frank Heyn, owner of Frank's Smokehouse in Amsterdam. "But a few months after the auction, it has lost its pizzazz."

At bustling harbor stalls, staggering numbers of plump filets are gobbled down with raw onions and pickles and chased with shots of *korenwijn*, a Dutch gin. The proper technique? Hold the herring aloft by the tail, and bite upward.

**PLANNING  Scheveningen** www.scheveningendenhaag.com, www.denhaag.nl. Dates for the Hollandse Nieuwe auction and festivities may change on short notice. For background on Flag Day, see www.vlaggetjesdag.com.

## BEST OF THE BEST
*Mauritshuis in The Hague*

The coastal scene at Scheveningen will have added meaning after a visit to the Mauritshuis museum in The Hague. Among the trove of 17th-century Golden Age masterworks is Johannes Lingelbach's "Departure of King Charles II from Scheveningen for England." The extensive collection of Dutch and Flemish paintings is spread over 16 rooms of this majestic, beautifully symmetrical 17th-century mansion overlooking the Hofvijver (Court Pond). Among its other highlights: Rembrandt's "Anatomy Lesson of Dr. Nicolaes Tulp" and Johannes Vermeer's "Girl With a Pearl Earring." (Due to renovations, select paintings will move to the Gemeentemuseum through mid-2014; others will be on tour.) www.mauritshuis.nl

Their name may be the "common starling," but there's nothing ordinary about the sight of a million starlings flying against a sunset backdrop.

DENMARK

# WADDEN SEA NATIONAL PARK

**Witness one of nature's most kinetic phenomena when waves of starlings form in the springtime skies.**

A tangle of salty, squelching reed beds on the western coast of Denmark, wafer-thin Wadden Sea National Park—the country's largest nature reserve—is perfectly placed on a migratory superhighway. For birdwatchers, the prime slot is mid-March to April, when the tall, woody grasses turn a beautiful, tender green, just in time for a mesmerizing aerial ballet known as the *sort sol*, or "black sun."

The spectacle occurs at dusk, when swarms of more than a million starlings erupt from their feeding grounds and etch amazing patterns into a darkening sky. Hawks, eagles, and other birds of prey on the hunt prompt the starlings to take on especially dramatic, ever-changing formations—a beautiful but potentially deadly show.

The best place to go is the coastal Tønder Marsh in southern Jutland, not far from the German border. While pinpoint accuracy isn't possible, a savvy tour guide can narrow the odds of spotting the flocks. "We have people in the field who find the starlings ahead of time," says Iver Gram, owner of Dansk Natursafari, which leads 25,000 visitors into the UNESCO-listed region every year. "Then we crouch in the reeds around sunset to watch and wait."

PLANNING **Denmark** www.visitdenmark.com. **Wadden Sea Center and starling tours** www.vadehavs centret.dk. **Danish national parks** www.danmarksnationalparker.dk.

## BEST OF THE BEST
*Møgeltønder Church*

While waiting for dusk and the starlings to dance, pay a visit to Møgeltønder, a well-scrubbed hamlet about 5 miles (8 km) from Tønder Marsh. The town's 13th-century Møgeltønder Church boasts one of Denmark's most lavish interiors. In the beautiful Romanesque nave, a creaking wooden ceiling is the canvas for biblical events framed in billowing clouds, while the elaborate four-winged altar (ca 1500) shines with gilt detail. Amid the riches, a sly wit emerges: The carved pulpit is held aloft by cherubs, while impish faces peer from pipes on the organ, the country's oldest.

# MONTE-CARLO

**Rub elbows with *tout le monde* at the weeklong Grand Prix, when speed and glamour mix along the French Riviera.**

I t's not the screaming metal demons that make the Monaco Grand Prix such a singular motor-racing experience; it's the ability of mere mortals to walk the track—and perhaps mingle casually with the world's greatest drivers—just hours before and after the furious Formula One action each May.

The whole of race week in the tiny principality is that way. You might find yourself sitting next to racing champ Sebastian Vettel at the trackside Chez Bacco restaurant or sharing elbow room at the bar with Will Smith in the posh La Rascasse nightclub, a darling with drivers and celebrities who populate the annual race turned see-and-be-seen event.

Duane Penner, who arranges customized Grand Prix trips, calls it a "truly iconic event." He elaborates: "It's got royalty and beautiful people parties. It takes place on the French Riviera. It's got Ferrari and Mercedes-Benz. Just walking around you feel like you're part of something."

Get a feel for the 2.1-mile (3.3 km) course by walking or biking the sinuous street circuit on one of those blue-sky spring days that add to Monte-Carlo's glitter. And watch Sunday's race from a private terrace perched high above the track—sipping Dom Pérignon, of course, because during race week in Monaco, only the best will do.

**PLANNING Monaco** www.visitmonaco.com. Customized tours of the Grand Prix *(www.roadtrips.com)* include private party invitations, helicopter transfers to and from Nice Airport, and race viewing from a private balcony at the Hôtel de Paris.

## IN THE KNOW
### *Europe's Other Great Races*

● **ISLE OF MAN TT:** Since 1907, public highways have been used for this hard-core spring motorcycle event on this island in the Irish Sea. Racers reach speeds exceeding 130 mph (210 kph) on the 38-mile (61 km) circuit. www.iomtt.com

● **LE MANS:** First held in 1923, Le Mans is the world's oldest and most prestigious endurance race, lasting 24 hours. High-performance cars compete on an 8.5-mile (13.7 km) circuit in western France. www.lemans.org

● **RALLY FINLAND:** Raced in Jyväskylä on gravel roads in souped-up versions of ordinary street cars, Scandinavia's top auto race spans three days in late July or early August. The course is known for its high-speed turns and big air jumps. www.nesteoilrallyfinland.fi

City driving takes on a whole new meaning as the Monaco Grand Prix roars around Monte-Carlo's narrow streets.

One of Paris's 37 spans across the Seine, the Alexander III Bridge commemorates friendship between Russia and France.

FRANCE

# PARIS

**Renew your spirit with the city's irresistible spring display—in gardens, restaurants, and cafés and on the court.**

Paris radiates a special glow in spring, when flowers decorate the streets and parks, people-watchers luxuriate in sidewalk cafés, restaurant menus take on a lighter touch, and the season seems to actually sing—with an utterly Parisian accent.

To appreciate the best of the season, take to the streets. As you promenade from one *quartier* to the next, you'll admire clouds of fragrant color—daffodils, tulips, hyacinths, wisteria, lilacs, roses, peonies—framing ancient arches, columns, and stone walls. "Strolling the city's parks and streetlets when the almond trees pop into minty bloom, you feel like you've wandered into a Jean-Jacques Sempé illustration," says *National Geographic Traveler* magazine writer Olivia Stren, who has visited family in Paris all her life.

One favorite floral spot is little Square Vert Gallant near Pont Neuf, where manicured flower beds decorate a Parisian scene of plane trees and grass-framed promenades surrounded by the Seine. Another is the Musée Rodin's spectacularly fragrant rose garden (where picnics are allowed).

For something even more special, head to one of the city's many painstakingly maintained parks and gardens. Whispers of France's departed royals linger in the Left Bank's Jardin du

*As you promenade from one* quartier *to the next, you'll admire clouds of fragrant color— daffodils, tulips, hyacinths, wisteria, lilacs, roses, peonies —framing ancient arches, columns, and stone walls.*

The Eiffel Tower is an amazing site any time of year, but in spring, flowers are painstakingly groomed around its base to add a photogenic touch.

While away the hours at Les Deux Magots discussing the works of former regulars Hemingway and Sartre—or give over to people-watching.

Luxembourg, where you'll find statue-dotted formal gardens and an orchard filled with apple and pear trees glorious in their peak bloom. Relatively unknown, the Parc Floral de Paris is a gorgeous botanical garden in the Bois de Vincennes, showcasing 3,000 manicured plant varieties from around the world, including magnificent roses; stroll its grassy paths, then settle down in an Impressionist landscape to enjoy a *pique-nique* in the sun. And don't miss the Promenade Plantée, a defunct elevated railway line beginning near the Bastille where springtime cherry trees, chestnut trees, and colorful flower gardens accent an afternoon stroll.

To bring some blooms home (or at least to your hotel room), visit one of the many flower vendors along the Seine, perhaps Marché d'Aligre on the Place d'Aligre, Cler Fleurs *(46 Rue Cler),* or the picturesque Marché aux Fleurs near Notre-Dame (a flower market that on Sundays switches to a sweet-sounding bird market).

## SPOTS FOR A PERFECT PICNIC

A picnic in Paris in springtime is a must. Be authentically Parisian in the huge Bois de Boulogne, on the western edge of the 16th Arrondissement: Rent a boat and explore the islets dotting the lake. Commissioned by Emperor Napoleon III, the Parc des Buttes Chaumont is a hilly landscape, with trails and winding pathways, located in the 19th Arrondissement. And the famed Jardin des Tuileries outside the Louvre is replete with a series of graceful sculptures, fascinating bronze works, and wonderful urban views. Don't forget to bring a bottle of wine. Three wonderful selections for the season: a sparkling Tissot Crémant du Jura rosé; a 2010 Domaine du Bagnol cassis, another rosé; or a 2009 cabernet, Gauthier Bourgueil Soif de Jour. These wines go with any food. *Santé!*

## THE CAFÉ SCENE

When all is said and done, there's no better way to celebrate the end of the winter doldrums than at an outdoor café—take a book, order a coffee, and bask beneath the bright blue sky. You'll find suitable cafés throughout the city; for some of its most famous, head to the Carrefour Vavin (renamed Place Pablo Picasso) and seek out Le Select, Le Dôme, La Rotonde, La Coupole, or even the Dingo American Bar, where in April 1925 Ernest Hemingway introduced himself to F. Scott Fitzgerald.

In this city of gourmands, Parisian restaurants update their menus with the season's finest ingredients—including spring lamb, plump strawberries, bright green beans, white asparagus, morel mushrooms, spring chèvre, and daily catches of John Dory, cod, and turbot. You can enjoy a chef's take on the season or peruse a farmers' market for your own feast. Julia Child frequented the market on Rue Cler; other excellent markets include Bastille and Place Monge.

PLANNING  **Paris** www.viator.com. **Guided tours** www.toursbylocals.com. **Food and wine** www.foodandwine.com, www.eatinparis.com, www.localwineevents.com.

Champions often take flight at the French Open, aka Roland-Garros, named for an early French aviator.

# Top 10

# SPRING VINEYARDS

**Savor the pleasures that come with a spring visit to these outstanding wineries.**

### INNISKILLIN WINES

*Niagara-on-the-Lake, Ontario, Canada*

Canada is the epicenter of ice wine, which is made from grapes harvested in subfreezing temperatures, which concentrates their flavor, complexity, and sugars. Inniskillin helped pioneer the process in Canada, and its tastings show surprising range. Its on-site restaurant pairs food expertly.

*inniskillin.com*

### PENNER-ASH WINE CELLARS

*Newberg, Oregon*

Oregon's Willamette Valley has become one of the world's celebrated wine destinations. The reason: Pinot Noir. While you'll find dozens of notable producers, Penner-Ash Wine Cellars may be one of the prettiest (and friendliest). With bands of windows and a floating roofline, the tasting room and its views are as memorable as the wines.

*www.pennerash.com*

### JUSTIN VINEYARDS AND WINERY

*Paso Robles, California*

Even beer drinkers know that Napa and Sonoma produce great wines, but recently attention has turned south. Paso Robles on California's Central Coast produces rich reds, including Cabernet Sauvignon and Syrah. At Justin Vineyards and Winery, you'll find a striking Tuscan-style tasting room, restaurant, and B&B, along with its Cabernet-based Isosceles blend.

*www.justinwine.com*

### PEDERNALES CELLARS

*Stonewall, Texas*

The Texas Hill Country, with its rolling countryside and spring-fed rivers, once evoked images of the Wild West. But now it has vineyards, too, and Pedernales Cellars offers one of the prettiest places to take it all in. Come at sunset to sip award-winning Viogniers and Tempranillos. John Wayne never had it this good.

*pedernalescellars.com*

### LAURA HARTWIG

*Santa Cruz, Chile*

About two hours south of Santiago, vineyards crowd the compact Colchagua Valley between the Andes and the Pacific. By all means, taste the Carménère, Chile's signature grape long misidentified as Merlot. At the boutique winery Laura Hartwig, visitors pass polo fields and tennis courts before arriving at a traditional-style bodega.

### CAVAS RECAREDO

*Sant Sadurní d'Anoia, Spain*

Spain calls its sparkling wine Cava because the French have claim to the more familiar name Champagne. But the bubbly produced in the Penedès region south of Barcelona is just as festive. Unlike the area's industrial-scale wineries, Cavas Recaredo still produces by hand and uses Earth-friendly biodynamic methods.

*recaredo.es*

### DOMAINE DU DALEY

*Lutry, Switzerland*

You'll marvel at the Lake Geneva view, but don't forget the vineyard. Swiss wines are often overlooked because the country keeps most to itself and exports very little. Domaine du Daley, which dates from 1392, grows 12 grape varieties. Make sure to sip the Chasselas, a dry, fruity wine perfect with raclette cheese.

*www.daley.ch*

### VECCHIE TERRE DI MONTEFILI

*Greve in Chianti, Italy*

"Super Tuscan" sounds like a comic book hero, but it's a type of Italian wine that once flaunted the regulations governing blends and labeling. Sample some at family-run Vecchie Terre di Montefili, south of Florence. In addition to the super Tuscans, try the Chianti Classico—it's a pure 100 percent Sangiovese, instead of a blend.

*vecchieterredimontefili.it/eng*

### CRAMELE RECAS

*Recas, Romania*

The Roman god Bacchus supposedly came from Romania, and even now Cramele Recas, among the hillside vineyards in the Transylvania region, produces surprisingly good but inexpensive Cabernet Sauvignons and white blends. And its vampire and werewolf labels are just fun.

*www.recaswine.ro*

### SERESIN ESTATE

*Renwick, Marlborough, New Zealand*

Sauvignon Blanc put New Zealand on the wine map—and gave visitors another reason to visit the country's scenic South Island. At Seresin, grapes grow without pesticides and are harvested by hand. The vineyard offers tastings at outdoor tables among the vines and a chance to sample the internationally trained winemaker's olive oil as well.

*seresin.co.nz*

Switzerland's Dézaley wine region, planted since the 12th century, overlooks Lake Geneva from breathtakingly steep cliffs.

With banners aloft and their faith strong, Romanies honor St. Sara, who is said to have arrived on these shores by boat.

FRANCE

# SAINTES-MARIES-DE-LA-MER

**Join a colorful springtime celebration of ancient miracles as the region rejoices with a colorful Romany pilgrimage.**

A marshland frontier that lies in France's Provence region between the ancient city of Arles and the Mediterranean, the Camargue is famed for its long-horned bulls and magnificent white horses with flowing manes. A supreme bird reserve, it's home to nearly 300 species, the most famous denizen probably being the great flamingo. To watch these lanky pink birds gliding effortlessly in the pure blue sky is one of Provence's most memorable sites.

### AN ANCIENT LEGEND

The landscape's quiet mood changes dramatically in spring. On May 24 and 25 every year, bedecked in colorful skirts and scarves with the jingling of silver jewelry filling the air, thousands of Romanies flock here for baptisms, family reunions, and to pay homage to their revered St. Sara, the Egyptian servant girl who accompanied a boatful of early Christians here around A.D. 40.

Legend has it that soon after Jesus Christ was crucified, three Marys—Mary Magdalene; Mary Jacobé, the Virgin Mary's sister; and Mary Salomé, mother of the Apostles James and John—along with their servant Sara, were shoved out to sea without sails or oars. They

## IN THE KNOW
*Bull Games*

Throughout the Camargue in summer, the region's semiwild long-horned bulls are rounded up, destined for the bullring. In the *courses camarguaises,* as the bullfights are called, the bull is never killed. Instead, the events are a thrilling cat-and-mouse game between the bull and *raseteurs,* who attempt to unhook strings and tassels from the animal's horns with handheld rakes. Points are awarded for retrieving different items. The crowd erupts in screams and shouts as the men egg on the bull, trying to make him charge. The most prestigious games—July's Cocarde d'Or—occur in Arles, with others taking place in Nîmes, Tarascon, and Saintes-Maries-de-la-Mer.

drifted and finally washed ashore here, where the settlement became known as Saintes-Maries-de-la-Mer ("Saint Marys of the Sea"). The grateful Marys built a chapel, where the relics of Mary Salomé and Mary Jacobé are said to be preserved. Beside them stands a statue of their honorary saint Sara, covered with a huge layer of dresses provided as offerings.

## PROCESSION TO THE SEA

On May 24, Romany pilgrims partake in a Catholic Mass inside the Église des Saintes-Maries, followed by a grand, cacophonous procession that transports Sara's statue from the church to the sea, escorted by elegant white Camargue horses. The pilgrims strain to touch and kiss the statue, believing they will receive health-giving properties in return. "Being there was magic," says Delazad Deghati, a film student who has spent time shooting the festival. "All these people, most of whose lives are not easy, were enjoying themselves immensely. Colors, dresses—everything—was warm and happy."

The statue is bathed in the sea as pilgrims dance and throw flowers to bless the water. The singing crowd then accompanies Sara back to the church amid cheers and the peal of church bells. The festivities continue late into the evening, with the procession repeating itself the next day. "To be a part of this celebration made me nearly cry from happiness," Deghati says.

PLANNING  **Saintes-Maries-de-la-Mer** www.saintesmaries.com. **Provence** www.beyond.fr. The ancient city of Arles, 45 minutes north, has many options for lodging *(www.avignon-et-provence.com).*

## GREAT STAYS
*The Camargue*

● **L'AUBERGE CAVALIÈRE DU PONT DES BANNES:** Individual lodges constructed with traditional adobe walls and thatched roofs. Inside, though, are handsome, modern interiors. www.auberge cavaliere.com

● **MAS DE LA FOUQUE:** A traditional Camargue hotel, with large rooms, tiled floors, and wooden beams. Private terraces overlook the lagoon and park. www.masdelafouque.com

● **MAS DE PEINT:** A working ranch in the center of the Camargue, offering horseback rides through the wild countryside, this farmstead is a remarkable combination of elegance and authenticity. www.masdepeint.com

In a land that's also home to hundreds of varieties of birds, pilgrims pay homage at the Church of Saintes-Maries-de-la-Mer.

The terraced gardens fronting Lake Como at Villa Monastero showcase sculpture-ornamented promenades and a collection of citrus trees.

ITALY

# LAKE COMO

**Surround yourself with the sweet, spring-scented life amid grand villas and perfectly tended gardens.**

From the water at night, the lake seems to have stepped out of time. The mansions along the shore cast their lights, glittering like stars in the ferry's wake. The faint tinkle of fine stemware and laughter spills out an open hotel window, patios full of people shaking off winter like they've just come out of hibernation. Como, about 30 miles (48 km) long, is Europe's deepest lake, dropping more than 1,300 feet (410 m). But it's a lake to be on, not in—a famous actor's house swallowed up the one good public beach—and the water has paid the price for the region's industry and agricultural runoff. Still, that's meant nothing to the views: Ripening vineyards stretch up the hills, and each lakefront house looks like it's simply waiting for the return of a slower, quieter time when servants were cheap and cocktail hour went on all through the long spring twilight, scented by countless blossoms.

Comfortable, efficient ferries connect every section of the lake, and that's the best way to see Lake Como; yes, there's a road, but it's more an apology than a good way to get around. From the water, Como best reveals its secrets: Villas hidden from land by trees and vines show their secret faces over fresh lawns; hotels that have hosted royalty and rock stars, honeymoons and golden anniversaries; glimpses of gardens in new spring bloom; fountains

*From the water at night, the lake seems to have stepped out of time. The mansions along the shore cast their lights, glittering like stars in the ferry's wake.*

One area, an endless supply
of gifts: Varenna's lake views,
spring produce, and a general
understanding that, here,
there is no reason to rush

Perched on the
edge of Lake Como,
Varenna's winding
lanes and rustic
fishermen's houses
have views to the
Italian Alps.

unleashed from winter's freeze; and artwork through loggias. The warming spring air is like a caress from the water, as the lake again invites exploration.

## INDULGE ALONG COBBLESTONE STREETS

On the south-central shore, nestled on the peninsula where the lake splits like a "Y," lies Bellagio, a small village of twisted cobblestone streets and stairways hiding pastry and gelato shops that seem to appear like welcome buds among the high-fashion boutiques. The gray stones of the 12th-century Church of San Giacomo peer over blazing white luxe hotels down toward the lake's smooth, blue water. Restaurants fight for attention with the spring's first produce, and around it all, villas show what a couple hundred years of paying attention to the gardens can do with hillsides, now solid colors. No view ever seems to appear twice, as if each corner brings a new lake into being. The town has been famous as a resort since Roman times. After a walking tour or an afternoon strolling its charming, winding streets, it will be easy to see why the town's nickname is the "Pearl of the Lake."

## TAKE IN THE VIEWS

Bellagio isn't the only town on the lake; the city of Como still has its ancient walls and a town center as twisted as a maze. There, you can catch a funicular and ride up into the Alps to Brunate, almost a half mile (0.8 km) above the lake, for a view of scenery clear to Switzerland. Heartier souls can take one of the hiking trails on the edge of town, catching the last patches of snow in shadowed groves. Como's also famous for silk, with a museum that shows what Marco Polo was after in China, and shops where the silk patterns form their own gardens of color.

## LIVE VICARIOUSLY: THE HEIGHT OF LUXURY

But maybe the best thing to do on Lake Como is simply see what it was like when the living was easy. Check out the mansions, grand villas surrounded by landscape that looks like it's been tended by tweezers and tiny scissors, the fragrant blossoms of *gel-somino* (jasmine) climbing walls like ivy. The 17th-century Villa Carlotta has an expanse of perfect, perfumed gardens, where the season's dazzling rhododendrons, azaleas, and an array of rare plants will be showing off now. The Villa del Balbianello started as a Franciscan monastery, was turned into a luxury home in the late 18th century, and ended up as the backdrop in a *Star Wars* movie.

That's Lake Como in the spring: anything you dream, surrounded by flowers.

PLANNING **Lake Como** www.discovercomo .com. **Ferry service** www.navigazionelaghi .it. **Bellagio** www.bellagiolakecomo.com. **Villa Carlotta** www.villacarlotta.it. **Villa del Balbi-anello** villabalbianello.com. The area is best reached by train from Milan (*www.trenitalia.com*).

Ancient busts at Villa Melzi in Bellagio encourage visitors to step outside into the sunshine.

# GIRONA FLOWER FESTIVAL

"The medieval city of Girona overflows with creativity during its annual spring flower festival, the Temps de Flors. Surprising floral creations spill down cathedral steps and bloom-inspired art installations fill city squares and stone-walled courtyards."

—ABIGAIL KING, *NATIONAL GEOGRAPHIC TRAVELER* WRITER

The northeastern Spanish city of Girona transforms annually between May 7 and 15 into one enormous garden, covered with colorful floral arrangements for the Girona Flower Festival, known in Catalan as the Temps de Flors. *Pictured:* Floral artists put finishing touches to a festival street mural.

# SEVILLE

**Revel in Holy Week and the romantic spirit of flamenco that envelops this Andalusian city each spring.**

A click, a stutter step, a stomp. Some cities have a heartbeat, others a pulse. But Seville is one of the few that comes with its own full-blown musical score, with flamenco pouring out of every open doorway.

Dancing to its own music, Seville has always been "a romantic city that looks away from the rest of the country," says National Geographic photographer Jad Davenport, who grew up in Spain. "It's the New Orleans of the peninsula. You could always go to Seville, forget reality for a few days, and soak up the sense of romantic adventure that permeates Andalusia."

And there's no better time than spring: Come Holy Week, leading up to Easter, the entire city turns out for processions, carrying *pasos* (portable shrines) through the streets. The oldest of these parades go back nearly 500 years. Kids beg for candy, while locals improvising flamenco songs line the routes.

Just two weeks later, the streets fill yet again, this time with costumed revelers for the Feria de Sevilla, the Spring Fair. Decorated tents line the banks of the Guadalquivir, and Manzanilla wine flows faster than the river itself. It's just another part of what locals will tell you is the *dulcera de vivir:* the sweet life of Seville.

**PLANNING  Seville** www.turismosevilla.org, www.sevillaonline.es. **Flamenco** www.sevillaflamenco.com. For Holy Week and the Spring Fair, plan far ahead for hotels.

---

### BEST OF THE BEST
*Flamenco Dance*

Taking the flamenco out of Seville would be like taking the hot dogs away from Coney Island—it simply can't be done: Guitars and castanets are everywhere. In springtime, as restaurants open their doors to the warm evening breezes, the music pours out, with dozens of shows to choose from. Wander from one to the next, noshing tapas along the way, or head to the Museo del Baile Flamenco. Tour the exhibits for a history of the art before the show starts. Better yet, stick around for a class to start stomping yourself; then you're not just visiting Seville in the spring, you're a part of its very heartbeat. www.flamencomuseum.com

---

Nazarenos—wearing pointed hoods called *capirotes,* symbolizing repentance and grief—lead an Easter Week procession to the Seville Cathedral.

A squacco heron takes flight in Murighiol, Romania, not far from where the Danube spills into the Black Sea.

## ROMANIA
# THE DANUBE DELTA

**Spy on spring's nesting pelicans and scores of other birds at the mouth of Europe's famous river.**

The Danube, Europe's second longest river (after the Volga), wends some 1,770 miles (2,850 km) through a dozen countries before finally emptying into the Black Sea at Romania's port of Tulcea. Here, nine diverging channels sprawl for hundreds of square miles, creating a vast marshy wetland home to an unrivaled ecosystem.

In spring, enough rare communities of birds convene to make even the nonbirder's heart race. "Birding in the Danube Delta during springtime is one of the most spectacular events," says tour guide Daniel Petrescu. "The huge number and variety of birds present is unique in Europe: colorful rollers, bee-eaters, hoopoes, and red-backed shrikes."

April marks the start of the bird migration season, when new birds arrive and nest among the many reeds and inlets until September's cooler winds send them on their way again. Come May, the rains are gone and the air is warmer, making it prime time for visitors.

Much of the delta is closed to vehicle traffic, so the best way to observe the birds is by ferry from Tulcea to remoter inland destinations such as Sulina or Sfântu Gheorghe that are closer to the sea. The tiny hamlet of Sfântu Gheorghe lies at the end of the southernmost channel and abuts a pristine beach. It's a favorite haunt of the white pelican.

**PLANNING Bird Watching in the Danube Delta** www.ddbra.ro. The Danube Delta Biosphere Reserve Authority (DDBRA) is charged with protecting the delta. Its website is an excellent starting point for getting your feet wet.

### FOR FOODIES
*Danube Delta Fish Soup*

The delta usually is presented as an adventure or outdoor destination, with hiking, birding, and boating the big lures. But its vast waters also offer food lovers something to savor. Throughout the region, cooks pride themselves on serving what just might be the best fish soup there is. The local, seemingly infinite variety combines both fresh- and saltwater species, including carp, turbot, sturgeon, and *somn*, a giant catfish native to the region. The soup is served with garlic sauce and a hearty side of Romanian-style grits called *mămăligă*.

Even the Dutch would have to admit that Istanbul knows a thing or two about tulips. Here, blooms welcome visitors to the Hippodrome.

## TURKEY
# ISTANBUL

**Discover the eternal city in spring when its ancient stone streets light up with flowers and festivals.**

Thousands of years of history bridge East and West in this Islamic city, set in both Europe and Asia. Today Istanbul—once Constantinople, the capital of the Eastern Roman Empire, Byzantium, and the Ottoman Empire—is the social and economic heart of modern Turkey. One of the greatest joys for visitors is getting lost in its twisting neighborhoods and hearing the call to prayer echo against the stone buildings. But in spring, you will find this ancient metropolis on the Bosporus delivers many bonuses, from the kaleidoscope of brilliant flowers to a series of welcoming festivals.

### COLORFUL TULIPS

A highlight is the Tulip Festival, when Istanbul bursts with these colorful flowers, native to the Asian steppes. "April is a great month in Istanbul, with the whole city in bloom and everyone heading to all the outdoor cafés and outdoor venues," says Turkey travel expert Earl Starkey of Sophisticated Travel. "In a city of 13 million people, there is something happening all the time, but spring is always special."

Visitors will find Istanbul's creative juices blossoming in the spring, too, as art gallery openings and events proliferate, a perfect way to know the city a little more deeply than merely by its monuments. The Istanbul International Film Festival takes place from late

### BEST OF THE BEST
*Topkapi Palace*

This sprawling palace complex, once the seat of Ottoman power, dates back to 1459 and overlooks both the Bosporus and the Golden Horn. Referred to by many as a paradise on Earth, its mix of styles reflects the height of Ottoman construction. Visitors get a sense of palace intrigue touring rooms where heads of state met the sultan, or where his harem of women was kept. The concubines could only gaze onto the gardens—especially beautiful in spring—through windows and balconies where wooden slats, it is said, barred any man but the ruler from laying eyes on them. topkapipalace.com

March to mid-April, bringing a cross-continental flare and a chance to add intellectual conversation to your vacation. National Sovereignty and Children's Day will help you understand the country's unique history, with its balancing act between a solemn remembrance of the founder of Turkey's republican government and a festive, countrywide show of pride in its children—and future. (In Ankara, the capital, kids even sit in parliament for the day and "govern.")

## MUSIC, MOTION, AND SPRING WISHES

Among Starkey's favorite spring events is the Hidrellez Festival, in the first week of May, which honors a prophet whose history dates back over 3,000 years. Visitors who come will find themselves surrounded by music and motion, with the action centered in Ahirkapi Park near the waterfront. Turkish, Balkan, and Romany musicians entertain the throngs who come for the event, with people eating *döner* kabobs, *kokoreç*, grilled sheep intestines, and other Turkish specialties and drinking lemonade and tea served from samovars—all to provide energy for dancing throughout the streets of the city. A highlight is attaching notes with wishes and dreams to the festival's *nahil*, or "wish tree." You'll want to ask to return again to Istanbul in the spring, or in any season.

PLANNING  **Istanbul** www.goturkey.com. **Istanbul Tulip Festival,** www.visitistanbul.org/istanbul-tulip-festival.html; **Hidrellez Festival,** hidrellez.org/english.asp; **Istanbul International Film Festival,** film.iksv .org. Sophisticated Travel *(www.sophisticated-travel.com)* offers custom trips to Istanbul and other parts of Turkey and surrounding countries.

Put a sound track on your exploration of Ahirkapi Park with the help of the bands that strike up tunes during the Hidrellez Festival.

## SINAI AWAKENING
# *Bruce Feiler*
## St. Catherine's Monastery

I bolted upright the first time I heard the bells. I held my ears when I realized the clamor was just outside my door. And when the ringing showed no signs of stopping, I stuffed my head back under the covers. A carillon 15 centuries old; a wake-up call older than the clock.

St. Catherine's Monastery, in the southern mountains of the Sinai Peninsula, was founded 1,500 years ago by monks who believed it was where Moses heard the voice of God. The dozen or so monks who still live there today hold services five times a day in Byzantine Greek.

The night before, I decided to go for a stroll in the dark. I tiptoed down a set of stairs, past a room that contains all the skulls of all the monks who've ever lived at the monastery. They spill out of a crypt like Cheerios onto the floor. At the end of the alley is a large, raspberry bramble about 10 feet (3 m) tall. The monks say this particular bush has been here since Moses passed by 3,200 years ago.

I sat down to reflect. With the light from gas lamps and the shadow of the mountain above that some believe is where Moses received the Ten Commandments, I felt a sense of awe. But then I noticed something by the base of the bush. It was a fire extinguisher. At first, I thought it was just an eyesore, and then I realized: Is this in case the burning bush catches on fire?! And if it does, should I put it out or look for the face of God?

I tried to put the image out of my mind, but then a white cat with a brown patch over its eye jumped out of the bush, landed at my feet, and screeched. I ran back to my room to brush up on my Byzantine Greek.

Spring is Passover, when the Israelites are said to have left Egypt and walked this route. Spring is Easter, filled with symbols of renewal. In almost 20 years visiting sacred sites around the world, I find St. Catherine's the holiest place I've ever been. It defies centuries. It houses an impressive cross-section of different architectural and religious traditions. And to me, it defines spring.

*Bruce Feiler* (www.brucefeiler.com) *is the author of the international best-seller* Walking the Bible *and host of the PBS series* Walking the Bible *and the forthcoming* Sacred Journeys with Bruce Feiler. *His latest book is* The Secrets of Happy Families.

*"In almost 20 years visiting sacred sites around the world, I find St. Catherine's the holiest place I've ever been."*

In the stone kitchen of St. Catherine's, priests and Bedouins gather to shape bread dough into loaves.

# FEZ

### Take in far-flung sounds in Morocco's spiritual and cultural capital.

Twelve-hundred-year-old Fez, Morocco's intellectual, artistic, and spiritual heart, has forever beguiled with its collision of the medieval and the modern (this is the sort of place where you'll find mule-cart drivers busy texting on their mobiles). The weeklong Festival of World Sacred Music, like Fez itself, also enchants with its colorful contrasts. The summertime event woos visitors with its musical rencontres, collaborations between artists hailing from wildly diverging cultures and traditions—such diverse talents as Icelandic rock star Bjork, American folk legend Joan Baez, and Congolese-French rapper Abd al Malik.

In the daytime, find cool reprieve from the city's sun-torched summer streets in the Andalusian gardens of the Musée Batha, a 19th-century sultanate palace. Here, afternoon recitals—where you might hear *qanun*-accompanied Aramaic songs, the sounds of Tuareg nomad groups, Koranic phrases set to gospel harmonies, Senegalese *mbalax* rhythms, or Blue Note–style jazz—are set to storybook effect under the shade of an enormous Barbary oak tree. Post concert, wander through the museum, now home to a formidable collection of Fassi embroidery and 14th-century ceramics. By night, head to the Bab al Makina, the gold-plated gates of the Royal Palace. Grand and moonlit, the palace doors serve as romantic and moody backdrop to the festival's nighttime concerts.

**PLANNING  Fez Festival of World Sacred Music** www.fesfestival.com

## GREAT STAYS
### La Maison Bleue

Festivalgoers who spent the evening at the threshold of a palace can also bid *bonne nuit* in one. In the heart of the city's labyrinthine medina, the Maison Bleue is the lavish former home of renowned Moroccan judge, professor, and astrologer Sidi Mohammed El Abbadi (the place was restored by his grandchildren). If the palatial decor (blue *zellij* tile work, carved cedar doors, spouting fountains, canopy beds) pampers them, guests here can also indulge in history: A library houses antique bound books, texts, and oil paintings. www.maisonbleue.com

With hot pink lights setting off the night sky, the Belen Maya Spanish Dance Company takes to the stage at the Festival of World Sacred Music.

Hikers survey the scene from the peak of one of the Atlas Mountains in Imilchil, Morocco. Next stop, the 13,671-foot (4,167 m) peak of Jebel Toubkal?

MOROCCO

# ATLAS MOUNTAINS

**Explore the strongholds of Berber culture in the villages and valleys when the spring thaw clears the way.**

Berbers proudly call themselves Imazighen, or free people. Meet these fiercely independent tribes in settlements tucked below one of the Atlas Mountains's highest peaks, Jebel Toubkal. Whether you plan a rigorous overnight hike to the top at 13,671 feet (4,167 m) or make a day trip from Marrakech to villages like Imlil, the spring thaw makes the season the most exhilarating time to visit. Melting snow rushes through the streams of the Ourika Valley and budding trees make an unforgettable contrast as you ascend from the arid landscape of the city. Overhead, massive cumulus clouds drift over the hills, alternating with brilliant sunlight.

Village life revolves around Islamic icons: the mosque, madrassa, bread oven, public fountain, and hammam, a communal steam bathhouse. Days are punctuated with chants echoing among the stone valleys of muezzins calling worshippers to prayer. And in this traditional culture, you will rarely glimpse a woman's tattooed face, a mark of her tribe; most stay far from sight.

"It's what I would call the real Morocco," says Mike McHugo, owner of Kasbah du Toubkal, an Imlil guesthouse. Be sure to pack an extra bag, along with your bargaining skills; you'll want to shop for brilliant, handwoven wool carpets.

**PLANNING  Atlas Mountains** www.visitmorocco.com. Western High Atlas operators offer custom tours of the Toubkal National Park region by foot, mule, or camel. The area is an easy 37-mile (60 km) drive from Marrakech.

## GREAT STAYS
*Kasbah du Toubkal*

A former mountain fortress, or casbah, the Kasbah du Toubkal offers modern, comfortable lodgings with unforgettable views of the High Atlas. Spring's longer, warmer days allow you to relax on its sunny terrace or to spend a day trekking rocky paths. In the evening, the Kasbah offers warming tagine stews and conversations with other travelers around a blazing fireplace. As you return to your en suite room, stop to appreciate the frosty night sky, studded with stars. The Kasbah devotes some of its profits to Education for All, a charity that supports secondary education for girls. www.kasbahdutoubkal.com

# MAGNIFICENT GARDENS

**Inhale spring's breathtaking perfume in extraordinary landscapes that range from vast to intimate.**

### BUTCHART GARDENS

*Vancouver, Canada*

This former limestone quarry was transformed into magnificent gardens in 1904. Located on Vancouver Island, its rolling landscape features more than a million bedding plants from 700 varieties for uninterrupted blooming from March through October. Wander through the Sunken Garden in the original quarry and the Japanese Garden facing Butchart Cove.
*www.butchartgardens.com*

### BROOKLYN BOTANIC GARDENS

*Brooklyn, New York*

Founded in 1910, this sprawling garden in the heart of Brooklyn highlights more than 6,000 plant species. The Bonsai Museum showcases some 350 carefully sculpted trees, one of the largest collections on public display outside Japan. In late April, more than 45,000 bluebells burst into flower and picnickers gather beneath the Cherry Esplanade's blooming trees.
*www.bbg.org*

### JARDIM BOTÂNICO DE CURITIBA

*Curitiba, Brazil*

Located in the capital of Brazil's southern Paraná state, these French-style botanical gardens center around a towering greenhouse reminiscent of London's 19th-century Crystal Palace. In the Garden of Sensations, visitors stroll blindfolded, experiencing the surrounding foliage and trickling waterfalls through sound, smell, and touch.
*www.visitbrasil.com*

### KEUKENHOF GARDENS

*Lisse, The Netherlands*

With more than seven millions tulips, daffodils, and hyacinths in bloom from March to May, this 79-acre (32 ha) spread southwest of Amsterdam is considered the world's largest flower garden. View the tulip fields from "whisper boats," electric-powered boats that glide almost silently through the Dutch landscape.
*www.keukenhof.nl*

### MONET'S GARDEN

*Giverny, France*

Many of Impressionist master Claude Monet's most famous paintings were inspired by the flower and water gardens he cultivated around his home northwest of Paris. Open from April to November, the gardens burst with narcissus, jonquils, and wisteria. Stroll around the pond in May, when sunlight and shadow play over Monet's beloved water lilies.
*fondation-monet.com/en*

### VILLA D'ESTE

*Tivoli, Italy*

A Renaissance masterpiece of Italian gardening, this sprawling complex northeast of Rome features grottoes, waterfalls, and ancient statues. Explore the ruins of the Villa Adriana, built by the Roman emperor Hadrian, and the spouting animal heads and lilies along the Avenue of the Hundred Fountains.
*www.villadestetivoli.info/storiae.htm*

### KIRSTENBOSCH

*Cape Town, South Africa*

Set against the eastern slopes of Cape Town's Table Mountain, this 89-acre (36 ha) garden was established in 1913 to conserve fynbos, southern Africa's unique plant life. Visit in the South African spring, between August and November, to view the fynbos at its best and see the greatest number of plants in flower.
*www.sanbi.org/gardens/kirstenbosch*

### SEYCHELLES NATIONAL BOTANICAL GARDENS

*Victoria, Seychelles*

Established more than a century ago in the island nation's capital, the Botanical Gardens is one of the Seychelles's oldest national monuments. Look for native orchids, rare spice trees, roosting fruit bat colonies, and giant tortoises from Aldabra, some of which are more than 150 years old.
*www.seychelles.travel*

### SINGAPORE BOTANIC GARDEN

*Singapore*

Founded in 1859, the Botanic Garden displays lush bougainvillea, bamboo, palm trees, and other native tropical plants over 128 acres (52 ha). Visit the Healing Garden for a peaceful walk among plants traditionally used in Southeast Asian medicine, then hike to the 7.5-acre (3 ha) National Orchid Garden at the park's highest point, where more than 60,000 orchids bloom.
*www.sbg.org.sg*

### KENROKU-EN

*Kanazawa, Japan*

Developed by feudal lords in the 17th century, Kenroku-en is considered one of the most beautiful gardens in Japan. The strolling-style landscape features artfully designed ponds, hills, and teahouses. In March, hundreds of plum trees show off dark pink and white blossoms while irises flower along the garden's winding streams.
*www.pref.ishikawa.jp*

For more than a century, Butchart Gardens has offered residents and visitors of Vancouver Island 50-plus acres (20 ha) of tranquillity, beauty, and photo ops.

An already impressive sight, Victoria Falls' beauty goes into overdrive as a rainbow throws itself across the scene.

ZAMBIA/ZIMBABWE

# VICTORIA FALLS

**Soar over the world's "greatest sheet of falling water" and touch its rising mist.**

"Scenes so lovely must have been gazed upon by angels in their flight," said Scottish explorer David Livingstone, bringing Victoria Falls poetically to the attention of the outside world. Described by the UNESCO World Heritage Committee as Earth's "greatest sheet of falling water," the falls are at their most thunderous around April and May, after the rainy season. To stand in front of the mighty, 300-foot-high (90 m), mile-wide (1.6 km) falls is to realize the combined power of geology, vast amounts of water, and time.

Victoria Falls straddles the border of Zambia and Zimbabwe, and each country claims the best views. But visitors don't need to choose sides. It's easy enough to walk across the border and do both. Even better, a bird's-eye perspective from high above in a two-seat microlight avoids the argument altogether; flying in the open aircraft means passengers feel the wind in their hair as they take in the unforgettable sight of the Zambezi River, Livingstone Island, and surrounding wildlife on plains that stretch to the horizon. "In the right conditions, you can reach out and touch the spray as it rises from the raging torrent," says pilot Kevin Macquish. But you're far enough from the massive mist to shoot a picture of this natural wonder (indeed, one of the World's Seven).

**PLANNING  Victoria Falls** www.zambiatourism.com, www.zimbabwetourism.net. Most hotels and lodges can arrange visits to the falls. Microlight flights are available from Livingstone's Adventure (*www.livingstonesadventure.com*).

## BEST OF THE BEST
### *Rafting the Zambezi*

Names like "oblivion" and "devil's toilet bowl" make it clear the rapids on the Zambezi River aren't exactly mild. Rafting the Zambezi has a reputation as one of the most exciting river adventures in the world, especially in April and May when water flows are high. The classic one-day trip covers about 16 miles (25 km) and 20 rapids, around half Class V giants. For added excitement, there are crocs in the water (though only small ones). It's also possible to take longer trips, with days of paddling broken up with riverside lunches and finished off with nights by a campfire. www.zambezirafting.com

# YANGON

**Immerse yourself in a Buddhist celebration surrounded by gold and flowers.**

Though the country was previously known as Burma, some things in Myanmar never change: You still don't need an alarm clock, because the monks will start chanting about sunrise and wake you up anyway, and fishermen still catch spring hatchlings from low sampans like they were time machines. Rudyard Kipling once said, "This is Burma, and it will be quite unlike any land you know about."

When the full moon rises in March, a visitor can begin to find out why. Burmese families from all over the country travel to Yangon to pay homage to the shimmering gold and gemstone-encrusted Shwedagon Pagoda. The temple contains eight strands of the Buddha's hair, and some people believe it to be 2,500 years old. As a visitor, it is easy to lose yourself among the thousands who circumambulate the halls for the annual celebration—banned for most of the past few decades—amid half a million flowers decorating the grounds.

The mood is decidedly festive, as the sacred mixes with the delightful. Watch a puppet show or traditional *zat* dancing that tells stories of the Buddha's life. For dinner, when the spring air fills with prayers, follow the charcoal scent to street vendors hawking *mohinga*, a fish stew, or *hta min thouk*, a traditional rice salad. Don't forget to save some Burmese *kyat* to buy a bit of gold leaf. You'll want to join the celebrants and make a donation to renewing the sacred grounds each spring.

**PLANNING  Shwedagon Pagoda Festival** www.myanmartravel.org. The official tourism site can be found at www.myanmartourism.org. However, the country is still new to online planning, so you'll get a lot farther phoning hotels and tour operators.

## BEST OF THE BEST
### *Cool Off at the Water Festival*

In Myanmar's tropical weather, any reason to cool off is a good one. During spring's Thingyan Water Festival, that means chucking water at anything and everything that moves. The first day is filled with traditional Buddhist observances, but by sundown, the fun starts: performances on highly decorated stages, music, and dance. Then it's time for the water. Start by sprinkling some on the ground as a prayer. After that, everybody's fair game: Try squirt guns, water balloons, or anything else that can help douse a passerby. Forget drying off for the next several days, as the country throws its biggest party of the year. www.myanmartravel.org

Not all that glitters is gold on the Shwedagon Pagoda. The exterior also gleams brightly with sunlight bouncing off encrusted gemstones.

# HOLI FESTIVAL OF COLORS

"All along the roads the air is filled with singing and drum beating. Everything is colored yellowish red and rendered dusty by the heaps of scented powder blown all over."

—*RATNAVALI*, SEVENTH-CENTURY DRAMA

After the first full moon in March, Holi celebrations bring India to life, as people throw colored powder to commemorate the coming of spring. The northern city of Jaipur enhances the celebrations further with its Elephant Festival.

# Andrew Evans
## May Days in Kiev

Cannon fire with a magnificent boom, followed by gentle white wisps of gun smoke that flutter skyward. The air is warm and the music loud—a military brass band marches the mile (1.6 km) of Khreshchatyk, and thundering drumbeats echo off the imposing gray facades that line Kiev's central boulevard.

The crowd swarms like honeybees, making way for the white-haired veterans who wear their polished medals with pride. Timid children in their best clothing hand pink carnations to the aging heroes. Over and over, I watch this touching gift between generations and I am moved.

Victory Day falls on May 9, a day to remember the end of the Great Patriotic War, World War II. Though families are here for the pony rides and hot dogs and Mylar balloons, the Ukrainian nation will never forget the time when Nazi armies marched down this same boulevard.

May is my favorite time in Ukraine's capital, when the long winter ends abruptly and the city stops to party for a good ten days. The fun begins on Labor Day, the first of May, when an old Soviet habit still grants all workers the day off. Though a few red stars still linger in the city, today's May Day is a joyous shout to the pagan rites of spring.

The snow is gone and in its place, the lacy white blossoms of chestnut trees cover the city's steep hills that slope down into the fast-flowing Dnieper. From this flowering forest poke the shiny golden domes of Kiev's Pechersk Lavra, a thousand-year-old Orthodox monastery built over a labyrinth of deep and natural caves.

Though this city is ancient, Ukraine is still a young country. The May holidays mark a youthful change of pace, leaving indoors for outdoors, moving from darkness into light. Each new day lasts a little longer. And, in the weeks that follow, the rich black earth will turn into brilliant green—in Ukrainian, the word for May is *traven,* or "grass."

All of this is cause for celebration—a reminder that no matter the upheaval of war, no matter how cold and terrible the winter, the rhythm of nature will continue, bringing new life each spring.

*Andrew Evans is a contributing editor at* National Geographic Traveler *magazine as well as National Geographic's "Digital Nomad," traveling the globe to create interactive travel experiences for readers. He is also the author of best-selling guidebooks to Ukraine and Iceland.*

*"May is my favorite time in Ukraine's capital ... a joyous shout to the pagan rites of spring."*

Founded during the early 12th century, Kiev's St. Michael's Cathedral—devoted to the city's patron saint—kicked off the trend of gilding domes.

# OSAKA AND TOKYO

**Experience the thunderously popular ancient sport of sumo wrestling.**

S pringtime in Japan may be better known for its vaunted cherry blossoms, but its annual flesh-to-flesh pounding sumo tournaments are no less thrilling. Watching these 300-pound (140 kg) humans fight is a strange experience, best viewed in its native Japan, where sumo is the Japanese NFL, albeit more than a thousand years older than football.

Springtime draws sumo fans and Japanese tourists enjoying Golden Week, a seven-day period from late April to early May containing four national holidays, including the former emperor's birthday, Greenery Day, and Children's Day.

The two, 15-day springtime sumo tournaments—in March in Osaka and May in Tokyo—are epic events that draw rowdy crowds, the antithesis to Kyoto's gentle flower-snapping set. Osaka's tournament is held at Osaka Prefectural Gymnasium (aka the Bodymaker Colosseum) and is nicknamed the "Rough Spring Tournament." It features matches between lowest to junior-grade wrestlers that are not usually televised.

Tokyo's tournaments are bigger spectacles, where grand champions are bestowed their titles. Visitors also will find the Sumo Museum there and peruse everything from woodblock prints and *banzuke* (rankings) to ceremonial aprons worn by champion wrestlers of the past.

**PLANNING  Sumo tournaments and the Sumo Museum** www.sumo.or.jp. Japanese sumo is run by the Nihon Sumo Kyokai (Japan Sumo Association). Visitors may buy tickets online a month before the tournaments.

## IN THE KNOW
### *Sumo: A Primer*

S umo wrestlers, called *rikishi* or *osumo-san,* lose when any part of their body (besides their feet) touches the *dohyo* (circular ring) or when they are pushed or thrown outside of it. Hair pulling, ear boxing, choking, closed-fist punching, and crotch hitting are forbidden. There are more than 60 official *kimarite* (winning techniques), but only a dozen are seen regularly. Of course, weight matters; nicknamed the "Dump Truck," Konishiki Yasokichi's peak was 630 pounds (286 kg), the heaviest on record. Wrestlers have their own official dish, *chanko nabe,* a protein-rich stew made from chicken, beef, daikon, and tofu, served with rice and beer for maximum caloric intake.

Professional sumo wrestlers, dressed in their ceremonial *kesho-mawashi,* circle around the referee during the ring-entering ceremony, the *dohyo-iri.*

Meijyo Park's cherry blossoms frame Nagoya Castle to perfection.

## ASIA
# JAPAN

**Join in the country's cherry-blossom-viewing frenzy that kicks off the spring season.**

Cherry trees are found throughout the temperate world, but only in Japan have the pink blossoms that usher in the start of spring risen to the level of a national obsession. Tokyo resident and marketing consultant Debbie Howard, a confessed "freak about cherry blossoms," describes two schools of *hanami* (flower viewing) in Japan: "walk-through" advocates who try to see as many cherry groves as possible during the peak time, and "Zen" viewers who max out their experience at one especially good spot. She prefers the latter approach: "It's very special to sit down and party under the cherry blossoms with friends."

Hanami nomads should pack a good pair of walking shoes and a map or GPS showing the best blossom-viewing spots in a given city. Those who prefer to picnic should bring a blanket to their chosen spot, plus fresh food (like sushi or sashimi) from a local market and a flask of preheated sake to take the edge off the spring chill. Howard advises viewing both in daytime and after dark, when many groves are artfully illuminated. Among her favorite hanami spots are Tokyo's Meguro River and Ueno Park, where you can float through the pink landscape on a rented boat.

**PLANNING Japan** www.jnto.go.jp. **Cherry Blossom Festival** For the official annual forecast for major cherry blossom destinations, go to www.jnto.go.jp/sakura; another good source is www.japan-guide.com/blog/sakura12, written by local correspondents.

---

### BEST OF THE BEST
*Floral Fortresses*

The parks and gardens of Japan's great medieval castles are among the best spots for cherry blossom viewing.

● **HIMEJI CASTLE:** This sprawling medieval bastion near Kobe is almost perfectly preserved. The parkland on the north flank is flush with cherry trees. www.himeji-castle.gr.jp

● **HIROSAKI CASTLE:** Little remains of the original medieval citadel, but the castle's 120 acres (49 ha) in northern Honshu contain more than 2,600 cherry trees. www.hirosaki.co.jp

● **TAKADA CASTLE:** Surrounded by a moat, the grounds of this 17th-century castle in Joetsu on the Sea of Japan boast more than 4,000 cherry trees. The scene is especially magical at night when the blossoms are lit by thousands of lanterns. www.jnto.go.jp/eng

# SUM

FIREWORK EXTRAVAGANZAS, WILD
HORSES, NEVER-ENDING SUNSHINE,
AND FESTIVALS GALORE

# MER

Even in midsummer, surfers rely on wet suits to ward off the chill of England's waters.

# VANCOUVER

**Witness a global symphony of exploding lights during summer's international fireworks competition.**

For a few evenings every July, thousands of rockets burst in the sky over Vancouver's English Bay, trailing sparkling plumes and thrilling throngs of spectators. The festival (called the Honda Celebration of Light) attracts the world's leading fireworks artisans, who strut their stuff above the city. No small-town show, the event offers a rare chance to catch these princes of pyrotechnics in one place. And like Olympians, they're inspired by the competition.

The festival runs three nights, each featuring a different country. Festival producer Andrea Dowd-Dever says Vancouverites have become fireworks connoisseurs, learning different styles. "China has big shows, really big shells," she says. "Italy is a bit more known for complexity and artistry."

It's not all visual, either. While crowds of up to 400,000 gather around the bay enjoying the evening breeze and the show above, the air surges with hip-hop, samba, Vietnamese folk songs, or Canadian rocker Neil Young, all synchronized to the pyrotechnics.

Still, Dowd-Dever says her favorite part is watching the city get fireworks fever every year. "You see so many people watching one event. It's a shared experience."

**PLANNING** **Vancouver's Honda Celebration of Light** www.hondacelebrationoflight.com. The festival takes place annually in late July, sometimes carrying over into early August.

## FOR FOODIES
*Vancouver's Asian Eats*

Fireworks originated in China, so why not explore Vancouver's substantial ties to the East? The city is one of the most vibrant Asian enclaves on the continent, with neighborhoods where English is rarely heard. Jade Seafood Restaurant (*jaderestaurant.ca*) serves updated dishes like mushroom dumplings with truffle oil or Grandpa's smoked chicken. Cattle Café (*cattlecafe.ca*) features Hong Kong–style street food like bubble waffles or Laksa seafood hot pot, a coconut-curry soup. Or wander the Night Market (*richmondnightmarket.com*) for everything from satay skewers to dragon's beard, ancient China's cotton candy.

Vancouver's Burrard Bridge—an art deco structure that opened to the public on July 1, 1932—underscores the drama of a fireworks display.

Modern-day hand-beaded coin purses showcase artist Judy Lafferty's attention to detail and devotion to traditional crafts and designs.

NORTHWEST TERRITORIES, CANADA

# INUVIK

**Engage with a vibrant creative community at an arts festival in one of the world's most unexpected places: the Arctic Circle.**

World-class art is not typically associated with Canada's Arctic North. Each July, however, during summer's brief window of midnight sun and warm temperatures, a small town just two degrees above the Arctic Circle becomes a hub of artistic creativity.

A professional lifeline for artists separated most of the year by hundreds of miles and extreme weather, the ten-day Great Northern Arts Festival explodes with a unique energy born when great minds, who have been waiting all year to share their latest ideas, finally meet. Visitors can take in the work of a hundred visual artists and performers, from landscape painters and glassblowers to traditional wood-carvers and bead workers. "It's like a homecoming," says executive director Sasha Webb. "These artists come from different communities and cultures, but they all share common skills and similar experiences."

To gain a sense of the vast distances, dramatic landscapes, and geographic barriers that simultaneously isolate artists while shaping the creativity and cultural traditions at the core of their work, drive to Inuvik via the Dempster Highway, a 417-mile (671 km) route that's largely devoid of people, towns, and gas pumps. "It's like driving to Mars," observes Webb. But it's a road filled with some of the richest landscape—and artistic inspiration—in the world.

**PLANNING** **Northwest Territories** www.spectacularnwt.com. **Great Northern Arts Festival** www.gnaf .org. Flights to Inuvik arrive from Whitehorse via Air North or Yellowknife via Canadian North. Driving from Dawson City is also an option.

Don't surprise the locals. Keep the conversation, or at least a "Hey bear, hey bear" mantra, going on your walk to Anan Creek's bear-viewing area.

# ALASKA

**Get a goose-bumps good look at some of Alaska's most famous and magnificent residents.**

Biology demands it: If you want to see Alaska's bears, summer is a must. Once the season hits, both black bears and grizzlies (called brown bears on the coast) come out of hibernation, intent on mating, teaching their young essential life skills, and bulking up for their next long winter's nap. During Alaska summers, all the world becomes a bear's pantry as the waterways begin to crowd with salmon and, later, bushes hang heavy with blueberries, crowberries, and soapberries.

When it comes to wildlife viewing, there are, of course, no guarantees. But if you want a much better than average chance to see bears in their natural habitat, the state is loaded with opportunities. Hikers or strollers out wandering the in-city trails of parks right in Anchorage have even been known to get their fair share of up-close-and-personal experiences with bears.

Brenda Schwartz, a Wrangell, Alaska–based artist and bear-viewing and river guide, grew up going out to Anan Creek, a "really rich ecosystem" that's a popular fishing spot for both brown and black bears, eagles, and more. Though it's now highly regulated by the Forest Service, that hasn't dampened Schwartz's enthusiasm: "It's a great place to watch people's eyes just light up."

*During Alaska summers, all the world becomes a bear's pantry as the waterways begin to crowd with salmon and, later, bushes hang heavy with blueberries, crowberries, and soapberries.*

A bear cub tests out its climbing skills in its efforts to get a good look at visitors on the nearby viewing stand.

A bed of geraniums provides an ideal resting place for two bear cubs at Kodiak National Wildlife Refuge.

Keep in mind: Just because it's summer, that doesn't mean Alaska will always feel summery. Fleece and rain gear are essential Alaska equipment all summer long.

## ANAN CREEK

After a boat ride from Wrangell, follow your guide down the trail to meet up with a ranger and then to the viewing platform. There's a good chance for bear sightings all along the way. After all, the Forest Service may have laid down a wooden walkway here, but they did it over existing bear trails—and the bears still use the paths. Out on the viewing platform—and in a photo blind below—you'll often find yourself surrounded by bears hungry for the fatted salmon coming up the creek. (Don't hang your toes over the edge of the platform or you could end up with a grizzly sniffing at your tootsies.) "Just watching their daily lives at that closeness is an amazing treat," Schwartz says.

## KATMAI NATIONAL PARK

There's no road into Katmai. You day-trip into the park, across the Gulf of Alaska from Wrangell, by floatplane. Your pilot and guide (at times, one and the same person) will watch for bears from the air and, once spotted, set down on the water in areas with wonderful names like Geographic Harbor or Hallo Bay. Then, follow your guide's every instruction—she knows bear behavior and will keep you safe as your group tracks grizzlies, getting as close as 50 yards (46 m). For platform viewing or overnight accommodations in Katmai, book a trip to Brooks Camp (see sidebar).

## KODIAK NATIONAL WILDLIFE REFUGE

While a ratio of 3,000 Kodiak brown bears to 1.9 million acres (769,000 ha) might not sound overly impressive, it is. Kodiaks like to keep a little space from their neighbors, so the wildlife refuge actually has a fairly sizable population—and each member is of incredible size. The bears can grow as large as 1,400 pounds (640 kg).

Hire a guide and head out to Frazer Lake by floatplane to see these behemoths in action. But, while there, keep your eyes open for the area's other mammals; there's a chance you'll spot some red foxes and river otters, or a tundra vole or two. Other living thrills abound. Fingers crossed, you'll get to see flocks of puffins speed on by; it's nearly impossible to keep from getting giddy when that happens.

PLANNING **Alaska** www.travelalaska.com. **Anchorage Park Foundation** www.anchorage parkfoundation.org. **Anan Creek** www.fs.usda .gov. To book a tour with Brenda Schwartz, www.alaskaupclose.com. For information about visiting Wrangell, www.wrangell.com. Learn more about Anan's bears at Wrangell's annual summer BearFest (www.alaskabearfest .org). **Katmai National Park** www.nps.gov/ katm. **Kodiak National Wildlife Refuge** www.fws.gov/refuge/Kodiak. For day trips into Katmai or Kodiak Refuge, consider Kodiak-based Sea Hawk Air (www.seahawkair.com) or Homer-based Bald Mountain Air Service (www.baldmountainair.com).

Salmon beware—it's feeding time at Katmai National Park.

# WHALE AND DOLPHIN VIEWINGS

**Visit great mammals of the sea in their summer getaways.**

### SAGUENAY–ST. LAWRENCE MARINE PARK

*Quebec, Canada*

The meeting point of the St. Lawrence River and the Atlantic Ocean is a safe haven for large marine life. In addition to the world's largest mammal, the 100-foot (30 m) blue whale, the St. Lawrence estuary is home to 1,000 belugas. For a closer look, take a sea excursion by boat or kayak.

**www.quebecmaritime.ca**

### BAY OF FUNDY

*New Brunswick/Nova Scotia, Canada*

The Bay of Fundy attracts the largest population of North Atlantic right whales—one of the most endangered whale species. With some of the world's highest tides, the bay amasses large quantities of zooplankton, attracting up to 12 different kinds of whales. Each summer, the Grand Manan Basin becomes the right whale's primary nursery and feeding ground.

**www.bayoffundytourism.com**

### BAFFIN BAY–DAVIS STRAIT

*Nunavut, Canada/Greenland*

Every summer, the ice in the North Atlantic's Baffin Bay melts away to become a marine feeding ground, welcoming one of the longest-living animals on Earth—the bowhead whale. Reaching ages exceeding 100 years, bowheads follow a migration pattern in association with ice floes. Characterized by their large heads, bowheads are capable of breaking through sea ice at least eight inches (20 cm) thick.

**www.polarcruises.com**

### CHANNEL ISLANDS NATIONAL PARK

*California*

Close to 30 species of cetaceans (whales, dolphins, and porpoises) visit Channel Islands National Park, providing numerous opportunities to encounter these majestic creatures. Hike to a lookout, scale the visitor center tower, or—for a closer look—book a boat tour.

**www.nps.gov/chis/index.htm**

### GULF OF MAINE

*New England*

After a long winter in the West Indies, humpbacks and newly born calves begin their journey to New England feeding grounds in the Gulf of Maine. By May, most have arrived and can be seen near the Stellwagen Bank National Marine Sanctuary's various locations in eastern Massachusetts.

**stellwagen.noaa.gov**

### INDIAN RIVER LAGOON

*Palm Bay, Florida*

North America's most diverse estuary system, the Indian River Lagoon is home to more than 2,000 species of plants and animals. The bottlenose dolphins found in the lagoon are smaller and have longer flippers than their ocean relatives. Encounter the fascinating behavior of these gentle and playful creatures on a daily Dolphin Discovery tour, guided by a certified Florida Coastal Naturalist.

**www.marinediscoverycenter.org**

### BAJA CALIFORNIA

*Mexico*

Gray whales travel 12,000 miles (19,300 km) in migration—the longest of any mammal on Earth—from the freezing feeding waters of Alaska's Bering Sea to the balmy breeding grounds of Mexico's lagoons, where they provide a prime destination for whale-loving vacationers.

**www.bajawhales.com**

### THE AZORES

*Portugal*

Aside from the Azores' magnificent mountain expanses and coastal scenery, this mid-Atlantic Portuguese archipelago is one of the world's best whale-watching destinations, attracting humpback, pilot, fin, minke, and blue whales. Pico Island ("the village of whales") offers an eight-day B&B package that includes several whale- and dolphin-watching boat excursions.

**www.steppesdiscovery.co.uk**

### RURUTU

*French Polynesia*

Surrounded by a barrier reef, Rurutu is known for being in a prime humpback whale migration pathway and plays host to much calving, nursing, and mating. Boats depart from Moerai for trips to whale-watch, witness mothers playing with their calves, and listen to the underwater opera amplified by the coral seabed.

**www.tahiti-tourism.com**

### DISCO BAY

*Greenland*

About 15 species of whales visit Greenland each year, but the narwhal—the unicorn of the sea—is among the stars. This elusive whale is known for its long, distinctive spiral tusk. At times, males can be seen surfacing the water mid-joust.

**www.greenland-travel.com**

A humpback whale's tail flukes disappear into the Pacific Ocean.

A bronco does its best to shake off a cowboy.

ALBERTA, CANADA

# CALGARY

**Kick up your heels at a Western-style combo platter of rodeo and festival fun.**

There's no better time to don a cowboy hat in Calgary. With the summer sun blazing overhead and the Calgary Stampede in town, you'll look downright out of place if you don't put on that most Western of chapeaus.

The incredibly modern, skyscraper-studded city of Calgary gets its yesteryear on when the century-old Stampede starts up every July. The ten-day event centers around one of the world's biggest rodeos and features an agricultural fair, Vegas-worthy shows, and big-name concerts. But it's those rodeo events that'll stick in your mind. Cowgirls charge full throttle on their horses as they loop around barrels and race to the finish line. Riders get thrown from broncos that, clearly, want nothing to do with them. And, perhaps the bravest of all, the rodeo clowns dash in (rainbow wigs and red noses a-blazing) to save the day when bulls try to make mincemeat of those they've dethroned.

Attending the Stampede stirs an intense desire to boot up and ride off into the sunset. So pair a Stampede trip with some horseback riding just west of Calgary in Kananaskis Country. Just don't forget that hat; the temps are cooler in the mountains, but the sun can still peel the skin right off an unprotected nose.

**PLANNING Calgary** www.visitcalgary.com. **Calgary Stampede** www.calgarystampede.com. **Kananaskis Country** www.kananaskis.com, www.albertaparks.ca.

## BEST OF THE BEST
*Alberta Boot Company*

Save your souvenir dollars for one grand purchase in Calgary. Stop into the Alberta Boot Company and have them size you up for a pair of custom boots. Keep them spare or bling them out—the choice is yours. Or buy them off the shelf. No matter. They'll quickly become your go-to footwear of choice, whether your daily ride is a horse, a pickup, or a Prius. The only boot company in the province and the official Western boot company of the Calgary Winter Olympics, Alberta Boot also makes boots for Canada's venerated Mounties. www.albertaboot.com

WASHINGTON

# SAN JUAN ISLANDS

**Browse the island's unique artwork and spectacular landscapes when the skies clear in summer.**

Filled with pine-covered mountains that slope toward the sea and miles of rocky shore, the dramatic landscape of mainland Washington State spills over onto the San Juan Islands. Nature's breeding ground for endangered species like bald eagles and orcas, the islands are also a fertile source of human creativity and art. The two often converge. "You are constantly in an environment that inspires you," says James Hardman, Orcas Island Artwork Cooperative member. "I never use it up."

Notorious for its gray and gloomy weather, the Pacific Northwest sees its highest concentration of warm, sunny days during the summer. Beyond wandering through art galleries and biking, hiking, or kayaking the land and waters that inspire them, each inhabited island is a community to be explored. Get off the main ferry route to smaller islands like Sucia, where the wind and tide carve unique shapes onto the shoreline.

May to October is also the best time to spot southern-resident orca whales. With the oldest estimated to be about 100 years old, many of the 85 whales have been around longer than the islanders. "People identify with these animals," says Eric Eisenhardt of Soundwatch, a whale protection program. "They get to know the individual whales and learn their life stories. It's a personal connection."

PLANNING **San Juan Islands** www.visitsanjuans.com. Four of the islands—Orcas, San Juan, Shaw, and Lopez—are accessible via the Washington State Ferry. Private water taxis service smaller islands.

There's no better way to get a whale's-eye view of the San Juan Islands (or a view of a whale's eye) than by kayak.

# *Sandra Bernhard*

## Lopez Island, Washington

Lopez Island is a wonderful spot out in the San Juan chain. The ferry trip over from Anacortes takes around an hour and a half, and on a sunny June day, you can feel all the strains falling away. I sat inside by the window watching whitecaps, but I could have stood out on the deck like my brother and his family did.

We caravanned out to MacKaye Harbor, where our friends, longtime residents of Lopez, loaned us their groovy getaway pad. Funky, simple, A-framed. We unloaded our gear and headed out for provisions. All over the island are farms that operate on the honor system; lockers filled with frozen beef and lamb, organic veggies are yours for the purchase without anyone to ring you up. Trust is big out in the San Juans.

We discovered Vortex, an organic café that serves up fresh juices, amazing salads, tostadas, and chocolate chip cookies for a pleasing lunch.

You keep moving, though. There are endless hikes, bike rides and beach exploration, wildflowers, driftwood, mosses, canopies of trees everywhere you turn taking you away into dreamscapes.

Plans came fast and furious: a brisk walk through the woods to a high bluff outlook known as Iceberg Point. "Magnificent" would not be an overstatement for the almost 360-degree views it provides. Time to sit on the rocks, staring out and clearing one's mind.

June weather can be unpredictable in the Northwest. Clouds may gather and disperse at will, but this did not deter us. We drove to Crowfoot Farm to pick organic strawberries. I kept my haul to two paper cartons' worth, but my family went a little nuts, clearing a row or two by themselves.

Without Internet connection, as the Lopezians have wisely forbidden the towers on the island, you are permitted to do all the simple things you would never entertain back home: sketching, wandering, creating a tiny wildflower bouquet to set on your daughter's pillow, or dozing off on a blanket in the high grasses of the backyard. You are off the hook.

Soon it would be back to the hustle and grind. I was already figuring out how to get back here next June.

*One-woman shows keep actor, author, comedian, and musician Sandra Bernhard on the road much of the year and reunited with old friends. Nothing like the smell of jet fuel in your hair.*

*"Without Internet connection . . . you are permitted to do all the simple things you would never entertain back home: sketching, wandering, creating a tiny wildflower bouquet to set on your daughter's pillow."*

Sunset at Lopez Island's Shark Reef Sanctuary offers a typical island respite from mainland life.

CALIFORNIA/OREGON/WASHINGTON

# PACIFIC CREST TRAIL

"Mile for mile, I can't think of another long-distance trail that rivals the Pacific Crest Trail. The trail is rarely crowded and almost always perfectly graded; in summer, the weather is consistently sunny, dry, and warm; and the scenery is world-class, highlighted by two of my most favorite locales, the High Sierra and North Cascades."

—ANDREW SKURKA, AUTHOR OF NATIONAL GEOGRAPHIC'S
*THE ULTIMATE HIKER'S GEAR GUIDE*

One of America's National Scenic Trails, the Pacific Crest Trail makes its way from Mexico to Canada, spanning 2,650 miles (4,265 km). The popular hiking and equestrian route snakes through California, Oregon, and Washington. *Pictured:* Upper Sardine Lake in California's Tahoe National Forest

COLORADO

# TELLURIDE

**Pick your pleasure when the canyon town becomes a summer playground of festivals and fun for big kids.**

Hit Telluride on a high summer day, and it's like landing in North America's Shangri-La: a perfect, protected box canyon, so narrow it almost seems as if you can reach out and touch both sides. At the end of the canyon overlooking Telluride, the 365-foot (111 m) Bridal Veil Falls looks like a prop for postcard photographers. The air smells of forest and altitude, like skiers whose clothes have dried after yet another epic winter.

On the streets of Telluride, which look about the same as they did in the mining heyday of the Old West, plan tomorrow by playing Telluride profiler, when you pick your hangout by the people on the open-air patios: Mountain bikers have bigger shoulders, mountain climbers bigger calves, rock climbers bigger mugs of beer, fishermen the biggest lies, and white-water rafters are still shaking river out of their ears. The spagoers are the relaxed ones, sipping an aperitif glass of wine.

No point in hurrying. Summer lasts until the closing credits of Labor Day's Telluride Film Festival. The altitude in this corner of southwest Colorado takes some getting used to, anyway. Maybe that's what's causing the heavy breathing. Or maybe it's just the sound of another group of mountain bikers coming in for the night.

**PLANNING Telluride** www.telluride.com. **Telluride Film Festival** www.telluridefilmfestival.org. For the film festival, advance planning for tickets and a place to stay are vital.

The lineup at the annual Telluride Film Festival gives fair competition to a hike in the surrounding mountains.

Though the area is famous for its tart cherries, Traverse City—and its National Cherry Festival—also welcomes fans of the fruit's sweet varieties.

MICHIGAN

# TRAVERSE CITY

**Bliss out on an endless array of cherry concoctions in the epicenter of cherry country.**

To enter the northwest corner of Michigan's Lower Peninsula in July is to land in cherry heaven: The region produces more than half of the U.S. tart cherry crop, not to mention plenty of the sweet kind, too. Traverse City celebrates the fruit with its National Cherry Festival, held in venues throughout the city.

"You're greeted with fresh cherries right when you arrive," says festival marketing manager Susan Wilcox Olson. Freshly picked ones.

Then plunge into cherry overdrive. Kids can do it face-first (read on). A slice of the event's signature pie, cherry crumb, is a must. Wash it down with a cold glass of cherry lemonade in the park at the foot of Grand Traverse Bay. Stock up on preserves and sample cherry barbecue, jerky, and mustard at the waterfront farmers' market. Assuage your guilt in a footrace along the coastlines of the East and West Bays. The runners' reward: a fresh cup of cherries as they cross the finish line.

And what would a cherry festival be without a cherry pie-eating contest? The ones here are for youngsters. "They're no-hands, face down into a slice of pie," Wilcox Olson says. "At the end, you've got all these kids with huge, happy red smiles."

**PLANNING** **National Cherry Festival** www.cherryfestival.org.

BEST OF THE BEST
*The Old Mission Peninsula*

The Old Mission Peninsula extends 22 miles (35 km) into Grand Traverse Bay, separating its east and west arms. Studded with wineries, orchards, antique shops, and cozy inns, the narrow stretch offers stunning views of rolling vineyards descending to azure waters on both sides. Take a leisurely road trip, pausing to snack on cherries and apples at roadside stands and farm markets. Stop in for ice cream or picnic supplies at the Old Mission General Store, which dates from the mid-1800s, then head for the water at Haserot Beach, tucked into a harbor near the tip of the peninsula. www.oldmission.com

# SHOWSTOPPING OUTDOOR MUSIC VENUES

**Listen, watch, and marvel at open-air stages as great as the performances on them.**

### GREAT STAGE PARK

*Manchester, Tennessee*

If you're after a really good time, then it's off to Bonnaroo, a music festival that takes over the 700-acre (285 ha) Great Stage Park every June. It is a giant party, though you'll need to get ready for crowds and the Southern sun. Maybe some mud, too. But it's all worth it: The lineup, from jam bands and rock royalty to bluegrass and funk, is a music lover's dream.

**www.bonnaroo.com**

### RED ROCKS PARK AND AMPHITHEATRE

*Denver, Colorado*

This one is nature made—big-time. The only acoustically perfect, naturally occurring amphitheater in the world, the well-named Red Rocks serves up the kind of audio experience engineers work a lifetime to perfect. And the visuals? Two brilliant red sandstone monoliths rise 300 feet (90 m) above the crowd.

**www.redrocksonline.com**

### THE GREEK THEATRE

*Los Angeles, California*

You'll go for the main act, but, thanks to the Griffith Park location and the stellar sound system, you'll remember the Greek. With just 5,800 seats, you'll never feel like you're out at sea (or, more importantly, can't see) at the Greek; it's one of the most intimate outdoor venues you'll ever experience.

**www.greektheatrela.com**

### DOWNTOWN MONTREAL

*Montreal, Quebec, Canada*

For ten days every summer, a wide swatch of downtown Montreal turns into one of the ultimate city music venues. All traffic comes to a halt once the annual Festival International de Jazz de Montréal kicks off. Then it's just people and music, from the namesake jazz to blues to rock.

**www.montrealjazzfest.com**

### SLANE CASTLE

*Meath, Ireland*

It takes a mighty backdrop to (just about) overshadow outsized performers like Madonna, U2, and the Rolling Stones. But if any venue can do it, it's Slane Castle, the current residence of Lord Henry Montcharles, Eighth Marquess Conyngham, whose family has called Slane home since 1701. The estate's natural amphitheater below the castle is worthy of rock royalty. With a history that includes King George VI and St. Patrick himself, Slane Castle is legendary—and so are its shows.

**www.slanecastle.ie**

### DALHALLA AMPHITHEATER

*Near Rättvik, Sweden*

There are few outdoor concert spots cooler (literally or figuratively) than an old limestone quarry. The terraced gray stone and pool of aqua water at the bottom create an arresting backdrop and add up to a striking photo op. Make your day at Dalhalla a double bill: Take one of the guided tours before the night's event begins.

### AUDITORIUM PARCO DELLA MUSICA

*Rome, Italy*

This modern, Renzo Piano–designed music complex actually recalls the theaters of ancient Rome. The 3,000-seat open-air space is, very much, of its city—and the acoustics aren't bad, either.

**www.auditorium.com**

### FLOATING OPERA STAGE OF THE BREGENZ FESTIVAL

*Vienna, Austria*

This is an opera stage on a lake. Every year since 1946, the Bregenz Festival creates amazing floating stages with sets as much a treat for the eyes as the music is for the ears.

**www.bregenzerfestspiele.com**

### SULTAN'S POOL

*Jerusalem, Israel*

The Ottoman sultan Suleiman the Magnificent brought this ancient pool of water back to life in the 16th century. Five hundred years later, during summers when it is dry, the area is put to use to refresh people in a different way: with music.

**www.gojerusalem.com/discover/item_30/Sultans-Pool**

### ETHNOMIR

*Near Moscow, Russia*

Every summer since 2008, this cultural complex hosts the Dikaya Myata (Wild Mint Music Festival) to become the Russian version of Max Yasgur's Woodstock farm. The open-air, multiday music festival, about a half hour outside Moscow, features musicians from Russia, Germany, the U.S., and elsewhere.

**eng.mintmusic.ru**

The floating stages built for Austria's annual Bregenz Festival heighten the drama of every opera performance. Here, a rehearsal of Umberto Giordano's *Andrea Chénier*.

Visitors get a sky-high, 360-degree view of the Iowa State Fair during a spin on one of the fairground's many colorful amusement rides.

IOWA

# DES MOINES

**Join the Iowa State Fair's classic American celebration of agriculture and community—and eat all your meals on a stick.**

As August's sultry summer days herald the home stretch of the growing season, rural and urban Iowans gather for a ten-day party to celebrate the state's rich farming heritage and to challenge visitors—and each other—to a bit of friendly, down-home competition. Held in historic Des Moines barns that have housed fairgoing livestock for more than a century, the Iowa State Fair attracts the biggest cows, the heftiest pigs, and the most successful harvests—all integral to a state whose engine is driven by agriculture. The spirit of healthy competition reaches beyond farming, too. Challenge yourself to a ride on the notorious double Ferris wheel, check out the world-famous butter cow, or take on the task of eating three meals a day—from breakfast eggs to pork chops—on a stick.

Livestock and produce contests, however, are the fair's lifeblood. Judging is done the old-fashioned way, with blue ribbons coveted by the best cattle breeders and tomato growers alike. "I love the animal judging," says historian Thomas Leslie. "When you watch sheep being judged, you start to learn why things like muscular balance are important to farmers and the rest of the state. We're all here because of the farmers."

**PLANNING  Iowa State Fair** www.iowastatefair.org. Flights arrive into Des Moines International Airport from around the country. Fair tickets can be purchased in advance online.

## IN THE KNOW
*Win a Blue Ribbon*

For those of us who may not have a best-in-class pig or a 3.5-pound (1.6 kg) tomato, there are plenty of other chances for Joe or Jane Fairgoer to make the cut. Each year, special events like chess tournaments, fiddling contests, spelling bees, and yo-yo competitions make it possible for anyone to participate and take home a prize. Sign-ups typically take place 30 to 60 minutes in advance. "There are competitions for everything," historian Thomas Leslie says. "It's about having fun and being a good sport." All part and parcel of the Iowa character. www.iowastate fair.org/competition/categories

# MONTREAL

**Surround yourself with silliness when this cultured capital turns itself inside out—and backwards—for July's Just for Laughs comedy extravaganza.**

Come July, Montreal removes all vestiges of its frosty mantle and gets its funny on—seriously. Absurdity fills the cosmopolitan streets around the Quartier des Spectacles, Montreal's cultural hub bounded by theaters, restaurants, and museums.

The Just for Laughs festival provokes bilingual chuckles throughout the month, when countless comedians and quirky acts in French and English take over the city. And where would the fun be if it were all hidden inside the city's many theaters and clubs? Much of the real craziness occurs *en plein air*. Explains festival president Andy Nulman: "We close off downtown and make it our playground. We've had big foam parties with thousands of pounds of soap suds."

In the swirl of the crowd, dodge can-can dancers on stilts and Les Grosses Têtes ("the Big Heads"), human caricatures with enormous noggins. Brace yourself for a ribbing from the smart-aleck Mauvaises Langues, street performers dressed as tongues who will give you a verbal lashing in French. And watch out for the occasional runaway bus. "We once wrapped a city bus to make it look like it was driving backwards," Nulman recalls. "Being a comedy festival, we can get away with things that would get other people arrested."

**PLANNING  Montreal Just for Laughs Festival** www.hahaha.com. For major savings on show tickets, pick up a passport on the site under "Special Offers."

All the world's a comedy stage—sidewalks and streets included—when the annual Just for Laughs Festival takes over downtown Montreal.

# Christopher Buckley

## Meteors Over Maine

Every early August, when my now-grown children were still growing and at an age when looking up at the night sky was more wondrous than looking down at the screen of an iPhone, we would start to count down the days until the start of the annual Perseid meteor shower. Thinking back on their genuine excitement over it makes me—now an old man of 60—a bit watery about the eyes.

We spent those summers in Maine, in a magical little coastal town called Blue Hill. The cabin that we rented was on a magical cove with the somewhat less magical name of Stinky Cove. I emphasize that it was no longer stinky by the time our era arrived.

Our view was to the north—ideal for meteor-shower viewing. And if we were lucky, there would *not* be a full moon to cast occluding light. In early August, no moon was best of all.

So just after dusk, we'd sit on the deck and tilt our chairs back so as not to get cricks in our necks and . . . watch. I would offer a reward for whoever saw the first one. When the kids were very young, a quarter would suffice, but as they got older and more mercenary, a dollar became the going rate.

And then one of them would cry out, "There!" And suddenly *there* would be a fiery little streak in the sky. Then another. And another. On a really good Perseid shower night, we'd might count, oh, 30 or more, depending on how long the kids were willing to postpone going back inside to watch *The Little Mermaid* or *The Adventures of Milo and Otis*.

You can see this amazing annual spectacle all over the Northern Hemisphere. But for us, there was no better observatory than the wooden deck and the still waters of Stinky Cove. If the water was really still that night, which in my memory it always is, you could actually see the reflection of the meteors on the mirror-surface of the cove, to the sound of loon call. Sometimes, added to that haunting, mournful sound track might come the raucous belching of seals, sated on a school of herring—a ridiculous, loud sound that always made us giggle.

*Christopher Buckley is the author of 15 books, most recently the novel* They Eat Puppies, Don't They?

*"My now-grown children were still growing and at an age when looking up at the night sky was more wondrous than looking down at the screen of an iPhone."*

Maine's night sky offers plenty of visual company as you watch for the Perseid meteor shower's speedy streakers.

# NEWPORT

**Hear legends and discover new sounds at the Newport Folk and Jazz festivals, living embodiments of America's musical history.**

In late July and early August, the population of Newport swells and the panorama of aristocratic white yachts seemingly painted into Narragansett Bay becomes the backdrop for a stage. Part of Newport's summertime resort tradition since 1954, the Jazz Festival has sprouted a six-decade legacy, bred the equally iconic Newport Folk Festival, and inspired an era of music festivals from Woodstock to Lollapalooza. "Name a legend—Bob Dylan, Joan Baez, Johnny Cash," challenges Folk Festival producer Jay Sweet. "They've all played Newport." The same goes for the Jazz Festival, where all-stars like Duke Ellington jump-started their careers.

International reputations dwarf the festivals' humble setting—a historic fort that maxes out at around 10,000 attendees. Fully concentrated days mean constantly hopping between tents. The Folk Festival's distinct iPod-shuffle feel, where bluegrass is juxtaposed alongside indie rock, broadens your ear and the boundaries of musical genres.

Beyond music, fans come for the sense of congregation that characterizes the lollipop of land sticking out into the harbor. "Singing 'This Land Is Your Land' along with 93-year-old Pete Seeger while all these people around you are bawling their eyes out," says Sweet, "makes you feel part of something way bigger than yourself."

**PLANNING Newport Jazz Festival** newportjazzfest.net. **Newport Folk Festival** www.newportfolkfest .net Tickets can be purchased online. The Newport County Convention and Visitors Bureau (*www.gonewport .com*) offers information about getting to Newport and accommodations.

## BEST OF THE BEST
*Newport Cliff Walk*

Sandwiched between the rugged, rocky Atlantic coastline and the backyards of mansions reminiscent of European aristocracy, the Newport Cliff Walk is a 3.5-mile (5.6 km) trail with stunning views. Largely built in the late 19th and early 20th centuries, Newport's mansions were summer "cottages" for some of America's wealthiest families whose investments during the industrial revolution paid off. Meandering over private property, the trail is protected as a sphere of public domain thanks to colonial-era edicts. Some of the historic mansions along the way are open to the public as museums, including the Breakers and Marble House, both of which belonged to the Vanderbilt family. www.newportmansions.org

It takes a stellar lineup to steal attention away from Newport's waterfront, but festivalgoers only have eyes (and ears) for the musicians.

Flags, back-in-time costumes, and plenty of smiles pave the way for a not-politics-as-usual feel during Washington, D.C.'s Fourth of July celebrations.

UNITED STATES

# WASHINGTON, D.C.

**Immerse yourself in the capital's celebrations of independence—and other cultures—for the Fourth of July.**

Not too surprisingly, the nation's capital puts on a really big show for the Fourth of July. And the thousands who gather there know it. The sense of community is palpable in spite of—or maybe because of—the crush of people sweating together on the National Mall's grassy expanse under the iconic dome of the U.S. Capitol as the sticky summer sun sets. "People from all over the world were gathered," marvels Pavel Romanenko, a Russian-born expatriate who says the celebration made him feel "part of American history."

In the afternoon, top musicians, accompanied by the National Symphony Orchestra, put on a free concert. Then, after the sun sets, the crowd's attention turns to the pointy tip of the Washington Monument as fireworks create an explosive dialogue in the sky above it.

Another nice bonus of the July spectacle is the Smithsonian Folklife Festival, also on the Mall. The ten-day event features music concerts, dance programs, and hands-on workshops showcasing worldwide cultural traditions—in recent years, the festival has featured everything from folk music in Central Asia and storytelling in Appalachia to body and street art in New York City. You'll find the two outdoor celebrations are a natural fit. As Smithsonian curator Betty Belanus notes, "Programs about independence traditions from around the world relate to the festival's goal of celebrating and humanizing diversity."

**PLANNING  Washington, D.C.** washington.org. **Smithsonian Folklife Festival** www.festival.si.edu.

# Top 10

# LOCAL FOURTH OF JULY CELEBRATIONS

**Feel the Independence Day spirit at these quintessential American festivities.**

### INDEPENDENCE, CALIFORNIA

Venture to the remote eastern Sierra east of Kings Canyon National Park to celebrate the small town of Independence's favorite day. Watch fireworks glow against the snowcapped mountain backdrop, chow down on pancakes and homemade pie in the park, and join the floats and fire engines in the community parade.

*www.independence-ca.com*

### TELLURIDE, COLORADO

Save room at the Volunteer Fire Department's July 4 barbecue for the free root beer floats on tap at the Telluride Mining Museum. Located in southwestern Colorado's San Juan Mountains, this historic gold-rush town turned world-class ski resort goes all out for Independence Day with F-16 flyovers, fireworks, and a quirky Main Street parade.

*www.visittelluride.com*

### BISBEE, ARIZONA

The longest and fastest running Fourth of July tradition in this former Old West copper mining camp is a 1.5-mile (2.4 km) coaster-car race down Tombstone Canyon Road. Cheer on the young drivers (ages 9–16), then, after the town's parade, head over to Brewery Gulch to watch traditional mining contests like mucking (shoveling broken rock into a bucket) and hard rock drilling.

*www.discoverbisbee.com*

### SEGUIN, TEXAS

Follow the flag-waving crowds 40 minutes northeast of San Antonio to downtown Seguin, home to the "Biggest Small Town Fourth of July Parade in Texas." This multiday celebration includes a food-and-music Freedom Fiesta and a Fiesta Swim at the Wave Pool.

*www.seguintexas.gov*

### SEWARD, NEBRASKA

Named "America's Fourth of July city–small town USA" by congressional proclamation, this former prairie settlement city about 30 minutes west of Lincoln has hosted a star-spangled Independence Day celebration since 1868. Student and civic groups coordinate the day's events, ranging from a grand parade and Wild West shoot-out to apple-pie-eating contests and clogging.

*www.julyfourthseward.com*

### HANNIBAL, MISSOURI

National Tom Sawyer Days add a Mark Twain twist to the Fourth of July in Missouri's beloved river town. The multiday event (typically four days, including July 4) features the National Fence Painting Contest, live music, mud volleyball, and a competitive frog jump for little kids and their favorite amphibians.

*www.visithannibal.com*

### MACKINAC ISLAND, MICHIGAN

Hire a horse-drawn taxi to clip-clop between Independence Day activities on car-free Mackinac. The island's simply patriotic July 4 pastimes typically include old-fashioned three-legged races, an egg toss, and the All-American Picnic at Revolutionary-era Fort Mackinac. At dusk, spread a blanket at the shore to watch the fireworks.

*www.mackinacisland.org*

### CLINTON, TENNESSEE

Step inside the Museum of Appalachia's split-rail fences to experience the pioneer-era July 4 Celebration and Anvil Shoot. There's bluegrass music, bell ringing, rail-splitting, and dulcimermaking, but the highlight is seeing (and hearing) 100-pound (45 kg) iron anvils jettisoned into the air by exploding gunpowder. The living history village-farm is 16 miles (28 km) north of Knoxville.

*museumofappalachia.org*

### MURRELLS INLET, SOUTH CAROLINA

In the laid-back "seafood capital of South Carolina," the Fourth of July parade is quintessentially low-country. At high tide, a flotilla of decorated fishing, shrimp, and pleasure boats—horns blaring and flags flying—floats down the Murrells Inlet shoreline. Stroll the Marsh Walk to see the procession and the fireworks that follow.

*www.murrellsinletsc.com*

### BAR HARBOR, MAINE

This historic resort gateway to Acadia National Park rolls out the red, white, and blue bunting for a sunrise-to-starlight community celebration. Festivities begin with an outdoor blueberry pancake breakfast and end with evening fireworks over Frenchman's Bay. In between, there's a town parade, a seafood festival, concerts, and lobster races.

*www.barharborinfo.com*

America's small-town celebrations—like Hannibal, Missouri's Tom Sawyer Days—practically demand that every man, woman, and child get in on the fun. Costumes are optional (but recommended).

# CHINCOTEAGUE PONY SWIM

"It's one of those sights that stays with you—a flock of ponies veering into the sea, suddenly waterborne. You can't really tell if they can see the distant shore, but they're paddling like fury in that direction, so you've gotta believe they'll make it just fine. And they always do, tugging onto the sand as if they were pulling the chariot of Poseidon behind them."

—K. M. KOSTYAL, NATIONAL GEOGRAPHIC AUTHOR

**During the Chincoteague Pony Swim, wild horses make their way across Virginia's Assateague Channel. This event occurs on the last Wednesday of July when the tide is calm enough to allow even the youngest ponies to make the trip safely.** *Pictured:* **Chincoteague horses race through the Assateague marshes.**

There's no shame in passing an hour—or four—just sitting on a Pawleys Island dock, watching the day slip away.

SOUTH CAROLINA

# PAWLEYS ISLAND

**Luxuriate on unspoiled beaches, net your own shellfish, and relish summertime's warm coastal breezes.**

Step back into a simpler time on Pawleys Island, a sandy Atlantic coast barrier island about 3 miles (5 km) long, separated from the real world of South Carolina's mainland by a tidal creek. Here, even high summer season brings an unspoiled calm to the open shoreline. The pace is relaxed and the atmosphere rustic but comfortable, unmarred by development or pretension.

A summer retreat on Pawleys means basking on beautifully preserved beaches, wandering among antebellum homes in the historic district, fishing for flounder in the marshes, or kayaking in the creek. There are restaurants, shops, and diversions aplenty just across the causeway, but it's better to stay on the island and do almost nothing at all.

Rent an oceanfront house that backs onto the creek, and catch your own seafood for a low-country boil, advises Lauren Cobb, whose family started vacationing on Pawleys more than 40 years ago. "Catch the shrimp in the creek with a cast net, throw out a crab trap, run to the market for kielbasa and corn on the cob, and throw it all in a pot," she recommends. The result: a fresh seafood dinner savored on the back porch of your island quarters with the ocean steps away and a tangy salt breeze stirring the air.

**PLANNING  Pawleys Island** www.townofpawleysisland.com. Contact Pawleys Island Realty Company (*www.pawleysislandrealty.com*) for information about vacation rentals.

## FOR FOODIES
*Palmetto Cheese*

Palmetto cheese, a savory pimento cheese blend of sharp cheddar, jalapeños, mayo, and a carefully calibrated mix of spices, was born at the historic Sea View Inn on Pawleys Island. The owners initially featured their creation as an appetizer for the weekly low-country shrimp boils they held each summer at the inn. It became so popular with visitors that it is now distributed more widely—and has its own website—but is nonetheless a delicious, locally crafted hors d'oeuvre for your own shrimp boil. You can pick up some Palmetto cheese at any supermarket on the mainland. www.pimentocheese.com

# COPPER CANYON

**Travel back in time with a breathtaking and nostalgic train ride across Mexico's sprawling Copper Canyon.**

The rugged, red mountains and vast stretches of desert scrub of Copper Canyon, scattered with giant candelabra cacti, cattle, and sombrero-wearing farmers, presents a classic vision of Mexico. And though new roads and airports may be built, there's only really one way to travel into such a landscape: on the Chihuahua-Pacific Railroad, affectionately known as El Chepe. During July and August, moderate temperatures and cooling rains irrigate waterfalls and landscapes, and greenery and wildflowers pop up on the slate vistas as the train makes the steep climb from the canyon floor to mountain ridges.

Start the 406-mile (653 km) train journey from Los Mochis to avoid passing through scenic sections at night. "You get on and feel disconnected from everything, from work and stress," says Ivan Fernandez, local guide with Amigo Trails tours. "You have to slow down and just look at the views. The rhythm of your heartbeat changes."

Deeper and larger than the Grand Canyon, Copper Canyon is one of Mexico's great undiscovered regions—warm and welcoming, rich with history and culture, and home to the Rarámuri Indians, famous for their stamina in long-distance running. Disembark at stops along the way to zip-line and rock-climb at Divisadero's Adventure Park, visit unspoiled canyon villages, or take in epic views.

**PLANNING Mexico** www.visitmexico.com. **El Chepe** www.chepe.com.mx. Tickets can be bought at stations in Los Mochis, Chihuahua, and other stops. Amigo Trails (*www.amigotrails.com*).

## BEST OF THE BEST
*Batopilas*

Get off El Chepe at Batopilas, one of Mexico's *pueblos mágicos* ("magic towns"), meaning that its laid-back character has been well preserved. It's a quiet, friendly little place. Local guides lead travelers up into the rust-colored hills to explore abandoned silver mines. The silver from this area, hauled out by mules, helped create Mexico's banks and build the modern country. The area around Batopilas is good for hiking and challenging downhill mountain biking. Also worth a look is the nearby "Lost Cathedral," a grand cream-colored church in a dramatic valley setting on the banks of the river. www.visitbatopilas.com

During July and August, waterfalls spill down into Mexico's Copper Canyon and the land erupts with an endless supply of greens.

CHILE

# LA TIRANA

**Witness the dance of the devil and acts of devotion at Chile's hot desert fiesta, La Tirana.**

The little desert town of La Tirana in northern Chile has just 600 inhabitants. But once a year, this low-key village is overwhelmed by a blitz of color, music, passion, and dancing as 250,000 celebrants descend for La Fiesta de La Tirana. Named after an Inca princess-warrior nicknamed La Tirana (The Tyrant), the July celebration lasts seven days and nights. Midnight fireworks kick off the biggest party on July 16, the feast day of the Virgin of Carmen.

Join with the crowds as they clamor through the hot, dry streets, sometimes on their knees, to attend Mass and make offerings in the chapel, thought to be the site of La Tirana's grave. Then witness a fantastic display as more than 400 masked and costumed dancers and musicians whip up a storm, performing the powerful *diablada*—the dance of the devil—to dispel bad spirits.

The town also becomes an open market, selling religious souvenirs and models of festival characters, including El Diablo himself. Refuel for late nights of dancing with sizzling *anticuchos* (llama meat on a stick) and doughy, deep-fried sopaipillas. Leave the booze behind, though; selling or consuming alcohol is prohibited at the festival. La Tirana may be a big party, but it's also a time of serious devotion.

**PLANNING  La Tirana Festival** www.visitchile.com. Book ahead. Buses and taxis to La Tirana leave from the hub city of Iquique. Go prepared for desert conditions, with a sun hat, water, and lots of sunscreen.

Though the streets grow crowded when La Tirana's festival adds nearly a quarter million people to the town, the costumes always stand out.

Hard-hatted spelunkers explore Caverna da Torrinha, the limestone caves of Brazil's Chapada Diamantina National Park.

BRAZIL

# CHAPADA DIAMANTINA NATIONAL PARK

**Sneak away from the season's busy beaches to explore this little-known region of forests, mountains, caves, and waterfalls.**

Meaning "diamond highlands" in Portuguese, Chapada Diamantina National Park boasts incredible hiking trails through the Atlantic Forest, featuring table mountains, cave systems, hundreds of waterfalls, and incredible canyons laced with rivers and streams, rich greenery tracing up their walls. The advantage of traveling during North America's summer is that it is Brazil's winter, a dry season in this region of the state of Bahia, meaning the trails are more easily hiked and caves are dry and accessible. Tourists flocking to Brazil's beaches during this season drain the laid-back region of any crowds. Chapada provides an inland oasis: cliffs of multilayered sediment hues, lush overlying vegetation, and crystal clear waters.

The landscape invites exploration. "The mountain region offers some of the best hiking in Brazil, as well as mountain biking and other outdoor sports activities," says Brazilian travel author Alexandra de Vries. You can use the cobblestoned historic town of Lençóis as a base, with its pastel-colored houses, excellent restaurants and cafés, and quaint arts-and-crafts shops. From here, adventures can easily begin. Day trips will take you to waterfalls, caves, and famous lookouts such as Pai Ignacio, a short hike to 360-degree views, ideal for a sunrise or sunset photo.

**PLANNING Chapada Diamantina National Park** www.guiachapadadiamantina.com.br. Borello Travel (*www.borellotravel.com*) provides a specially planned trip to the region.

# INTI RAYMI FESTIVAL

"The festivities culminated at the Sacsayhuamán ruins above town with Inti Raymi, a massive and tightly choreographed reenactment of the Inca Empire's most sacred rituals. Among the ancient rocks, modern-day Inca took on their ancestors' roles as kings, courtiers, provincial chiefs, and warriors, all of whom would travel from the far reaches of the empire to call Inti, the Inca sun god, back to the southern skies."

—TOM CLYNES, *NATIONAL GEOGRAPHIC ADVENTURE* MAGAZINE, NOVEMBER 2007

**The celebration of Inti Raymi, the Festival of the Sun, is held annually on the Southern Hemisphere's winter solstice—the shortest day of the year. The festivities include dancing and other rituals to mark the beginning of the new year.**

# BUENOS AIRES

**Get your sensual Latin groove on at the tango dance world cup when the dancing spills into the streets.**

Visiting Buenos Aires during the tango dance world cup in August is like seeing the city dreaming about itself. Hundreds of events are scattered all over the city during the two weeks of competitions, heating things up during South America's cooler winter season. The city bursts with an unprecedented energy, with major avenues like Avenida de Mayo near the famed Casa Rosada presidential palace closed to traffic, allowing hundreds of couples to literally dance in the streets. Theaters and cultural centers along Avenida Corrientes host some of the most important performances and contests. The plaza surrounding the city's main symbol, the Obelisco, where Corrientes joins with Avenida Nueve de Julio, the world's widest road, often becomes an open-air *milonga,* or tango salon.

"This is the mecca of tango," declares tango teacher and Icelandic transplant Helen Halldórsdóttir, nicknamed La Vikinga, "the best place to dance and understand it." She notes that the championships allow foreign tango enthusiasts to meet Argentine and other tango dancers from all over the world. Visitors who join in will find "a closeness in the embrace, and the beat of tango," she says. Those who feel timid about participating can simply watch and enjoy its vicarious pleasures.

**PLANNING  Tango Buenos Aires Festival and Dance World Cup** www.welcomeargentina.com/tango/tango-world-cup.html.

## IN THE KNOW
*A Brief History of Tango*

The history of Argentina's people is encapsulated in the sad, slow dance called tango. Tango's earliest roots are in African *candombe* moves (pronounced can-DOME-bey) brought over by slaves in Argentina's colonial period. The modern dance began to take shape in the late 1800s. The sounds of Africans, Spanish creole Argentines, and the millions of European immigrants arriving on the shores of the Rio de la Plata began mixing in the milongas of the poorest neighborhoods. Italian immigrants and Germans in particular, who brought over accordions like the *bandoneón,* the most important instrument used in modern tango, embraced tango. Today, tango is an art form recognized by UNESCO.

Few cities are as deeply associated with a dance style as Buenos Aires and the tango. The city goes into tango overdrive every August.

Modern golf may have teed off in Scotland, but Iceland—and its endless supply of summer sun—grabs the glory for golf courses per capita.

EUROPE

# ICELAND

**A game of endless golf, anyone? Tee up where the summer sun always shines.**

A quick hit of brennivín from your caddie's flask and you're ready to whack the ball down a fairway flanked by jet-black volcanic rocks. You check your watch. Yes, it really is midnight, and there's enough light to play a round of 18. Along with alternative rock and Nordic sagas, Icelanders are obsessed with golf. That's especially true during the summer months, when you can tee off 24/7 thanks to the midnight sun.

It's estimated that this North Atlantic isle has more golf courses per capita than any other nation—roughly a course for every 4,500 souls. "Older players say that golfing in the winter extends your life," says Hördur Arnason, coach of the country's national junior golf team and resident pro at the Keilir Golf Club near Reykjavík.

Start your midnight sun quest at championship courses like Keilir, with its undulating volcanic landscapes, or Akureyri Golf Club in the far north, where the Arctic Open unfolds each June. But leave time for some of the more remote courses, like the Geysir course in the middle of a geothermal field and the spectacular Westman Island course in a dormant volcano.

**PLANNING  Iceland** www.visiticeland.com. **Golfing** www.golficeland.org, www.arcticopen.is, www.keilir.is.

---

### IN THE KNOW
*Iceland's Black Magic*

Long before they were besotted by golf, Icelanders had another obsession: sorcery. Given the long winters and extreme isolation, many folk turned to witchcraft to solve their problems. By the 17th century, the Westfjords region was the hub of Icelandic black magic, leading to a bloody backlash of witch trials and burnings at the stake. Locals had a spell for raising the dead and used a blend of blood and ink to paint magic symbols on their foreheads to ward off evil. The Icelandic Museum of Sorcery and Witchcraft in Hólmavík collects relics and stories from that dark era. www.galdrasyning.is

# SUMMER SUNSETS

**Let Nature's greatest light show cap the perfect end to a warm summer day.**

### HALEKULANI RESORT
*Honolulu, Hawaii*

It's a Hawaiian classic. Take a seat on the veranda. Let the breeze coming off the water, a mai tai (a house specialty), and the music start to convince you that, somehow, you should live here. Forever. The sunset—which will likely match your drink—will finish the job.

*www.halekulani.com*

### ANTELOPE ISLAND STATE PARK
*Syracuse, Utah*

Sunset blooms big around the Great Salt Lake's largest island. Whether you're standing near the causeway or pulling out your camera to catch the sunset behind the island's namesake herd, you'll feel surrounded by the evening's big event.

*stateparks.utah.gov/parks/antelope-island*

### NEW YORK HARBOR
*New York, New York*

Lady Liberty looks just that much more elegant with the sunset at her back. Take it all in from the deck of a classic tall ship, the sails raised high and a glass of Champagne in your hand. The views east dazzle as well, as the sun's fading light reflects softly off the glass and steel skyscrapers of Lower Manhattan.

*www.manhattanbysail.com/sails*

### KEY WEST
*Florida*

No town puts on a better sunset-related shindig than Key West. Every night, starting about two hours before the disappearing sun paints the sky, head to the waterfront for some shopping and food cart delights. Then, turn toward the Gulf of Mexico and watch the natural artwork break out.

*www.sunsetcelebration.org*

### TORRES DEL PAINE NATIONAL PARK
*Chile*

The park's geographic range offers a million different sunsets. But, one mental snapshot: Imagine the park's granite peaks and the glacial lakes below glowing pink. All around, spots of green moss send the blushing landscape into overdrive.

*www.torresdelpaine.com/ingles*

### OIA CASTLE
*Santorini, Greece*

It's just a giant postcard. As the sun starts to slip below into the Aegean Sea, the sky all around the traditional village and castle of Oia, on the very northern tip of the island of Santorini, gives itself over from the day's magnificent blue to crimson to . . . every sunset color imaginable. Beware: It's a popular spot. But once that color starts to break out, you won't notice. It is breathtaking.

*www.greeka.com/cyclades/santorini/index.htm*

### CLIFTON BEACHES
*Cape Town, South Africa*

White sand. Aqua water. Brilliant sunset sky. There's a reason Clifton is home to some of Cape Town's wealthiest residents: that view. But a shuttle ride to the area—parking is dreadful—makes it easy to take in without the house payment. Head straight to one of Clifton's four beaches. Take up temporary residence on a blanket and watch Nature's fireworks explode over the South Atlantic Ocean.

*www.capetown.travel*

### KENTING NATIONAL PARK
*Hengchun Peninsula, Taiwan*

High above Kenting's western shore, this viewpoint on Taiwan's southern tip looking out over the Taiwan Strait is, surprisingly, not one of the park's most popular sights. For you, this is a good thing; you may end up with the sunset all to yourself. Keep an eye out for some of the park's other natural beauties: thousands of varieties of tropical plants, birds, and butterflies.

*www.ktnp.gov.tw/eng*

### VAIROU BAY
*Bora Bora, Tahiti*

Park yourself on a deck at your resort. And just wait. As the sun meets the horizon, the world glows brilliant. Though the area's hotels are all high-end—there's a price to pay when you head to the quintessential tropical island paradise—the free evening show may be the best amenity of them all.

*www.tahiti-tourisme.com*

### ULURU (AYERS ROCK)
*Northern Territory, Australia*

As the sun dips and the sky swirls through its color show, the sandstone of Uluru, a massive monolith rising 1,150 feet (350 m) from the plains of the Australian outback, glows red—nearly stealing the sky's thunder. Before choosing a spot to watch the view, consider taking a hike around the sacred site. It's farther than it looks—the rock is nearly 6 miles (10 km) in circumference.

*whc.unesco.org/en/list/447*

Bora Bora's postcard-perfect good looks get bumped up a notch (or 30) during every evening's sunset. Even the water seems to soak up the color.

The only thing to expect at the Fringe Festival: the unexpected. Here, the Kataklo dance theater group gets their bikes in on the act.

SCOTLAND

# EDINBURGH

**The capital city discards its dreary coat for a summer filled with music, comedy, dancing, and golf.**

I t's a sunny summer afternoon in Edinburgh and thousands of people are roaming the streets of the Scottish capital. Some are strolling the revitalized waterfront, others are bouncing from circus show to comedy act at the city's famous summer Fringe Festival, while still others clamber over the stout walls of Edinburgh Castle—perched atop an ancient volcano. About an hour down the coast, golf pilgrims tee off at grassy seaside links where the game was born hundreds of years ago.

### ENJOY THE SHOWS: FROM THE WACKY TO THE RIDICULOUS

Edinburgh's action reaches fever pitch over the last month of summer. In August, the world's single largest arts festival—the Edinburgh Fringe—takes the stage in hundreds of venues large and small all over the city. Offbeat and obscure comedy, music, dance, and drama are the forte of this wacky parallel to the highbrow Edinburgh International Festival, which takes place at the same time. The scale of the Fringe is enormous: nearly 2,700 shows at more than 250 venues attended by around two million people each year. The program alone is nearly 400 pages long, featuring acts from around the world. Many of the shows are free, all of them unusual, and some so far out they seem to come from another planet.

*In August, the world's single largest arts festival—the Edinburgh Fringe— takes the stage in hundreds of venues large and small all over the city.*

A bonus summer festival: More than 200,000 attend Edinburgh's Military Tattoo (an international show of military bands, color, pageantry, and theater) during its three-week run at Edinburgh Castle every year.

St. Andrews is the town that, in many ways, gave birth to today's Scotland. It's where both modern-day golf and Scotland's universities got their start.

Start with the Royal Mile. It's chockablock with buskers—fire-eaters, mimes, escape artists—strutting their stuff on the cobblestones. But it's the eclectic stage acts that bring people back to the Fringe year after year. You'll find break-dancers competing for the Scottish championship in a club near the old North Bridge, while acrobats dive into a circus-style adaptation of Dante's *Inferno* near the city's celebrated castle. Just try keeping a straight face at a musical-comedy version of the Spanish Armada at a small theater or at the somber reinterpretation of *Grease* at another.

The best way to approach the megafestivities? It's up to you. Buy tickets in advance or, suggests American musician and Fringe aficionado Matthew Peterson, just "walk around without a plan and experience all sorts of things."

## WANDER THE WATERFRONT

Edinburgh's waterfront also comes alive in summer. The once hardworking port has transformed itself into a historical and cultural hub. Scramble aboard the royal yacht *Britannia* to see how the "other half" once lived. The 412-foot (126 m) steamship was the Queen's floating palace until 1997 and is now a museum (recalling its own regal history) permanently docked in Edinburgh. Then, drink in a little cultural enrichment: Learn the difference between Highland and island Scotch while lounging on a leather sofa in the wood-paneled vaults at the Scotch Malt Whisky Society.

## CATCH A ROUND ON LEGENDARY GREENS

Escape the madding crowds at one of Scotland's legendary golf courses, like the storied Royal and Ancient Golf Club in St. Andrews, about 56 miles (90 km) up the east coast from Edinburgh. Founded in 1754, the club is generally regarded as the governing authority of global golf. There, you can realize the fantasy of many a golfer and play in the footsteps of Bobby Jones, Ben Hogan, Arnold Palmer, Jack Nicklaus, and Tiger Woods on the scenic Old Course, one of seven public links in the seaside city, where 12th-century shepherds knocking stones into rabbit holes with crooks and canes allegedly invented the game.

At first glance, the links look deceptively easy. But don't be lulled into a false sense of bravado: The greens are huge and notoriously tricky, more than 100 bunkers are waiting to swallow your ball, and over the back nine you'll need to conquer legendary Old Course features like Hell and the Valley of Sin.

Before you drive back to the capital, pop into the British Golf Museum with its 17,000 artifacts, including early clubs and the original 18th-century hand-written rules of golf.

**PLANNING Edinburgh** www.visitscotland .com, www.edinburgh.org. **Edinburgh Fringe Festival** www.edfringe.com. The website gives a complete rundown of the acts, the venues, and how to buy tickets. Festivalgoers often purchase tickets months in advance. **Waterfront** Royal yacht *Britannia,* www.royal yachtbritannia.co.uk; Scotch Malt Whisky Society, www.smws.co.uk. **St. Andrews** Royal and Ancient Golf Club, www.randa.org; Old Course, www.standrews.org.uk. **British Golf Museum** www.britishgolfmuseum.co.uk.

## FOR FOODIES
*Scottish Food in Edinburgh*

When you're out and about, these restaurants are excellent, convenient eating options near Edinburgh Castle:

● **ELEPHANT HOUSE:** Haggis (the national dish), neeps (turnips), and tatties (mashed potatoes) are among the favorites at this café on George IV Bridge. J. K. Rowling is among its celebrated habitués. www .elephanthouse.biz

● **GRAIN STORE:** A cozy, medieval granary known for its nouvelle Scottish cuisine. Among the standouts: Orkney scallops ceviche and Aberdeen Angus steak with ox tongue. www .grainstore-restaurant.co.uk

● **NUMBER ONE:** With a Michelin star, this upscale restaurant in the Balmoral Hotel is one of Scotland's finest. The menu ranges from simple seafood to venison with blackberries. restaurantnumberone.com

Tao samurai drummers leap into action at a recent Fringe Festival.

# SUMMER THEATER

**Catch the season's best shows, from musical premieres to world-class Shakespeare productions.**

### STRATFORD FESTIVAL

*Stratford, Ontario, Canada*

The largest classical repertory theater in North America stages productions on a thrust stage where the finest Shakespearean actors perform the bard's great comedies and tragedies. Open May to September.

*www.stratfordfestival.ca*

### NEW YORK MUSICAL THEATRE FESTIVAL

*New York, New York*

Each July, dozens of original musicals premiere at this festival, held in the heart of New York City's theater district. Many of the event's new musicals go on to successful Broadway or off-Broadway runs, including the Tony Award–winning *Next to Normal.*

*www.nymf.org/index.html*

### FESTIVAL INTERNACIONAL DE TEATRO

*Caracas, Venezuela*

For more than 30 years, the premier theater festival in Latin America has brought together scores of performance companies from around the world to act in Venezuela's capital. Performers take to the streets, plazas, and theater venues throughout the city for two weeks each April to stage classics such as Anton Chekhov's *The Cherry Orchard,* Henrik Ibsen's *Hedda Gabler,* and Dante's *Inferno.*

*fitcaracas.blogspot.com (use your translator)*

### EDINBURGH INTERNATIONAL FESTIVAL

*Edinburgh, Scotland*

Founded soon after the end of World War II, Edinburgh's annual August fest ranks as one of the leading arts celebrations in the world. Theater productions range from *Electra* to a modern-day retelling of *Macbeth.* Visit the festival headquarters in the Hub, an iconic city landmark whose spire dominates the Royal Mile between Edinburgh Castle and Holyrood Palace.

*www.eif.co.uk*

### OPEN AIR THEATRE

*Regent's Park, London, England*

Vivien Leigh and Judi Dench both trod the boards of this London landmark, the oldest permanent outdoor theater in Britain. More than 130,000 spectators attend each season's four productions between May and September. Bring a hamper and sip Pimm's on the picnic lawn while enjoying the theater's signature piece, *A Midsummer Night's Dream.*

*openairtheatre.org*

### FESTIVAL D'AVIGNON

*Avignon, France*

At least one new show opens every night at this festival in the south of France. Every July, Avignon becomes a "city-theater," with 20-odd historical venues transformed into performance spaces. The heart is the Cour d'Honneur, the main courtyard of the Pope's Palace, where spectators gather for performances during the Provençal summer nights.

*www.festival-avignon.com/en*

### ZÜRCHER THEATER SPEKTAKEL

*Zurich, Switzerland*

Dozens of independent theater companies put on cutting-edge productions each August in one of Europe's most important contemporary performing arts festivals. Performances take place in the parklike Landiwiese on Lake Zurich, where venues include an open-air stage and a shipyard for creative staging possibilities.

*www.theaterspektakel.ch*

### NATIONAL ARTS FESTIVAL

*Grahamstown, South Africa*

Bundle up for performances at Africa's largest cultural event, held in June and July in South Africa's Eastern Cape region. The children's arts festival offers drama workshops for kids ages 4–13, while street theater productions carry the festival spirit throughout the city.

*www.nationalartsfestival.co.za*

### IIDA PUPPET FESTA

*Nagano Prefecture, Japan*

Known as the "city of puppet shows," Iida, located between Tokyo and Nagoya, hosts the largest puppetry festival in Japan every August. Some 150 troupes perform shows ranging from traditional Bunraku puppetry to modern acts in dozens of sites throughout the city, from Puppetry Hall to the grounds of parks and shrines.

*www.city.iida.lg.jp/puppet*

### PERTH INTERNATIONAL ARTS FESTIVAL

*Perth, Australia*

Each year, Perth celebrates the oldest annual, international, multiarts festival in the Southern Hemisphere. Founded in 1953, the three-week-long celebration includes the National Play Festival, which showcases new plays written and performed by Australia's finest theater artists. Venues include His Majesty's Theatre, the only working Edwardian theater in Australia.

*www.perthfestival.com.au*

During the esteemed Festival d'Avignon, the Cour d'Honneur at the Place du Palais des Papes hosts an actor with Charlie Chaplin on the brain.

Did King Arthur ever stand on this beach? Ponder the question as you gaze out upon the Atlantic and watch modern-day knights on their surfboards.

ENGLAND

# THE CORNWALL COAST

**Swim and surf with seals or hike the headlands on the region's dramatic Coast Path.**

Eighteenth-century smugglers and pirates rode the rough waves by the coves and cliffs near Land's End, Cornwall. Today, surfers in wet suits follow their lead. Ride the coast's most challenging swells with hardy adventurers near Fistral Beach, off Newquay.

"There are lots of good beaches in Cornwall, but Fistral is the main hub of surfing because it's most consistent," explains Ben Ridding, who runs Surfing Is Therapy below the Headland Hotel. "The shape of the wave is created by the headlands. Fistral picks up the Atlantic swells along a beach that's a kilometer [half a mile] long at low tide. And, of course, there's the infamous Cribbar"—a legendary 30-foot (9 m) wave that breaks only once or twice a year. Joining you are seals that skim the swells, then bask on rocks in the surf.

For walkers and hikers, the South-West Coast Path offers a well-marked long-distance trail punctuated with villages and guesthouses. For shorter strolls, Ridding recommends the beach at Porthcurno. "The light there is totally different, really beautiful and dramatic," he says. Anywhere along the coast in these northern latitudes, summer sunsets linger late, bathing the headlands in the season's golden light. Toast the moment with Camel Valley sparkling wine made from local Cornish grapes.

**PLANNING Cornish Coast** www.visitcornwall.com. Trains depart for the five-hour journey to the West Country from London's Paddington Station. Frequent flights from London Gatwick to Newquay cut travel time to 70 minutes.

SWEDEN

# GOTLAND ISLAND

**Get into a Gothic groove at a raucous Swedish summer homage to its Middle Age roots.**

To visit the island of Gotland is to travel back in time—way back. In 1361, it was the site of one of Scandinavia's greatest battles, when Denmark's king invaded and conquered the island, the largest in Sweden.

The bloody face-off inspired myths of long-ago Norseman and knights, as well as Medeltidsveckan (Medieval Week), a weeklong time trip that takes place each August. The action centers around the Viking town of Visby, considered the "best-preserved fortified commercial city in northern Europe," according to UNESCO.

Immerse yourself in the festivities clad in period clothing (brought from home or purchased there). Go Gothic at outdoor markets and moody local taverns. You can also eat your way through grandiloquent banquets, dance at medieval music performances, and listen to Nordic sagas spun by people who look like they actually might have been there.

The biggest ancient action comes at jousting tournaments featuring armor-clad warriors on horseback. "The best knights in Sweden compete for honor with thousands of people cheering and mocking them to great deeds," says Bjorn Sundberg, a festival director and owner of a medieval-themed restaurant. "Archers and jesters entertain, trumpets are sounding, and flags are raised to keep the scores—the biggest medieval sports event you can imagine."

**PLANNING  Gotland** www.gotland.info. **Medeltidsveckan** www.medeltidsveckan.se. Kapitelhusgarden, Sundberg's restaurant, is near the cathedral in Visby.

The quietude of Visby, Sweden's medieval churches and red-roofed cottages gives way in August to the annual Medieval Week.

# NORWAY
# SVALBARD

"Through binoculars he stared over the pack ice off Svalbard, that rugged Arctic archipelago between Norway and the North Pole. These bleak islands, the largest of which is Spitsbergen, are one of the strongholds of a magnificent animal we Norwegians call *isbjørn*—ice bear."

—THOR LARSEN, *NATIONAL GEOGRAPHIC* MAGAZINE, APRIL 1971

**Glaciers cover more than half of the Svalberg archipelago in the Norwegian Sea. Despite that, 2,500 people and 2,500 polar bears call this chain of islands home.**

# THE BALTIC SEA

**Stay in the region's great cities while indulging in all of the niceties of a romantic cruise.**

Leaving Stockholm, the ship cuts across steel-blue waters through a cottage-dotted archipelago straight out of Swedish fairy tale, headed for the Baltic Sea. In summer, the Baltic can still be gray and cool, but the seas are clear of icebergs, making the time right for a Baltic cruise.

The St. Peter Line connects St. Petersburg, Russia, with Stockholm, Sweden; Helsinki, Finland; and Tallinn, Estonia. There are two amazing things about this operation. First, you can disembark at each destination and stay for a few days, while passengers from other cruises have to head back to their cabins. And second, you can stay for 72 hours in St. Petersburg visa free; given the difficulties (and expense) involved in obtaining a Russian visa these days, this possibility is a godsend.

A bit of Baltic flair comes with this Russian-owned enterprise, including the shipload of Russians, Swedes, and Finns. During your time onboard, you can get a Russian-style massage, take a sauna, and enjoy a glittery stage show at night featuring both contemporary and Russian folk dancing. Indulge in caviar, Champagne, vodka (of course), and other delicacies in the restaurants. By morning, you'll be entering the harbor of one of the Baltic's great cities and headed for the next adventure.

**PLANNING  St. Peter Line** stpeterline.com.

Before embarking on a Baltic Sea cruise, explore the cobblestone streets and well-preserved medieval frescoes of Stockholm's Gamla Stan (Old Town).

Festivalgoers in St. Petersburg take time to enjoy fountains set up on the Neva River. There's no reason to rush: It stays light for two months.

RUSSIA

# ST. PETERSBURG

**Wander the midnight streets of the city's White Nights, a city kept awake by two months of unending twilight.**

From May until late July, St. Petersburg emerges from its long, dark winter into an almost endless twilight. During the course of these White Nights, sundown becomes elusive. As the summer solstice nears, the midnight sun—barely sinking below the horizon—streaks the sky with pink clouds and transforms it into translucent sapphire hues. "It was a wonderful night," Fyodor Dostoevsky wrote of his revered White Night walk 165 years ago. The Russian writer went on to lament the emptying of St. Petersburg during the summer as residents fled to countryside villas.

He'd probably like it more today, when this city of tsars pampers visitors with outdoor music concerts and round-the-clock discos. Tracing the Russian writer's footsteps, one of the best places to walk is along the Neva River, where the massive drawbridges rise in the early morning hush to allow cargo ships to pass. Though White Nights occur in northern cities around the world, they crescendo in St. Petersburg with world-renowned opera and ballet. The Stars of the White Nights, a classical festival programmed by the Mariinsky Theatre, features three months of performances by top Russian and international artists. Coupled with other citywide celebrations, the insomniac atmosphere is electric.

**PLANNING** St. Petersburg www.saint-petersburg.com. Flights from around the world land at Pulkovo Airport, including Aeroflot's daily jaunts from Moscow. **Stars of the White Nights** www.mariinsky.ru/en, www.balletandopera.com.

Venture farther north into the White Nights on an overnight cruise. Ships leave from St. Petersburg along the Neva River. As the urban sprawl dissipates, the river winds past small towns and wooden, onion-domed churches. Fall asleep as the Neva empties into Lake Ladoga, Europe's largest fresh-water lake, and awaken as the ship docks the following morning at Valaam Island. The site of a still-functioning Orthodox monastery that dates back to at least the 14th century, Valaam is thickly blanketed by aromatic pine trees, verdant ferns, and rocky ridges. Cruises are all-inclusive packages that include typically Russian meals and guided excursions. www.saint-petersburg.com

Explore the now-submerged village of Vilarinho das Furnas as a way to cool off after a day of hiking around Peneda-Gerês National Park.

PORTUGAL

# GERÊS

**Scale craggy promontories, cool off in a clear mountain stream, and, maybe, walk with the wolves.**

The northern Parque Nacional Peneda-Gerês is Portugal's first designated national park. Its rugged and wild landscape, harsh and foreboding during most of the year, is transformed during the warm summer months into a place of breathtaking natural beauty.

To get a true sense of the park, leave the car behind and strike out on foot. There is nothing quite like ambling along a cobbled Roman path with a rare golden eagle circling above; sticking your head inside the dark, cool interior of a 5,000-year-old dolmen; or simply stopping to watch granite boulders sparkle in the sunlight.

For the ultimate experience, hook up with a guide and immerse yourself in the mysterious world of the park's most endangered, predatory inhabitant: the much-feared Iberian wolf. "One of the best ways to experience the wolves' habitat is to take to the ancient shepherd paths," says local guide Pedro Alarcão. "In early July, the scenery is at its best."

Guides will teach you to recognize wolf tracks and follow their trails, show you disused traps, and regale you with local wolf legends. If your timing is auspicious, you may even be blessed with a glimpse of this rare and near-mythical creature.

**PLANNING  Parque Nacional Peneda-Gerês** www.visitportugal.com. For guided trekking through wolf habitats, consider Ecotura (*www.ecotura.com*).

### BEST OF THE BEST
*The Granite Grain Stores of Soajo*

To experience one of the park's most extraordinary man-made treasures, head to the village of Soajo and its remarkable grouping of 18th-century granite grain stores. *Espigueiros*, as they are known locally, can be found scattered across the region, but only here and in nearby Lindoso can they be seen in an impressive communal cluster. Try to visit at either dawn or dusk when the lighting is at its most atmospheric and best for taking photos. Climb up to the exposed granite outcrop, formerly the village threshing floor, and wander between the 24 granaries, with their protective rooftop crosses standing guard over the stored crops.

# THE PYRENEES

**Fly along on a hardy bike ride through medieval villages, fueled by clear mountain air and seasonal celebrations.**

Stretching from the Mediterranean to the Bay of Biscay, the Pyrenees mountains form the border between Spain and France. Bike trails linking hillside hamlets wind throughout the range. Bounce across the cobblestones of medieval hamlets like Castellar de n'Hug in Spanish Catalonia, and then cruise into pine-shrouded solitude on trails that hug the mountainside. Coast downhill past clusters of summer wildflowers while the valley far below, speckled with stone farmhouses, glows golden in the late afternoon sunshine. After pedaling up a steep incline, cool off with an icy dip in an alpine lake or shaded river gorge.

"They are mountains that, in addition to stunning scenery, have a great many villages, history, and wildlife ranging from brown bears to the tiniest creatures," says National Geographic photographer Tino Soriano, who lives in northern Catalonia. "In summer, the people hold many rural celebrations that still retain their timeless charm, when the people dance around bonfires."

Gaze upon finely worked stone and Romanesque bell towers as you bike through the narrow Vall de Boí, "full of churches and ancestral traditions," Soriano says. As evening falls, join cheering villagers celebrating late June's St. John's Day in Isil and watch flaming tree trunks flicker eerily in the darkness as they descend the mountainside.

**PLANNING  Pyrenees** www.spain.info. **Mountain biking** Cycle the Spanish Pyrenees to the Mediterranean with Easy Rider tours *(www.easyridertours.com)*.

## BEST OF THE BEST
### *Cadaqués, Spain*

Wander cobblestone streets lined with white houses in Cadaqués, a tiny Mediterranean fishing village on Spain's Costa Brava. Accessible only by a single winding road through the mountains, the isolated town on the rocky Cap de Creus peninsula inspired artists such as Picasso and Chagall and was the favorite haunt of Salvador Dalí. Visit the surrealist master's house turned museum to the north of town on Port Lligat Bay, then walk along the harbor where colorful boats bob at anchor. Stop in at the local gathering spot known as the Casino, where grizzled fishermen gather to play cards and while away the quiet afternoons. www.spain.info

A cyclist makes the most of a downhill section overlooking the Ossau Valley.

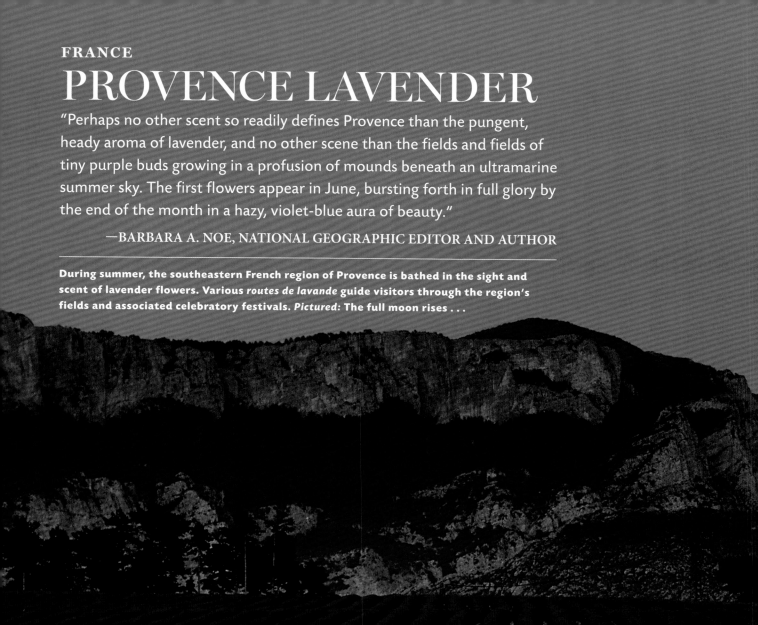

# PROVENCE LAVENDER

"Perhaps no other scent so readily defines Provence than the pungent, heady aroma of lavender, and no other scene than the fields and fields of tiny purple buds growing in a profusion of mounds beneath an ultramarine summer sky. The first flowers appear in June, bursting forth in full glory by the end of the month in a hazy, violet-blue aura of beauty."

—BARBARA A. NOE, NATIONAL GEOGRAPHIC EDITOR AND AUTHOR

During summer, the southeastern French region of Provence is bathed in the sight and scent of lavender flowers. Various *routes de lavande* guide visitors through the region's fields and associated celebratory festivals. *Pictured:* The full moon rises . . .

Lazing about in Lake Geneva often comes with an impressive view. Here, the Vaud's Château de Chillon keeps bathers company.

# SWITZERLAND

**Plunge into pristine turquoise lakes and the cobalt glacial Alpine rivers that feed them.**

The Swiss Alps conjure vivid visions of glittering white mountain peaks set against sharp blue skies. But the region's sparkling summer waters are no less alluring. Switzerland is home to hundreds of natural swimming areas, and every major city and small town has a lake, pond, or river to dip in. The warm months from June to September draw urban lappers, beach waders, post-hike plungers, and scuba divers who capitalize on the clarity of the Alpine waters for underwater archaeological excursions.

## CLEAR WATERS AMID ANCIENT CITY STREETS

Zurich alone is home to dozens of *badis,* thermal baths often enhanced with changing rooms, showers, sundecks, and cafés. Come July, it's more Rio than Europe. The entire social scene moves to a waterfront perch, where impromptu picnics give the city's bars and restaurants some competition. There are baths for gays, Hasidic Jews, women, and bankers, and baths where the city's large Google crew hangs out. In August, water revelers glide by Zurich's 14th-century bridges and ornate towers during Limmatschwimmen, when the city's Oberer Letten River opens for swimming.

Just south, Lake Zurich is dotted with beaches and badis on both coasts, the sunnier Gold Coast and the shadier, comically nicknamed but no less pleasant "flu coast." A bit farther, the Walensee glistens and lures visitors with its mighty Alpine wall backdrop.

Elsewhere, summer waters are no less dazzling. Lac Léman, or Lake Geneva, is dotted with parks and beaches, and on the water near Geneva floats a massive sauna. Chilly Lake Lucerne could pass for something in Middle-earth, with its sublime, primordial blue-green color. The Bodensee, or Lake Constance, along the German border, is wildly popular with German families and cyclists who bike a well-trodden waterside circuit.

## DIPS TO TEMPT THE DARING

Bern's milky, cerulean blue Aare River is bracingly cold but another favorite. Ditto for the überturquoise Verzasca mountain river. In the picturesque, Italian-speaking Alpine village of Lavertezzo, brave souls jump off medieval Ponte dei Salti ("Jumping Bridge") into the chilly green waters. Even the mighty Rhine, still trafficked by industrial barges, is swimmable. In Basel, where its powerful currents gave rise to the city's thriving industry, cordoned-off swimming areas invite urban dippers.

"The greatest thing about swimming in Switzerland," says Peter Brüwiler, a Bodensee lifeguard, "is that you never have to worry about water quality. You can just jump in any lake you feel like!"

**PLANNING  Swimming in Switzerland's lakes and rivers** www.myswitzerland.com. Swiss tourism's excellent swimming apps offer water temperatures and nearest swimming locations for numerous areas throughout the country.

Choose a lake. Hop in. Enjoy. In the Swiss Alps, the water's always fine.

# SALZBURG

**Bask in the summertime glow of Mozart masterpieces in his hometown.**

Ranked as one of the world's most important music festivals since its founding in 1920, the Salzburg Festival transforms the northern Austrian city into a glittering stage for classical concerts and dramatic art for five weeks each July and August.

"Every summer in Salzburg, the boundaries between daily life and stagecraft become blurred," says press officer Ulla Kalchmair. "The Salzburg Festival offers a certain flair. The entire city resembles a catwalk of high culture."

Born in Salzburg in 1756, Mozart gets top billing as the city's favorite son. Let the soaring melodies of his operatic masterworks like *The Marriage of Figaro* or *The Magic Flute* sweep you away in the golden House for Mozart concert hall, or soak in the haunting strains of his Requiem in the art nouveau splendor of the Mozarteum's Great Hall.

During the day, plunge into pristine glacial lakes that reflect pine-shrouded mountains in the surrounding Salzkammergut region, often called Austria's Lake District. As you head back into the city, snag a seat outdoors in the 17th-century Salzburg Cathedral's square. With an unmatched theatrical backdrop of twin white marble towers, watch the afternoon shadows advance upon the Everyman in the festival's annual performance of the medieval morality play *Jedermann*.

**PLANNING  Salzburg Festival** www.salzburgerfestspiele.at. Find insider tips on attending the festival, such as where to get last-minute Jedermann tickets, at Tourismus Salzburg *(www.salzburg.info).*

Part time machine, part feast, all Mozart—the Mozart Dinner Concert is a fitting tribute to Salzburg's favorite son.

Crowds pack into Siena's main square to watch bareback riders race through in an effort to snag local bragging rights for their neighborhood.

ITALY

# SIENA

**Catch the competitive fever that grips this Tuscan town as horses gallop around its famed medieval square.**

Twice every summer, the magnificent Tuscan city of Siena works itself into a collective frenzy during the Palio, a three-lap, bareback horse race around the main square. Dating from medieval times, the event is neither quaint museum piece nor tourist gimmick. The Palio is a very real, intense show of neighborhood rivalry, civic pride, and raw-throated emotion that strikes like a fever every July and August.

Tens of thousands of spectators jam every nook and cranny in and around the Campo di Siena, the gently tilted, shell-shaped central piazza. First up: the Corteo Storico, an elaborate pageant of drummers, flag bearers, and sword-wielding horsemen. Then, at the appointed evening hour, the air crackles with excitement as ten entrants line up. For a brief moment, you can hear a pin drop.

Suddenly the horses explode forward, hurling themselves around the dirt track, the jockeys furiously whipping their charges (or those of their rivals) before the ecstatic, pennant-waving crowd. It's one and a half minutes of high drama and potential tragedy—riders can be thrown and horses injured or even killed. The winning neighborhood holds riotous celebrations while the losers weep. Explains Elizabeth Minchilli, an area food and travel writer, "For the people of Siena, the Palio is everything."

**PLANNING   Palio di Siena** www.sienaonline.it. The Palio takes place on July 2 and August 16. Be sure to book tickets and accommodation well in advance.

# (WE ALL SCREAM FOR) ICE CREAM

**Savor the irresistible summer treat that comes in many languages.**

### MOOMERS HOMEMADE ICE CREAM

*Traverse City, Michigan*

The Plummer family opened Moomers near their dairy farm west of Traverse City in 1998 to help kids connect food and agriculture. Come summer, there's a perpetual line out the door for their 120 flavors. Get a scoop of Cherries Moobilee, a fudge-brownie concoction studded with local tart cherries.

*www.moomers.com*

### FOUR SEAS ICE CREAM

*Centerville, Massachusetts*

Four Seas has been an institution since opening in the 1930s. Generations of Cape Codders—the Kennedy clan among them—have made summer pilgrimages to the little white cottage for summer-only favorites such as fresh peach ice cream and refreshing frappés (localspeak for milkshakes).

*www.fourseasicecream.com*

### CAYUGA LAKE CREAMERY

*Interlaken, New York*

Cayuga Lake Creamery draws on the rich local bounty for some of its most memorable flavors, including Riesling orange sorbet, lavender, and maple bacon. Grab a cone for the short, scenic drive south to Taughannock Falls State Park, home to one of the largest single-drop waterfalls east of the Rockies.

*cayugalakecreamery.com*

### HELADOS SCANNAPIECO

*Buenos Aires, Argentina*

Buenos Aires is rife with *heladerías,* or ice cream parlors, but the most beloved is the tiny Scannapieco, opened by Italian immigrants in 1938. Family members carry on the handmade gelato tradition with flavors like limoncello and flan.

*www.heladosscannapieco.com.ar*

### BERTHILLON

*Paris, France*

The celebrated glacier on Île Saint-Louis is the first stop in Paris for ice cream enthusiasts from around the world. The tough part is deciding between *glacés*—with flavors like marrons (candied chestnuts), Earl Grey, and *chocolat noir*—and bright sorbets such as *frais de bois* (wild strawberry). Don't be disheartened to find the shop closed in late July and August; the ice cream is served at cafés citywide (just look for the Berthillon logo).

*www.berthillon.fr*

### IL GELATO DI SAN CRISPINO

*Rome, Italy*

Italian gelato purists head to Il Gelato di San Crispino, with a handful of locations throughout the capital city, including one near Trevi Fountain. The selection is limited according to seasonal availability—lemons from Amalfi, for example, or pistachios from Sicily.

*www.ilgelatodisancrispino.it*

### DOĞAL DONDURMA

*Bodrum, Turkey*

Soft, stretchy, and chewy, Turkish ice cream, or *dondurma*, is often thickened with salep, made from orchid roots. Vendors abound in Istanbul, but the legendary Doğal Dondurma in the coastal resort town of Bodrum is revered for its five-star licks and seasonal flavors. Don't miss the signature fresh mandarin lime sorbet.

### ICE CREAM CITY

*Tokyo, Japan*

A child's fantasy come true, the kitschy Ice Cream City is tucked into the Namja Town amusement area in Tokyo's Sunshine City shopping complex. Booth after booth of ice cream vendors peddle various styles—soft-serve, gelato, dondurma—in hundreds of flavors, including preserved cherry blossom and a salty-sweet eel.

*www.sunshinecity.co.jp (in Japanese)*

### TOM'S PALETTE

*Singapore*

A mom-and-pop ice cream shop in food-crazed downtown Singapore, Tom's Palette has developed a cult following with its homemade ethos and inventive flavors like mango sticky rice, durian, and salted egg. If these don't appeal, suggestions are welcome.

*www.tomspalette.com.sg*

### PASSIONFLOWER

*Melbourne, Australia*

Known for its exotic Asian flavors such as lychee rose and taro, Melbourne's chic Passionflower takes the sundae concept to new heights. Its Final Fantasy is loaded with scoops of black sesame and coconut ice cream and topped with black jelly pieces and a shot of evaporated milk.

*www.passionflower.com.au*

Never fresher: An ice cream maker finishes another batch to tempt passersby at a seaside town on the Turkish Riviera.

# Tony Hawk
## Santorini, Greece

I was peeking over my wife's shoulder at an email from our close friend requesting we go on vacation together. What followed was a link to a hotel website with images that looked too picturesque to be real. I noticed it was located on an island in Greece, so I muttered to my wife, "I've never been to Greece . . . ," and the ball started rolling.

We arrived in the heat of the summer. But the July skies were sparkling and the temperatures made the prospect of an island visit all the more appealing. On the way to Santorini, we spent a day like Griswold-type tourists in Athens. Which meant hiking in the hot sun to the top of the Acropolis with thousands of other tourists. As cliché as it seems, the view was stunning; all of Athens is laid out before you, with thousands of years of human history to gape upon.

With a few hours to kill, we decided to search out the legendary Skate House, a private home with a mini skate park inside. Through a series of emails and calls, we got in touch with the owner, a former skater who liked the aesthetic that ramps provided. We arrived five minutes later, moved her coffee table, and skated for 20 minutes, nearly hitting the flat-screen TV twice and falling into the bathroom after a misguided hand plant. It was just enough to get a short video clip: youtube/1FmQzAqKOY0.

We then flew to Santorini, a breathtaking flight in itself. We landed as the sun was setting, making the entire island glow in a golden hue.

On most travel sites, one of the top "things to do" in Santorini is "nothing." We took that advice for the most part, taking in the amazing views and Greek cuisine every day. We spent one day on a boat, exploring the island and visiting the hot springs. Santorini is essentially what's left of a huge volcanic eruption 3,600 years ago that is the basis of Atlantis folklore. But if Atlantis is an undiscovered paradise under the sea, Santorini is the terrestrial—and real—counterpart.

I highly recommend a trip there, especially in summer when you can experience clear skies and warm water. Once you arrive, do nothing as fast as possible, except cooling off in the beautiful Aegean Sea.

*Tony Hawk is arguably the world's most famous professional skateboarder and founder of the Tony Hawk Foundation.*

"[The] hotel . . . looked too picturesque to be real . . . so I muttered to my wife, 'I've never been to Greece.'"

Get on the fast track to lazy days in Santorini—where "sit in hot springs" and "eat local cuisine" are a reasonable day's to-do list.

Seeing an opera in Verona's open-air stadium may ruin you for all other operatic experiences—it turns an evening out into an extravaganza.

ITALY

# VERONA

**Enjoy one of Europe's most romantic settings when all the city's an ancient stage for great music and theater.**

Shakespeare couldn't resist the place: *The Two Gentlemen of Verona* was possibly his first play, and of course, this is the town where Romeo yelled up at a balcony and defined teenage love forever. It remains the place for culture, especially in summer.

Says Reid Bramblett, a longtime resident who met his own wife bellowing at a pretty girl on an Italian balcony, "Summertime in Verona is all about high culture in the open air, from classic Italian opera under the stars in the 2,000-year-old Arena amphitheater to Shakespearean plays in the ancient Teatro Romano just across the slow-flowing Adige River." Sit on the ancient amphitheater steps (cheaper than sitting closer, and a better view, anyway) for the performance, after getting everything you need for a picnic from local vendors. Not in the mood for opera? The Teatro Romano starts the summer with a jazz festival, then moves on to Shakespeare before closing out the season with modern dance.

And after any performance, the soft summer air almost begs a visitor to "tool down the side streets and slick-paved pedestrian shopping roads on a bicycle to browse the market stalls on Piazza delle Erbe," as Bramblett suggests. Or just cruise the streets and look for somebody you like leaning over a balcony. It's worked before.

**PLANNING Verona** www.verona.com/en. **Opera** www.arena.it/en-us/homeen.html. The city is 70 miles (113 km) west of Venice and 100 miles (160 km) east of Milan by train *(www.raileurope.com)*.

---

## BEST OF THE BEST
### *The Immortal Juliet*

Worldwide, the three fictional characters who get the most mail are probably Santa Claus, Smokey the Bear, and Juliet. Once you've taken in a Shakespeare show, why not drop a line to his most famous lover at Casa di Giulietta? The 14th-century house, complete with balcony (actually added in 1936 to draw tourists), is said to have been the Capulets'. Below is a tunnel studded with missives to dear Juliet, like a corkboard gone wild. The city does everything it can to keep the legend alive, with a staff of volunteers who answer the letters—something Smokey never bothered to do.

# OKAVANGO DELTA

**The swamp islands of the vast Okavango Delta become a mecca for wildlife during the summer floods.**

The guide cuts the outboard engine and you glide silently toward a fallen tree. Suddenly, he points to a crocodile sunning itself on an overturned trunk, now close enough to touch. Later, after dark, you tramp through the reeds on an isolated swamp island in the Okavango Delta and pitch camp. Sleeping out in the open that night, you spot the Southern Cross low on the horizon and listen to the deep-throated groan of a lion somewhere far off in the bush. When you awake the next morning, you see hippos emerge from the water's edge a short distance away.

In much of Africa, the dry months are the best time to view game, as that's the time when animals congregate around water holes. But in the Okavango of northern Botswana, the May–June flood season drives animals to islands in the middle of the vast swamps. "The quintessential Okavango experience," says safari planner Megan Ingoldby, "is the opportunity to watch wildlife at eye level while gliding silently in a *mokoro* [dugout canoe]." Those who don't want to rough it can overnight in luxury tented camps and lodges. "Mix different types of camps and environments to experience the full range of activities, flora, and fauna," Ingoldby advises.

**PLANNING Botswana** www.botswanatourism.co.bw. A number of outfitters offer guided safaris and accommodations in the Okavango Delta, including Expert Africa *(www.expertafrica.com)*.

## GREAT STAYS
*Okavango's Best Flood Season Digs*

● **EAGLE ISLAND:** This Orient-Express property is one of the posher places to sleep in the Okavango. Activities include mokoro trips, bush hikes, helicopter safaris, and village visits. www.eagleislandcamp.com

● **JACANA CAMP:** Located on a permanent island in the middle of the delta, this secluded camp features luxury tents on wooden platforms, mokoro excursions, and a plunge pool for cooling off. www.wilderness-safaris.com

● **LITTLE KWARA:** An intimate tented camp that offers a mix of land and water safaris, it's especially known for big cat encounters and expert guides and is one of the few Okavango camps that caters to families with children. www.kwando.co.za/circuit.html

Lions may be the biggest draw to Botswana's Okavango Delta, but the first sighting of zebras in the wild is an equally memorable experience.

# LAKE NAKURU

"The waters of Lake Nakuru aren't blue, nor do they shine gold or silver under the African sun. The lake is pink, a shifting, standing, flying, fluttering mass of hundreds of thousands of flamingos that feed here, a bird-watcher's paradise that the park's warden calls 'a chance to see God through His creation.'"

—GRAEME GREEN, NATIONAL GEOGRAPHIC WRITER

Located in central Kenya, the shoreline of Lake Nakuru is home to millions of flamingos. The prevalence of algae growing in this salty lake attracts a wide variety of species.

# RWANDA, UGANDA, AND THE LITTLE CONGO

**Commune with gorillas in the region's wild, misty mountains.**

Rwanda and the Republic of the Congo both provide visitors with one of the most profound animal experiences available. Their highly elusive and gentle mountain gorillas are fascinating; watching them in the wild is the very essence of understanding humanity. Winter months when the weather is dry are the best times for venturing out to spot these extraordinary, highly endangered animals.

Trek overland from Rwanda to the magical and arresting beauty of Uganda's Queen Elizabeth National Park and its mountain gorilla population. This is the same rain forest in which Dian Fossey lived, worked, and died while studying these enthralling creatures.

Rwanda's three national parks are must-sees, too. Akagera is home to savanna animals like giraffes and topi, while 13 primate species, including chimpanzees and long-haired colobus monkeys, live in Nyungwe. Volcanoes National Park teems with wildlife like gorillas—the park is home to one third of the worldwide mountain gorilla population—golden monkeys, and elephants, as well as one of Earth's most active volcanoes.

Or if you prefer flatter terrain and lower elevation levels, venture westward into the Republic of the Congo, aka the Little Congo, to visit the highest recorded density of western lowland gorillas in Odzala-Kokoua National Park.

**PLANNING  Queen Elizabeth National Park tours** Mountain Travel Sobek *(mtsobek.com)*. **Odzaka-Kokoua National Park tours** Wilderness Safaris *(www.wilderness-safaris.com)*.

## IN THE KNOW
### *The Vanishing Gorilla*

Fewer than 800 mountain gorillas remain in the wild. Traps set for other animals are the biggest killers. But gorillas also are killed for their body parts, which are sold to collectors. Baby gorillas—worth as much as $5,000 on the black market—are stolen and sold to zoos; in the process of kidnapping, an adult gorilla is usually killed. Sadly, much of the gorillas' habitat, especially Uganda and the Democratic Republic of the Congo, has been politically unstable and beleaguered by war and civil unrest. To help, go to the Dian Fossey Gorilla Fund International at gorillafund.org

About five pounds (2.3 kg) at birth, gorillas grow at a much faster rate than human babies—but they still stay close to their mothers for many years.

Hikers advance up the edge of a sand dune in Namib-Naukluft Park. Cooler temperatures from June to August make desert exploration comfortable.

AFRICA

# NAMIBIA

**Climb atop the big, red, rusty dunes and watch the fauna of Namibia's vast desert reserve.**

Namibia's iconic dunes have gained popularity as an ideal walking destination and caloric-burning alternative to more sedentary safaris. The lunar landscape reserve is home to ethnic Damara tribes, desert elephants, and wave after giant sinuous wave of red sand. From June to August, the unbearable heat passes and the desert cools, creating a short window for game viewing, when animals flock to water holes: Lions, rhinos, and the rare Hartman's zebra are frequently seen.

In this season, dawn and dusk become prime time for golden-hour hikes up the majestic dunes, Big Daddy (the king, with an elevation of 1,066 feet/325 m), Big Mama, and Dune 45. Come nightfall, the sky glitters with jewels and offers up fantastic views of the Southern Cross and Milky Way.

"To witness guests sliding down the roaring dunes for the first time is a most significant experience," says Chris Bakkes, Wilderness Safaris' Namibia area manager. "The sound emanating from underneath the rolling sand is like the drone of a squadron of bombers. People look up in disbelief, searching the skies, only then realizing that the sound is coming from below. To some it is the sound of creation itself. Others say it is the sound of the spirit of the desert."

**PLANNING  Namibia dune walking** Wilderness Safaris (*www.wilderness-safaris.com*) offers four types of wilderness camps; Travel Beyond (*travelbeyond.com*) features high-end safaris; and Country Walkers (*www .cwadventure.com*) has cheetah tracking by foot and golden-hour hikes.

## IN THE KNOW
### *The German Occupation of Namibia*

Home to the world's oldest desert (the Namib), Namibia became a pawn in Europe's colonial chess match during the 19th century. By 1884, Germany occupied the country. The spirited Herero and Namaqua people didn't accept colonialism without a fight, though, and the result was nothing short of genocide. From 1904 to 1907, as many as 100,000 indigenous Namibians died. Transition to a sovereign state finally began in 1988, and a constitution was adopted in 1990. Today, the country is one of Africa's most prosperous. Tidy, efficient Teutonic cleanliness is reflected in the streets of the capital, Windhoek, where you can still find beer gardens and overhear German being spoken.

The Spier Estate's Mojo restaurant pairs some of the Cape Winelands' stellar vintages with a shady alfresco setting.

SOUTH AFRICA

# CAPE WINELANDS

**Soak in mountain landscapes while sipping on wine with a 350-year history.**

Sheltered by lush mountains and nourished by rich valleys, the Cape Winelands region is steeped in a multitude of soil types perfect for grapevines, allowing South African winemakers to become some of the most prolific in the world. Though the first vines were planted just outside Cape Town in 1655, today the heart of wine country beats about an hour's drive east. Surrounding the towns of Stellenbosch, Franschhoek, and Paarl are hundreds of wineries, many located on centuries-old estates, where gabled mansions with bright white facades stand out against craggy, mountainous backdrops.

The region is linked via multiple wine routes that meander through rolling farmland. Arrive from late July to mid-September, as South Africa's winter dissolves into spring and the vines come to life with new growth. That way, you'll be surrounded by flowers under fresh, springlike skies instead of the crowds that populate the region during the hotter January to April summer months.

## CYCLE THE VINEYARDS OF STELLENBOSCH

Start out in Stellenbosch, where tree-shaded streets are lined with some of the most iconic examples of Cape Dutch architecture in South Africa—clean, whitewashed gables

*Surrounding the towns of Stellenbosch, Franschhoek, and Paarl are hundreds of wineries, many located on centuries-old estates, where gabled mansions with bright white facades stand out against craggy, mountainous backdrops.*

Savor Zorgvliet Wine Estate's Sauvignon Blanc in the tasting room housed in a building from 1692 or, better, in a room at their lodge.

Cape Winelands restaurants emphasize local produce, the perfect complement to local wines.

illuminating the same colonial Dutch influences that brought grapevines to the region. Today, Stellenbosch is the gateway into the Cape Winelands, with more than 200 wine and grape producers punctuating five different routes.

To best experience the verdant wineries and quiet farmland that characterize the region, go vineyard-hopping by bicycle. Rolling dirt paths take you so close to the vines you can hear the early spring wind rustling the leaves.

## THE FRENCH CONNECTION

About 20 miles (32 km) south of Stellenbosch, South Africa's French winemaking traditions are in full swing. Though the Dutch planted the first vines here, it wasn't until the French Huguenots, fleeing religious persecution, arrived in 1688 that a wine industry—and its surrounding culture—developed. Many of their original farms have developed into renowned wineries like La Motte, Chamonix, and Dieu Donné. Here, you'll also find a hub of high-end food. South Africa's top chefs will put spring's bounty of sweet berries and beets to savory use in newly opened gourmet restaurants.

In July, Franschhoek celebrates its French roots with its own Bastille Day Festival. Spend the afternoon tasting wine and the newest dishes by chefs armed with samples of their finest crafts. Or, if you're in town a bit later in the season, check out Franschhoek's Uncorked Festival in mid-September, when the wineries release their new vintages.

## THE LUSH WINERIES OF THE GREEN MOUNTAIN ECO ROUTE

South of the beaten paths of the Cape Winelands' more popular areas, vines throughout the Green Mountain Eco Route grow side by side with fynbos, the indigenous shrublike vegetation—now in full bloom—that characterizes the region. Part of the Cape Floral Kingdom, the area has some of the richest plant life on Earth.

The region's vines, which flourish in fresh Atlantic breezes that sweep off the coast and into the emerald valley, produce unique, cool-climate grapes. They are also a tool for curbing urban development and bolstering conservation. Visit the Paul Cluver Winery, where, in addition to sipping a perfectly chilled white with dramatic views of mountain-hugged vineyards, you can learn about Cluver's efforts to ensure the grapes and native vegetation coexist. Cluver is also involved in social initiatives such as Thandi Wines, a fair-trade winery and farm open to the public and owned, in large part, by 250 families, all members of South Africa's Black Economic Empowerment project.

**PLANNING  Stellenbosch** www.wineroute.co.za. Located about 30 miles (48 km) from Cape Town and accessible via regular train service or car. Bicycle tour information, www.bikesnwines.com. **Franschhoek** franschhoek.org.za. Accessible via taxi services from Stellenbosch or Paarl. Driving is also an option, either with a rental or a hired driver. Bastille Day Festival, www.franschhoekbastille.co.za. **Green Mountain Eco Route** www.greenmountain.co.za, www.elginvalley.co.za. The town of Grabouw is a central hub for exploring wineries.

Take a break from the vino to go on a wildlife safari.

# MONGOLIA

**Embrace the nomadic ways of the warrior during stirring countrywide summer celebrations.**

As sturdy Mongolian horses gallop across the open countryside, cheer along with the throngs of proud parents and onlookers—the riders are all young children, ages 5–13. Nearby, stocky wrestlers perform the honorary eagle dance before grappling with each other in a bid to win the title of *arslan*, "lion." The jubilant sounds of throat singing and *morin khuur* fiddling fill the breezy air around you.

This is Naadam, the annual festival celebrated throughout Mongolia from July 11 to 13, when the harsh winter snows recede and the steppes turn green, and nomads are free to come together and seek glory in the three proud sports of wrestling, archery, and horse racing.

In the capital city of Ulaanbaatar, the action takes place in a huge, packed, open stadium. Head west into the Arkhangai or Khövsgöl provinces to see local communities stage smaller, more intimate Naadams on rolling grasslands. "Mongolians are super hospitable and eager to share their culture," says National Geographic photographer Jeremy Schmidt. "They pull you right in as a spectator. You can ask people if you can try shooting a bow."

Gather your courage for the most daring national tradition: drinking *airag*, fermented mare's milk, one of many abundant dairy products available in summer. You can be sure once a friendly nomad invites you into his or her home, the host will present you with a cup.

**PLANNING Naadam Festival** www.mongoliatourism.gov.mn. View the Naadam Festival and ride horses across the steppes with Wild Earth Journeys *(www.wildearthjourneys.com)*. National Geographic *(www.nationalgeographicexpeditions.com)* also offers active tours.

## GREAT STAYS
*Steppe Nomads Eco Camp*

Join the hundreds of migratory birds that flock here in summer and live like a nomad in cozy, traditional, felt-wrapped Mongolian *gers*. Steppe Nomads Eco Camp, located about two hours outside Ulaanbaatar in the Gun-Galuut National Reserve on the banks of the Kherlen River, will help you enjoy your green surroundings with horse and camel rides across the grasslands in search of Siberian white cranes or argali—wild, big-horned mountain sheep. Try your hand at Naadam-style archery, then share a cup of milky tea with a nomadic family. www.mongoliagercamp.com

Competitors take aim in Mongolia. Legend has it that an archer, Erekhe Mergen, once saved the culture from drought by shooting down six suns.

Hong Kong's coastline offers plenty of respite from the heat. Here, the beachfront of Repulse Bay.

CHINA
# HONG KONG

**Stick your feet in the hot summer sand at Hong Kong's sexy, sizzling, and pristine beaches.**

Ditch the shopping bags and indulge in Hong Kong's natural side, which too often gets short shrift. White sandy beaches snake along the luxuriant green and mountainous roller-coaster coastline. Secluded bays, sheltered harbors, and more than 200 islands offer up a plethora of summer swimming and recreational opportunities—ideal places to cool down in Hong Kong's sultry summer heat.

With more than 100 beaches, there's one for every type of beachgoer. Lantau Island's popular Silvermine Bay is adjacent to the ferry port, but the more remote southern coast sands of Lantau along the Upper and Lower Cheung Sha beaches provide the longest stretches of sand in Hong Kong, backdropped by lush mountains that peak in color by midsummer. On Lamma Island, dip into the waters of Turtle Beach's tiny, quiet crescent bay or admire its gentle reptiles during summer breeding season from the turtle-watching cottage. Families flock to Shek O Beach, blessed with copper sands and small waves and protected by lifeguards and shark nets. For more action, follow the surf set to Big Wave Bay, Hong Kong's only officially recognized surf beach (or go "off piste" to Tai Long Wan, an unofficial surf beach offering wild waves and pristine mountains, an untouched side of Hong Kong rarely seen).

**PLANNING   Hong Kong beaches** Hong Kong's Leisure and Cultural Services Department *(www.lcsd.gov.hk)* provides a list of public beaches.

# MOUNT FUJI

**Climb the sacred mountain to watch dawn break over Tokyo and the Japan Alps.**

The Japanese have a saying: "A wise man climbs Fuji-san once, but only a fool climbs it twice." Another word to the wise: Ascending the world's most iconic volcano and watching the sun rise over Tokyo—and across the Japan Alps—is indeed a once-in-a-lifetime experience ideally undertaken during the July to August climbing season.

First know that Fuji-san is the almighty among mountains, revered by Japan's ascetic Shinto-Buddhists. Forbidden to women until the late 19th century, the sacred mountain is now ascended annually by more than 250,000 people of both sexes and all ages.

At 12,388 feet (3,776 m), Mount Fuji is Japan's highest mountain, yet you'll find yourself among many novice hikers. For the religious, climbing Fuji-san is the chance to commune with Amaterasu, the celestial sun goddess from whom the Japanese imperial family claims direct descent. But most make the trek to watch sunrise over Tokyo's never-ending metropolis. When the golden moment arrives, you'll hear a collective shout of "*banzai!—hurrah!*" as you enjoy the sweep of the clouds far below and the glittering lakes beneath them. Then descend by the Gotemba-guchi trail and race through soft volcanic sand. After climbing Fuji-san, you will actually feel like you're walking on air.

**PLANNING. Mount Fuji** For the latest weather forecasts and hiking information, www.city.fujiyoshida.yamanashi.jp.

## IN THE KNOW
*Climbing Mount Fuji*

Climbing Mount Fuji doesn't require special training or gear—there are chains to help you when the going gets a little rocky. But prepare well. Pack rain gear, a warm top, a hat, sunscreen, ¥100 coins for the bathrooms, and batteries for your headlamp. To avoid altitude sickness, take the advice of alpinist Ken Noguchi: "Go slow, drink lots of water, and sleep near the top to acclimatize." Huts (which you should book in advance) are available for a few hours' rest close to the summit. Look under "Mountain Lodges" at www.yamanashi-kankou.jp/english.

One of the world's most recognizable mountains, Mount Fuji is surrounded by five lakes, including Lake Kawaguchiko, the second largest.

It's high drama and big entertainment when Tahiti's female fire dancers light up the night.

FRENCH POLYNESIA

# TAHITI

**Immerse yourself in a sensuous summer dance celebration where ancient and modern traditions collide.**

Spend a night at Tahiti's summer dance festival, Heiva I Tahiti, and you will know why Fletcher Christian and his mates never wanted to go home. It wasn't just the blue lagoons or cloud-shrouded peaks that prompted mutiny; it was also Tahitian dance. Heiva I Tahiti is a three-week, pulsating homage to the sensual that unfolds on an open-air stage in To'ata Square in Papeete, the territorial capital. As a bonus, festivalgoers will arrive during the island's most pleasant month, July, when it's possible to explore Tahiti by day in ideal temperatures that hover in the low 80s°F (high 20s°C).

After dark, the real fun starts. It's time for an expressly Tahitian display of music and movement: quivering hips and hands, at a pace that makes hula seem slow motion; the bone-rattling, atavistic stomp and roar of the men; and a primal drumbeat that works its way into your soul and stays there long after the music has stopped.

Renowned dancer Tumata Robinson calls the festival a "voyage of discovery" through nearly 2,000 years of Tahitian culture. "Heiva is based on ancient traditions, but also modern times," Robinson says. Oddly, Hollywood's 1935 *Mutiny on the Bounty* helped spark the dance revival. Unlike the movie, the festival allows visitors to do more than watch: Feel free to offer a hand with rehearsals or making costumes before the shows.

**PLANNING Tahiti** tahiti-tourisme.com. Ask about joining in the Heiva I Tahiti festival preparations at the Manava Visitor Center by Papeete's cruise ship wharf.

## FOR FOODIES
*Tahitian Cuisine*

Polynesian and French culinary traditions collide in Tahiti in spectacular fashion with dishes that combine super-fresh South Seas ingredients and Gallic cooking methods. And the Heiva I display of Tahitian pride is one of the best times of year to sample them, when restaurants are likely to highlight local gastronomic delights. Among them: *poisson cru,* a tangy raw fish dish. Wash it down with Hinano beer. Round off the meal with Tahitian fruit *po'e,* or pudding. One of the best places to combine all three is the Pink Coconut *(tel 42 22 23)* on the western shore, with its views across the water to Moorea.

# GREAT BARRIER REEF

"Soft corals top hard ones, algae and sponges paint the rocks, and every crevice is a creature's home. The biology, like the reef, transforms from the north—where the reef began—to the south. The shifting menagerie is unmatched in the world."

—JENNIFER S. HOLLAND, *NATIONAL GEOGRAPHIC* MAGAZINE, MAY 2011

One of the seven wonders of the natural world, the Great Barrier Reef, located off the north-eastern coast of Australia, comprises more than 3,000 individual reefs and covers more than 134,360 square miles (348,000 sq km) of the Coral Sea. *Pictured:* A pink anemonefish peeks out from its sea anemone host.

More than 280 bird species call Kakadu home, from the comb-crested jacana to the rainbow bee-eater. Here, an egret lifts off across a park.

AUSTRALIA

# KAKADU NATIONAL PARK

**Explore Australia's premier national park when the air is clear and the wallaby and dingo encounters are frequent.**

Australia's version of the Serengeti, Kakadu National Park offers a vast, pristine wilderness almost the size of New Jersey. Located in the far north of the Northern Territory, it is home to copious wildlife: wild buffalo, huge saltwater crocodiles, wallabies, dingoes, sea eagles, and barramundi, to name a few.

Between mid-June and mid-August, triple-digit temperatures (40s°C) and monsoon storms give way to Wurrgeng—the local Aboriginal name for this cooler weather season—"with just enough heat to make you really appreciate a cool swim in the afternoons," says Tracey Diddams, the park's visitor services manager. "The skies overhead are a dazzling blue, and the bright yellow flowers of the Kapok trees can be seen across the park."

Drive yourself around, stopping at isolated billabongs (water holes) where animals gather for both food and water. Hook a barramundi in the South Alligator River. Plunge into the swimming hole at the bottom of Gunlom Falls or the rock pools on the escarpment above—both too far up the watershed for deadly saltwater crocodiles. Or hit one of the many ranger-guided walks and talks offered during this season. "One of the best ways to explore Kakadu during Wurrgeng," says Diddams, "is to see it through Aboriginal eyes by joining a tour run by one of our traditional owners."

**PLANNING** **Kakadu National Park** www.environment.gov.au/parks/kakadu. **Northern Territory** www.tourism nt.com.au. The main visitor services are in Jabiru, about a three-hour drive or one-hour flight from Darwin.

## BEST OF THE BEST
*Kakadu's Rock Art*

With more than 5,000 sites identified, Kakadu National Park boasts one of the world's greatest treasures of rock art. An expression of the local Aboriginal people's connection to the land and past, the paintings are rendered in ocher, black, and white in caves and beneath rock overhangs. Some are as many as 20,000 years old, while others were created by still-living artists. Nourlangie Rock is the most impressive site, its gallery punctuated by a massive figure of Namarrgon, the Lightning Man of Aboriginal creation lore. www.environment.gov.au/parks/kakadu (search "rock art")

# THE SNOWY MOUNTAINS

**Get your ski fix on world-class slopes in a rugged alpine setting—during summer's dog days.**

Come June, July, and August, as the U.S. bakes in summer heat, the Snowy Mountains range in New South Wales, affectionately known as "the Snowies," is blanketed in thick white powder and ski season is at its height. While Australia boasts several excellent bases for skiing, Perisher Ski Resort is the largest and offers the widest range of slopes and trails. The resort encompasses four ski villages—Perisher Valley, Guthega, Blue Cow, and Smiggin Holes—and each of their snowfields.

Base yourself at Perisher Valley, from which you'll have easy access to superb trails and each of the other three resort villages, suggests Andrew Horsley, coach of the 1984 Australian Winter Olympics cross-country ski team. Set in the stunning mountainous landscape of Kosciusko National Park, Perisher offers superb scenic opportunities as well.

If you want a break from the slopes, head to Guthega Alpine Inn, situated on the face of Blue Cow Mountain and adjacent to several ski runs. "Lunch at the Guthega pub has the finest views in the Australian Alps," Horsley notes, so stop in for a drink and take in vistas of the surrounding mountain range and valleys while you recharge.

**PLANNING  Snowy Mountains** Perisher Ski Resort, www.perisher.com.au; Guthega Alpine Inn, www.guthega.com. Ski season runs from early June to early October. Perisher is about a six-hour drive from Sydney or seven hours from Melbourne.

## BEST OF THE BEST
*Beyond Downhill*

If you want a break from downhill skiing and busy slopes, Perisher has more than 62 miles (100 km) of cross-country ski trails that take you farther into the wintery alpine terrain of Kosciusko National Park. The outfitter K7 Adventures offers lessons for those just starting out. Or try snow-shoeing with a half-day guided trip that leaves from the Nordic Shelter in Perisher Valley village and takes you up to the spine of the Crackenback Range; from there, you'll take in impressive views of Thredbo Valley as you enjoy a picnic lunch atop snowy ridges. www.k7adventures.com

There's more to Australian sports than surfing and football. In New South Wales, skiing's the thing, with some of the best at Thredbo.

Beat Northern Hemisphere heat by heading south—way south—to the X-Games meets Mardi Gras madness of the Queenstown Winter Festival.

NEW ZEALAND

# QUEENSTOWN

**The Southern Hemisphere's rowdiest snow resort takes après-ski—and heli-skiing—to new heights.**

While the Northern Hemisphere is sweltering through summer, Queenstown at the bottom end of New Zealand is chilling out beneath a mantle of fresh powder. The lakeside city may not have the largest snowfields or the longest season of the major cold-weather resorts below the Equator, but the others would be hard-pressed to say they offer more fun (and variety) than Queenstown when winter rolls around.

### ADVENTURE MEETS ABSURD

Snow season reaches fever pitch over the last ten days of June as the Queenstown Winter Festival blows into town. Snow sports and extreme adventures are the focus of the midwinter bash, but there are also masquerade balls, live music, fashion shows, and oddball events. "We don't take ourselves too seriously," says Jen Andrews of the local tourism association. "So over the ten days you see people dressed up in drag and racing against each other, mountain biking on snow, the Birdman competition where people try to 'fly' off the wharf into the lake. A lot of fun and a lot of laughs are had by all."

> ### BEST OF THE BEST
> *Glacier Trekking by Helicopter*
>
> Helicopters also whisk trekkers onto Franz Josef Glacier in the Southern Alps for day hikes amid a constantly changing landscape of ice caves, crevices, sun cups, moulins, and meandering streams. After taking off from Franz Josef village, the chopper makes its way up the Waiho River Valley, the mountain walls closing in on both sides as it nears the glacier facade. After getting dropped off at an icy landing zone, hikers use crampons and ice axes to scramble up, over, and around the frozen landforms. Heli-treks are also organized to nearby Fox Glacier. www.glacierhelicopters.co.nz

Locals as well as visitors may enter any of the competitions. Slide down a slippery slope in a steamer trunk during the Suitcase Race. See if your canine has the right stuff during the wacky Dog Derby, which entails (no pun intended) a chairlift ride with the dog at your side and then a pooch race down Coronet Peak. Or plunge into chilly Lake Wakatipu during the Splash and Dash along the Queenstown waterfront.

## GET-SERIOUS SKIING

It's not all fun and games. Queenstown also offers very serious skiing, especially on the slopes that you can reach only by helicopter. With multiple peaks over 10,000 feet (3,000 m), vast snowfields, and plenty of untouched terrain, New Zealand's South Island is considered one of the globe's top five spots for heli-skiing and snowboarding. "There is next to no human habitation in 99 percent of the total area, so it's remote and unspoiled," says Tarn Pilkington, chief guide at Southern Lakes Heliski. Late July to late August, when temperatures are cold and there is usually a great base, is best.

Top spots—like the Harris Mountains, Clarke Glacier, and Mount Cook—are only a short flight from Queenstown. Pilkington prefers the Forbes Mountains at the head of Lake Wakatipu. "Steep glaciated faces with views to the oceans and all at high elevations," he says. "It's Godzone!" Translation: God's own country.

PLANNING  **Queenstown** www.newzealand.com, www.queenstownnz.co.nz. **Winter Festival** www.winterfestival.co.nz. Southern Lakes Heliski (*www.heliskinz.com*) is one of several companies that organize helicopter skiing and snowboarding in the Southern Alps. Sessions range from two to eight runs and vary in skill level from intermediate to expert.

At Queenstown's Remarkables ski resort jagged peaks above the shores of Lake Wakatipu offer terrain for beginner to expert skiers and snowboarders.

# FALL

## HOT-AIR BALLOONING, BLAZING FOLIAGE, VIBRANT WILDFLOWERS, AND AN OKTOBERFEST OR TWO

Autumn color explodes in the vineyards of the Douro Valley, Portugal.

# KONA

**Sample sweet Kona coffee during the Big Island's high harvest—and low tourist—season.**

Hawaii's rich, volcanic soil—especially in the cooler upland slopes of its western coast—is ripe for growing coffee, as missionaries discovered back in the 1820s. And each fall, when coffee cherries ripen and summer crowds shrink, the Big Island kicks into high Hawaiian style with the Kona Coffee Cultural Festival. After all, here "November is coffee time," explains Malia Bolton, owner of the Kona Coffee and Tea Company.

Start things off at the Coffee and Art Stroll in Holualoa. In between perusing the village's many art galleries, chat with dozens of local farmers who set up booths for visitors to taste and buy their coffee. "The farmers will educate you on what makes it so special," Bolton says. "Kona coffee is really known for its mildness, with citrus and berry notes."

Cup in hand, wander under November's balmy skies along Kona's waterfront, where wind-whipped, massive waves crash against black volcanic boulders and locals strum ukuleles beneath the palms. Fall tangerines from the outdoor market make the perfect accompaniment for a breakfast beachside picnic. And for your second—and third—cup of morning coffee, hop on a scooter and head down the coast to the prestigious coffee cupping, or tasting, contest.

**PLANNING  Kona Coffee Cultural Festival** www.konacoffeefest.com. Visit the café of the Kona Coffee and Tea Company (*konacoffeeandtea.com*) to learn about the coffee harvesting and cultivation, from farm to cup.

A Kona farmer harvests the coffee crop by hand, a slow process but one that helps maintain the region's reputation for coffee excellence.

Fall's first frosts serve as a signal to Wyoming's elk herds that it's time to begin their winter migration. Here, they wade into the Snake River.

# WYOMING

**Track elk herds as they follow an instinctive call to brilliant pastures in northeastern Wyoming.**

The first frosts in the spectacular mountains of the Yellowstone region remind grazing elk that it's time to move to winter quarters. In early fall, bring binoculars to Wyoming's high country to watch the massive bulls clash for dominance. Their memorable cries, or bugling, cover a four-octave range, from basso profundo to ear-splitting shrieks.

"Migrations highlight the links, limits, and adaptability of the cast of characters who share the land," says Trey Davis, land management supervisor for the Wyoming chapter of the Nature Conservancy. The Conservancy's Tensleep Preserve, at the southern edge of Bighorn National Forest, protects migration routes from the fast pace of human development here. Even self-guided trails at Tensleep are occasionally closed as herds head to lower elevations.

Among the best places to watch the mating rut, says biologist Eric Cole of the National Elk Refuge, is Grand Teton National Park. "Try the turnouts of the inside loop around Lupine Meadows and Timbered Island," he suggests. After the cows are impregnated, in September and October, the herd descends to the outskirts of Jackson. This level valley, beribboned by the Snake River, provides ample food and shelter for nearly 12,000 elk each winter. You may also spy their predators: Wolves often hunt the herd.

**PLANNING  Grand Teton National Park** www.nps.gov/grte. **Tensleep Preserve** www.nature.org.
Snows and seasonal road closures may limit access to protected lands. Tensleep Preserve is open from early May to October.

---

### BEST OF THE BEST
*Laurance S. Rockefeller Preserve*

The Laurance S. Rockefeller Preserve is a 1,106-acre (448 ha) refuge within Grand Teton National Park on the southern end of Phelps Lake. The Preserve Center interprets local ecology and is the starting point for 8 miles (13 km) of minimal-incline trails—hikers are rewarded with magnificent landscape views. John D. Rockefeller bought the land, originally a ranch, for preservation. His son, Laurance, donated the land back to the park in 2001 with special preservation and maintenance restrictions. The preserve is open from late May to early September each year.

# INTERNATIONAL BALLOON FIESTA

"Every October, magic comes to Albuquerque as hundreds of colorful and whimsical hot-air balloons silently soar into the clear blue New Mexico morning. They fill the sky like brightly patterned ornaments. On the ground, adults and children wander among the rising behemoths, craning their necks and waving at the balloonists and saluting their adventurous spirit."

—NEALA SCHWARTZBERG, JOURNALIST AND EDITOR

The International Balloon Fiesta occurs annually in the first week of October at Balloon Fiesta Park in Albuquerque, New Mexico. Since its genesis in 1972, the festival has grown exponentially in size from 13 to more than 600 balloons.

A wrangler and his charges enjoy a calm moment during the annual bison roundup in the Black Hills of South Dakota.

SOUTH DAKOTA

# CUSTER STATE PARK

**Marvel at the thunderous drama of cowboys driving thousands of bison across the South Dakota prairie.**

Located deep in South Dakota's Black Hills, Custer State Park encompasses 71,000 acres (29,000 ha) of rolling prairie, pine-covered mountains, and sheer granite pinnacles. Some 1,300 bison, one of the largest publicly owned herds in the world, freely roam the park alongside bighorn sheep, mountain goats, and pronghorn antelope.

Late September marks the annual buffalo roundup, which culls the herd so it won't overwhelm the available rangeland. It's a sight straight out of the Old West, says Craig Pugsley, the park's visitor services coordinator. "The ground rumbles from 6,000 hooves, the dust billows into the air, you hear whip-cracking and yahooing from the cowboys as they drive them."

Join the nearly 14,000 visitors who gather on the prairie to watch cowboys and cowgirls in full regalia gallop alongside the herd, driving them toward holding corrals for branding, vaccinating, and sorting. The south viewing area offers a sweeping panorama of the thundering herd spilling down the hillside into the valley, but the north section brings the real excitement. "It's a head-on view of the entire herd being pushed through the gates to the east holding pasture, straight at the spectators," Pugsley says. "The bison go right by the fence. You could reach out and touch them."

**PLANNING**   **Custer State Park** gfp.sd.gov/state-parks. **South Dakota's Black Hills** www.fs.usda.gov/blackhills.

# GUADALUPE MOUNTAINS NATIONAL PARK

**Hike into the park to find the sepia-tone desert awash in autumn hues.**

Walk through the taupes and browns of the rocky desert where the iconic El Capitan peak looms just a short way away and follow stepping-stones across a creek. Come fall, a blazing oasis awaits.

Hidden in the shadow of Guadalupe Mountains National Park's McKittrick Canyon stands an unlikely trove of trees lit up for the occasion. Bigtooth maples create brilliant canopies of yellow, orange, and red, while shrubby flameleaf sumacs provide lower swatches of scarlet. Still more color comes from the green of the Texas madrone, its pink-and-red bark peeling to reveal a white canvas underneath.

The soundscape brightens, too: Listen for chirping songbirds that you wouldn't encounter a few miles away. "It's like discovering a whole different world that's hidden in this canyon," says park ranger Michael Haynie.

McKittrick's desert secret? Its canyon walls create shady pockets where vegetation thrives. The trees' roots sip surreptitiously from a water table fed by snowmelt and rain as it percolates through the mountains.

And while you'll find yourself surrounded by deciduous trees, you'll never really leave the desert behind. The autumn foliage eventually sheds, collecting around prickly pear and yucca, leaving the branches as barren as a desert.

**PLANNING McKittrick Canyon** www.nps.gov/gumo. McKittrick Canyon foliage typically peaks in late October and early November. Rangers can direct you to the brightest displays when you arrive.

## IN THE KNOW
*The Guadalupe Mountains*

This region was once underwater—part of a massive reef of lime-secreting organisms like coral and sponges. Over millions of years, the forces of climate and geology caused the sea to vanish and sculpted the modern-day Guadalupe Mountains. Geologists come from around the world to see the exposed layers of the ancient seabed, best viewed on the Permian Reef Trail. Of course, El Capitan and the rest of the Guadalupe Mountains aren't the only impressive formations to have emerged from the former sea. Nearby Carlsbad Caverns also owes its existence to the prehistoric reef.

A late fall color show frames El Capitan, the eighth highest peak in Texas.

VACATION WITH ICE BEARS

# *Boyd Matson*
# Churchill, Manitoba

Polar bears are like the supermodels of the Arctic, used by advertisers to sell everything from sodas to hybrid cars. As ubiquitous as their image is, most people never get a chance to see real live polar bears in the wild, because they live primarily in isolated, hard-to-get-to places. However, there's one place where, every fall, you're almost guaranteed a sighting—lots of them: Churchill, Canada.

The first time I went to Churchill, I was working with leading bear biologist Malcolm Ramsay. We had darted two polar bears and were taking measurements for his research when Malcolm pointed to his assistant and noted that he is the "world's foremost expert in polar bear posteriors." I turned to see his arm inserted halfway up the bear's backside, collecting a stool sample. At that moment I said, "I've never wanted to be that much of an expert about anything."

Fortunately, it's not necessary to be a posterior expert, or a bear researcher of any kind, to get a close-up look at polar bears in Churchill. The town bills itself as the "polar bear capital of the world," and every autumn the bears show up to welcome visitors like chamber of commerce greeters. Churchill is where the ice first forms on Hudson Bay, and these bears love ice, because it means they can finally eat after a summer of fasting. They start arriving in October eagerly awaiting the first freeze. By Halloween, there are so many bears around town, armed guards go out to protect the trick-or-treaters.

When I went back to Churchill as a tourist one November, we went out in tundra rovers, big buslike vehicles on giant five-foot-tall (1.5 m) tires. It insured I was both safe and warm, while I was still able to get amazing close-up pictures of the bears from three feet (1 m) away. I also spent three nights in the Tundra Buggy Lodge to avoid missing any action while driving back and forth to town. Staying at the lodge enabled me to go to sleep and wake up with polar bears. To make the experience even more memorable, one night there was also a stunning light show courtesy of the aurora borealis. Best of all, no one had to be an expert or get their hands dirty for these close encounters.

*Boyd Matson is a journalist and adventurer for National Geographic. He hosts the radio show* National Geographic Weekend *and is a contributing editor for* National Geographic Traveler *magazine.*

*"Staying at the [Tundra Buggy] lodge enabled me to go to sleep and wake up with polar bears."*

A polar bear and her cub walk across the thick ice that coats Hudson Bay.

# GREEN BAY

**Join the party for the autumn ritual brimming with pride and bratwurst: a Packers football game.**

Pick a Sunday when the Green Bay Packers are in town, kick your way through fallen leaves on the lawn near the stadium where you've managed to park, and watch Lambeau Field appear in its working-class neighborhood locale like a huge magic trick. Take a deep breath: Come fall football season, the streets smell like bratwurst and charcoal. As one of the team's owners, Stephen Sullivan, says, "You can smell the charcoal down the street, and it seems like the most natural thing in the world during autumn."

The Packers are the smallest market major sports team in the country. They're also the only one entirely owned by locals—which means Sullivan and 112,157 other fans have a personal stake in the team. In return, he says, "We get a team that's devoted to playing good ball and bringing entertainment and pride and trophies to Wisconsin and the fans."

A grateful fan base turns out in force for tailgating: laughing, eating, and listening to the pregame show. You might get hit with a little tailgate envy when you see the trucks tricked out just for the occasion, complete with grills and Wi-Fi connections for arguing about the stats. But you'll feel right at home, wishing, when the day is done, for yet another game.

**PLANNING   Green Bay** www.greenbay.com. Green Bay is about a 3.5-hour drive north of Chicago along the shore of Lake Michigan. **Green Bay Packers** www.packers.com.

---

## IN THE KNOW
### *Packer Snow Day*

Tailgating is one thing, but hard-core fans know snow is as common as falling leaves in autumn. And if it snows in the days before a game, join the party by showing up at the stadium, where locals armed with shovels clear the seats, bleachers—everything but the grass itself. The Packers shell out ten bucks an hour to whoever helps out—beer and brat money at the end of a ritual as serious as an altar boy lighting candles. That's a real fall day in Green Bay. That's how you become a true cheesehead.

Whether you're a Packers fan or devoted to a different team, football remains an inherent American fall tradition.

Among Berea, Kentucky's slew of artisans and craft shops, Bybee Pottery is the oldest pottery shop west of the Alleghenies.

## KENTUCKY
# BEREA

**Stroll through the southern Appalachian foothills to watch master folk artists and craftsmen at work.**

Berea's artisan tradition is rooted in the region's ancient past. From 200 B.C. to A.D. 400, these central Kentucky woodlands were home to the Hopewell, native crafters of intricately adorned jewelry and clay objects. Their spirit lives on in dozens of working studios located in and around Kentucky's folk-arts-and-crafts capital. Walk among the open workshops and galleries in Old Town and College Square, where you're always welcome to pull up a stool to listen to and learn from the master artisans.

On the second weekend in October, follow Berea's finest juried artists into the hills for the Kentucky Guild of Artists and Craftsmen's Fall Fair at historic Indian Fort Theater. The open-air festival grounds snake through Berea College Forest, showcasing southern Appalachian crafted baskets, blown glass, jewelry, fiber arts, and other one-of-a-kind pieces amid brilliant fall foliage.

"There's nothing quite like it in the world," says Kentucky Guild director and metals artist Jeannette Rowlett. "The fair winds up a pathway where you can see the hills hanging full of fall colors. Foot-stompin' pickers and fiddlers stroll and play while you watch the artists work. The art, the music, the foliage—it all makes you want to kick up your feet and dance."

**PLANNING** Kentucky Guild of Artists and Craftsmen Fairs www.kyguild.org. Learn more about Berea's self-guided studio walking tours, artisan workshops, and summer classes at www.berea.com.

---

### IN THE KNOW
*Berea College Crafts*

In 1893, a southern Appalachian trip helped establish Berea as a national folk-arts-and-crafts hub. On the outing, the president of Berea College, William Frost, witnessed industrialization's impact on the region's craft tradition. Instead of weaving homespun baskets, rugs, and blankets, mountain families were buying factory-made versions from the Sears Roebuck catalog and country stores. Frost returned to campus inspired to spark an Appalachian craft revival. He created a student weaving program (which today includes wood and furniture, ceramics, and jewelry), encouraged craftspeople to settle in Berea, and began marketing local textiles to the college's wealthy Northeastern donors.

PENNSYLVANIA

# HAWK MOUNTAIN

"Since 1934, more than a million people have visited Hawk Mountain sanctuary to watch the spectacular autumn flyby of 16 species of raptors, including Cooper's hawks, golden eagles, and merlins. Looking a hawk in the eye and seeing the individual feathers in its wings gives you a brief glimpse of its wild magnificence."

—RACHEL J. DICKINSON, *NATIONAL GEOGRAPHIC TRAVELER* MAGAZINE WRITER

Every fall, the changing weather requires hawks to migrate south for the winter in search of food. Hawk Mountain, in Kempton, Pennsylvania, is one of the best places to observe this migration, with about 18,000 hawks passing through each fall.

Prince Edward Island's famous lobster can be enjoyed in two fishing seasons: spring and fall.

CANADA

# PRINCE EDWARD ISLAND

**Dig into a fall seafood feast at one of the country's biggest festivals, held in its smallest province.**

The contestants raise their knives to signal their readiness to start, the master of ceremonies gives the signal, and off they go, shucking a dozen oysters as fast as they can and presenting them on a platter covered in coarse salt. A minute and 14 seconds later, the winner punches a fist in the air. His prize: $2,000 and the right to be called the world's fastest oyster shucker.

The fast and furious competition unfolds each September, in the thick of the fall oyster season, during the International Shellfish Festival on Prince Edward Island, the smallest of Canada's provinces. It's not just oysters that are celebrated: You can sink your teeth into lobster cooked more ways than you can imagine (ever tried lobster *frites?*) and a dozen different strains of seafood chowder, all the while listening to traditional Irish-Scottish Canadian Maritimes music and trading recipes with the celebrity chefs who have become a festival staple.

Irish émigré and local restaurant owner Liam Dolan started the festival in 1996, not realizing that it would become one of eastern Canada's biggest annual events. "It's grown huge," he says, "especially the oyster shucking competition and the chef's challenge. We have them in a tent with a big screen and 2,000 people watching, which is crazy."

**PLANNING  Prince Edward Island** www.tourismpei.com **International Shellfish Festival** peishellfish.com

## IN THE KNOW
### Green Gables

Extend your off-season, fall visit by a day—when hotel and inn rates are cheaper—to visit PEI's literary claim to fame. Green Gables was the farm that inspired Canadian author Lucy Maud Montgomery to write *Anne of Green Gables,* the children's literary classic about the red-haired orphan Anne. Visitors can tour Montgomery's white-and-green-trimmed home in Cavendish, as well as take a 45-minute walk on the Haunted Woods and Balsam Hollow trails of book fame. First published in 1908, the tale has sold more than 50 million copies worldwide. www.gov.pe.ca/greengables

# CAPE BRETON ISLAND

**Experience the island's music and food with the locals at the fall celebration of their Celtic roots.**

On Canada's craggy-rocked island of Cape Breton, the Celtic roots that feed its everyday music, food, and life converge at the Celtic Colours Festival. Held each fall as high-season crowds dwindle and colorful leaves enliven the island, musicians from the contemporary Celtic music scene arrive from around the world for concerts and community jams, spinning new collaborations alongside local artists and anyone who brings a fiddle. "Our culture has been kept alive in kitchens and community halls," explains artistic director Joella Foulds. "That didn't happen by people sitting and watching. People were involved."

Beyond concerts, the best way to experience the workshops and sessions programmed by towns across the island is to get off the main highway. In the rural commune of St. George's Channel, where Doug Begg and other locals host a Song Session and Supper, tunes echo impromptu jam sessions, and the jovial vibe among volunteers preparing fishcakes and beans for the group supper mirrors meals held regularly in the community hall. "When you get everybody together for the festival," says Begg, "you don't identify different cultures. British, American, Cape Breton, Canadian—we're all just singing together, chatting, and having a nice meal."

**PLANNING  Cape Breton Island** www.cbisland.com **Celtic Colours Festival** www.celtic-colours.com. Visitors can fly into Halifax, Nova Scotia, rent a car, and drive the 208 miles (334 km) to Baddeck on Cape Breton. Commuter flights are available from Halifax to Sydney, Cape Breton.

## BEST OF THE BEST
### The Cabot Trail

Encircling the northern half of Cape Breton, the Cabot Trail hugs the diverse and dramatic landscape that characterizes the island. The 186-mile (300 km), drivable trail lassos the Cape Breton Highlands and their panoramic views of the cliff-lined Atlantic coast. It then stretches southward, brushing the tip of the grassy shores of the Bras d'Or Lakes at its southernmost point. Stop along the way to whale-watch from MacKenzie Mountain Look-off or to visit the village of Baddeck and its tribute to former resident Alexander Graham Bell. www.cabottrail.com

From solo acts to full-on community jams, musicians at the Celtic Colours Festival all share a love of the old ways.

# GREAT HALLOWEEN HAUNTS

**Get totally spooked at these perfectly ghastly haunts.**

### THE STANLEY HOTEL

*Estes Park, Colorado*

At this Rocky Mountains hotel, people claim that ghosts tuck them in at night and play piano in the music room. The Stanley helped inspire Stephen King's *The Shining*, and today you can sleep in the suite that's named for him. Just be sure to book far in advance.

www.stanleyhotel.com

### LEMP MANSION

*St. Louis, Missouri*

This Victorian mansion boasts lovely hand-painted ceilings, stately mahogany mantles . . . and a history of untimely deaths and suicides. Now an inn, it hosts paranormal tours. The mansion sits above caves and tunnels once used for the family brewery business. Visit the brewery for Halloween, when the caverns are splattered with "blood" and you can descend into a subterranean haunted house.

www.lempmansion.com, www.scarefest.com

### EASTERN STATE PENITENTIARY

*Philadelphia, Pennsylvania*

Resembling a medieval fortress, Eastern State Penitentiary isolated prisoners to the point of madness. The last inmate left in 1971, and tourists now walk the crumbling cell blocks, some reporting ghostly screams. Every fall, the 180-year-old prison hosts a punishing haunted house.

www.easternstate.org

### TOWER OF LONDON

*London, England*

A place where queens were beheaded and young princes mysteriously disappeared, the Tower of London is steeped in tragic stories with gruesome outcomes. Today, Yeomen Warders, aka Beefeaters, lead twilight tours, taking visitors across cobblestone pathways and up spiral staircases after hours—when the Tower feels deathly quiet.

www.hrp.org.uk/toweroflondon/whatson/towertwilighttours

### EDINBURGH CASTLE

*Edinburgh, Scotland*

From an accused witch burned at the stake to a headless drummer, ghosts have been reported at Edinburgh Castle for hundreds of years. Some visitors say they've felt burning sensations and seen shadowy figures in the 12th-century Scottish fortress that towers over the Scottish capital.

www.edinburghcastle.gov.uk

### BARDI CASTLE

*Bardi, Italy*

A tragic legend of love haunts this northern Italian castle. He was a captain; she, the daughter of a lord. She saw enemy knights approaching, assumed her love had died in battle, and leapt from a tower. He was, in fact, donning enemy colors to celebrate victory. When he found his dead love, he killed himself, too. People say his ghost still searches for her.

turismo.comune.parma.it

### HOUSKA CASTLE

*Blatce, Czech Republic*

Built over a gaping crack in the ground, Houska Castle blocked a deep gateway to hell, according to local legend. Rumors say the 13th-century Gothic castle hosts a bleeding headless horse and a roaming gloomy figure called the "white lady." The chapel sits directly over the caverns, allegedly to prevent underworld demons from escaping.

www.ceskolipsko.info/dr-en/1230-houska-castle.html

### GOOD HOPE CASTLE

*Cape Town, South Africa*

Built by soldiers and slaves in the 17th century, Good Hope Castle didn't live up to its name for its dungeon's prisoners. Within the pentagonal fortress, torture was often used to extract confessions. Listen carefully: Some claim they still hear the screams of anguished souls.

www.castleofgoodhope.co.za

### BHANGARH

*Rajasthan, India*

Was this abandoned fortress and village in northern India cursed by a lovestruck tantric who didn't get his way? Or doomed by an arrogant king? Even if you prefer the more mundane explanations of drought and war, it's easy to sense why the ornate but crumbling 16th-century ruins are the source of myriad tales of hauntings.

www.rajasthantourism.gov.in/destinations/alwar/bhangarh.aspx

### MONTE CRISTO

*Junee, Australia*

A woman known to dress in high-collared black lace dresses is said to stalk this sprawling Victorian homestead in southeastern Australia. If you book a bed-and-breakfast ghost tour, the management suggests you come equipped with a flashlight—and that you arrive "prepared to be scared."

www.montecristo.com.au

Edinburgh Castle is rumored to have more than enough ghosts—including a "witch" who was burned at the stake—to unsettle even the biggest doubters.

Acadia's network of hiking trails takes in panoramic ocean views (like here at Beech Mountain), hidden ponds, and spruce-fir forests.

MAINE

# ACADIA NATIONAL PARK

**Embrace insomnia to stargaze where—and when—the Milky Way is at its best and brightest.**

I t seems ironic that Acadia National Park—one of America's most trafficked national parks on the densely populated East Coast—has prime conditions for stargazing. Too far north to be smeared by the light pollution marring skies above Boston and Portland, Acadia's celestial sphere can breathe. Fall provides visitors the ideal time for stargazing, as shortening days create longer windows of opportunity for stars to glitter. As the sun sets below a clear horizon and heralds a crisp autumn twilight, the Milky Way explodes, an oscillating contrast to the inky chasm of open ocean below.

## TAKE A NIGHTTIME HIKE TO THE STARS

Acadia's Cadillac Mountain, the tallest peak on the eastern coast of the United States, is the closest you get to touching Maine's sky. Join the relative few (a couple hundred or so) who gather at its summit for the star party, the highlight of the Acadia Night Sky Festival. Held each fall when Acadia's skies are sharper and crowds are thinner than in summer, visitors bundle up in blankets to ascend the 1,529-foot (466 m) crest at dusk. Stargazing buffs from astronomy clubs across Maine volunteer telescopes to share their views of the night sky. "I've been in Maine for 12 years," says Acadia park planner John Kelly, "and the sky still stops me in my tracks."

Stargazers' eyes will be open to another aspect of night-watching, too: Not everyone has access to a starry show like that found at Acadia—in fact, two-thirds of Americans don't. The festival aims to preserve the night sky by fostering dialogues on how to limit light pollution. Plus, "there's an important cultural side, too," Kelly points out. Hear the night-sky tales woven into our collective identity, from Native American creation stories to chronicles of Neil Armstrong's moonwalk. "Human interaction with the stars through folklore and astrology," Kelly believes, "can teach us about the sky as a resource."

## KAYAK WITH STARS ABOVE

When conditions are right—clear skies, calm waters, and not-too-cold temperatures—kayaking through Acadia's Bar Harbor at night reveals an otherworld only illuminated up close. When ambient light is minimal, the senses turn to sound. "A few birds call at night, and sometimes you hear a porpoise or a seal," says local kayak tour guide Brescian Lander. "But mostly there's a deep sense of silence." Shimmering bioluminescent organisms in the water that glow when disturbed by the sweep of a kayak paddle mirror the twinkling of the Milky Way. "If you are lucky," Lander says, "you can see fish swimming underneath the kayaks."

**PLANNING** **Acadia National Park** www.nps.gov/acad. **Night Sky Festival** www.acadianightskyfestival .com. The town of Bar Harbor *(www.barharborinfo.com),* located on Mount Desert Island next to the park, is a central place to stay. **Kayaking** Evening kayak tours are offered during the Acadia Night Sky Festival by Acadia Park Kayak Tours *(www.acadiaparkkayak.com).* Other local kayak companies lead tours into October, depending on the weather.

Maine's night sky leaves visitors feeling like they're very happily trapped under a bell jar made of stars.

NEW YORK
# FALL FOLIAGE

"When people think of autumn in upstate New York, they usually think of a snapshot, not a succession. But a succession it is. The maples with their feet in the water redden and vanish first. Then come the dry-ground maples and the hickories, the hardwoods that seem to set the hills on fire. And when they're gone, the oaks remain, which light up the hollow, blank woods of November."

—VERLYN KLINKENBORG, AUTHOR AND *NEW YORK TIMES* CONTRIBUTOR

The spectacular fall foliage of upstate New York peaks in September and October. The Adirondack Mountains are an ideal and well known spot to view the shock of autumnal colors, attracting thousands of visitors a year. *Pictured:* Adirondack Park's High Peaks region

# Cokie Roberts
## Washington, D.C.

Ah, late summer in Washington—the time to schedule that trip to the nation's capital. No, I'm not kidding, despite the weather's rotten reputation. In late September (technically the first days of fall, but hot days have a way of ignoring the calendar in this city) tents pop up on the National Mall, bracketed by the United States Capitol at one end, the Washington Monument at the other. In that great ceremonial space for two days you can hear people . . . reading—yes, reading and talking about books at the National Book Festival.

Then First Lady Laura Bush introduced this excellent addition to the capital's calendar in 2001, working with the longtime head of the Library of Congress, Jim Billington. Mrs. Bush felt certain that people would actually show up to listen to authors, ask them questions, stand in line for their signatures, and buy their books. She guessed right: Hundreds of thousands now celebrate the festival, even when it rains.

And if readers love it, authors love it even more. The first year I participated, I was stunned to find my tent stuffed to the flaps with people eager to hear more about women in American history, women who would be amazed to see how nicely the capital city they first settled has grown up. History's a natural subject for this spot, but there's a genre for everyone: mystery writers, cookbook chefs, novelists. Jules Feiffer came one year, Heloise another.

Sports figures draw crowds, but so do children's book authors. That's one of the great things about this festival—it's a family affair. Kids jab and jostle each other to get closer to their favorites, spellbound by Rick Riordan, titillatingly terrified by R. L. Stine, cracked up by Mo Willems.

For the 1,200-plus volunteers who help staff the complex event, it's all about getting kids into the tents, literally and figuratively. Watching youngsters listen and learn and then pester their parents into buying a *book* makes the sometimes sweaty work worth it. And once kids get hooked, they beg to come back year after year. I know. When his mother was busy one year, my grandson announced confidently, "Cokie will take me." And so I did, happily.

*Cokie Roberts is a political commentator for ABC News and National Public Radio. She has appeared at the book festival several times to talk about her best-selling books and to accompany her grandchildren.*

*"I was stunned to find my tent stuffed to the flaps with people."*

# KANCAMAGUS SCENIC BYWAY

**Discover New Hampshire's fall foliage along a road less traveled and soar above the dazzling canopy.**

Two hours north of Boston, any remaining vestiges of urban life give way to an imposing wilderness, the White Mountain National Forest. Spanning nearly 800,000 unspoiled acres (3,200 sq km) in north-central New Hampshire and western Maine, the forest—home to the Northeast's highest mountains—embodies the Granite State's rugged individualism.

Zigzagging east up, over, and through the "Whites" from Lincoln to Conway, the 34-mile (55 km) Kancamagus Scenic Byway (Route 112) *is* New Hampshire. While neighboring Vermont is quite rightly famous for its spectacular fall foliage, the mid-September through mid-October views along the "Kanc" rival any on more frequently trodden leaf-peeper paths. Snow-dusted, 6,288-foot (1,917 m) Mount Washington crowns the resplendent beech, birch, and maple canopy. Rocky gorges, covered bridges, and pristine waterfalls beckon.

"If you were to design a laboratory for perfect fall foliage, the Kanc would be it," says Greg Kwasnik, a manager at Loon Mountain Resort in Lincoln. "Consistently high elevations ensure cool nights and warm days, producing shockingly vivid reds, yellows, and deep purples. Ride the gondola to the Loon summit to see the vibrant colors stretching all the way to Mount Washington, or zip-line over the Pemigewassett River to fly through one of the most breathtaking autumn landscapes on Earth."

**PLANNING  Kancamagus Scenic Byway** byways.org. Loon Mountain's *(www.loonmtn.com).* Gondola Skyride and Aerial Forest Adventure Park zip line are open through mid-October.

---

### IN THE KNOW
*Old Man of the Mountain*

The actual Old Man of the Mountain face-shaped rock formation fell ignominiously from its Cannon Mountain perch in May 2003. But the iconic Granite State symbol endures—on everything from license plates to maple syrup bottles. After surveyors spotted the 40-foot-tall (12 m) granite profile in 1805, wealthy tourists—and the hotels to house them—followed, helping establish the White Mountains as a summer vacation mecca. With a slight squint, it's still possible to "see" the Old Man in Franconia Notch State Park. Here, huge, uniquely chiseled steel rods re-create the beloved view formed—and erased—by Nature.

A drive down the Granite State's quiet Kancamagus Scenic Byway takes in breathtaking views of the White Mountains and Swift River—and affords plenty of stellar leaf-peeping opportunities.

As gentle as they are large, whale sharks make wonderful swimming companions for skin divers in the Gulf of California.

MEXICO

# BAJA CALIFORNIA

**Join the world's largest gathering of giant whale sharks, which congregate each fall in the peninsula's gulf waters.**

In the translucent water beside your kayak, you see something huge rising from the blue-green depths. Resisting the urge to paddle for your life, you wait patiently (with camera at the ready) as the creature nears the surface—a 30-foot (9 m) whale shark glides beneath your boat as it gently scoops another mouthful of plankton.

Autumn is when the world's largest fish gather by the thousands in the Gulf of California—the only place on Earth where the genial giants congregate in such large numbers for so long each year, says Carlos Godinez, director of Islas del Golfo de California nature reserve. "You can go and swim with them, and there is not the risk [like] other places where you are in the open sea," Godinez says. They stick around to mate, give birth, and raise their young before migrating back into the open Pacific by the end of November.

On the Bay of Los Angeles (Bahía de los Angeles), you can rent kayaks and take motorboats to interact with the whale sharks, or take multiday voyages that afford an opportunity to see such other local denizens of the deep as humpback whales, squid, and nearly 900 tropical fish species.

**PLANNING  Baja California** www.discoverbajacalifornia.com. **Bahía de Los Angeles** www.bahia delosangeles.info.

### IN THE KNOW
*Where Else the Whale Sharks Roam*

● **DONSOL, THE PHILIPPINES:** Perched near the southern tip of Luzon Island, Donsol overlooks the Ticao Pass where whale sharks gather between November and June. Local operators offer scuba and snorkel trips. tourism.albay.gov.ph

● **ISLA HOLBOX, MEXICO:** Whale sharks gather in the warm waters around this Yucatán island between mid-May and mid-September. Day trips to swim with the creatures run from Holbox, Cancun, and Isla Mujeres. holboxisland.com

● **NINGALOO REEF, WESTERN AUSTRALIA:** Whale sharks migrate to this 160-mile-long (257 km) reef between late March and mid-July. Outfitters run whale-watching and swimming trips from the mainland towns of Coral Bay and Exmouth. www.westernaustralia.com

A traditional Catrina—the best-known Day of the Dead symbol—joins in the celebration at Mexico's National Autonomous University.

MEXICO

# OAXACA

**With a swig of mescal and a dash of the macabre, celebrate the Day of the Dead, the country's impassioned autumn gathering.**

Well after midnight on the morning of November 2, thousands gather in a cemetery on the outskirts of Oaxaca. Here, Catholic traditions blend with ancient Olmec customs to create a Day of the Dead that is at once ghoulish and a celebration of life. The same ritual is played out in cemeteries all over Mexico on the Día de los Muertos, but no place with as much gusto as Oaxaca. With summer's heat and humidity now a distant memory, the weather is perfect for the outdoor rite of autumn.

Many visitors polish tombstones or assemble intricate candle displays to honor their dear departed. Those tasks complete, they settle into graveside meals, curled up beneath richly woven blankets as they eat homemade tamales washed down with mescal and familiar songs.

The week prior, you can fall in with sinuous parades of brass bands and dancers clad in outrageous costumes as they make their way through the cobblestone streets. Along the way, vendors may lure you into eating *pan de muerto* (bread emblazoned with skulls or crossbones) or drinking a sour cactus moonshine called *pulque*. You might even be inspired to pen your own *calaveras*—sardonic poems eulogizing living celebrities and family members. All this leads up to the overnight cemetery rendezvous.

**PLANNING Oaxaca** ciudaddeoaxaca.org. **Día de los Muertos activities** oaxacalive.com/muertos.htm.

---

## BEST OF THE BEST
### *The Ruins of Monte Albán*

Perched on a mountaintop above Oaxaca is the ancient city of Monte Albán, one of the best preserved, most impressive archaeological sites in the Western Hemisphere. From around 500 B.C. to A.D. 750, the sprawling metropolis was one of the largest urban areas in the Americas as well as the political, economic, and cultural hub of the Zapotec empire. Among its iconic structures are several large pyramidal platforms, an astronomical observatory, and perhaps the finest example of an ancient ball court in Mexico. Many of the treasures discovered here are on display at Mexico City's National Museum of Anthropology (*www.inah.gob.mx*) and Santo Domingo Church in Oaxaca.

# GALÁPAGOS ISLANDS

**Walk through the unique animal kingdom that spurred Charles Darwin to conceptualize evolution.**

Few places are as striking for their beauty and impact on scientific knowledge as the Galápagos, the island chain some 600 miles (almost 1,000 km) off Ecuador. The islands' most famous fan was Charles Darwin, who famously studied the Galápagos's rich animal and plant life in developing his theory of evolution. About 140 years later, the Galápagos were declared UNESCO's first Natural World Heritage site.

The islands straddle the Equator, and in the fall, the Humboldt Current intensifies, bringing cold, nutrient-rich waters along with an intense array of wildlife. Scientific cruises with exploratory excursions by Zodiac and canoe are the best way to explore. Once on land, visitors walk among the blue-footed booby birds, marine iguanas, green sea turtles, and other creatures, differing by island. Best of all, evolving without human occupation or natural enemies, the animals show no fear of their guests, allowing close-range viewing as if in an exotic zoo; the creatures are as curious about you as you are about them.

Returning to the ship is an energizing retreat, allowing stimulating conversation with your guides and fellow passengers about what you've just seen. Bring a bathing suit, too. Scuba diving and swimming can be a refreshing after-dinner option.

**PLANNING  Galápagos Islands** www.ecuador.travel. Two excellent scientific cruise companies are Klein Tours (*www.kleintours.com*) and Galapagos Legend (*www.galapagoslegend.com*). National Geographic (*www.nationalgeographicexpeditions.com*) also offers tours.

A member of the only turtle species to nest in the Galápagos Islands, a green sea turtle goes for a deep-sea swim near Darwin Island.

# LUJÁN

## Witness fall's stunning Gaucho Pilgrimage, when millions journey to a sacred site on horseback and foot.

It could easily be a century ago or more: Hundreds of riders and their horses spread out along a road through the pampas, a line that's punctuated every so often by carriages, buckboards, and even ox carts with family members at the reins. Some are singing or waving Argentine flags, others lost in silent prayer as they make their way to the sacred city of Luján, about an hour's drive from Buenos Aires.

The occasion is the annual Peregrinación Gaucha (Gaucho Pilgrimage), a procession that culminates with Mass at the Luján Basilica, as many as 5,000 horses filling the huge plaza outside. And that's just the start of an autumn pilgrimage season that includes both individual odysseys and massive group treks to Argentina's most celebrated church, dedicated to the country's patron saint. The largest pilgrimage gathering comes a week after the gaucho ride, when a million teens and children hike the 40 miles (65 km) from Buenos Aires.

Even if you don't ride or walk to Luján, you can get into the pilgrimage spirit by attending a basilica service, eating at one of the pilgrim-packed *parrillas* (barbecue restaurants) that flank the square, or volunteering at one of the water and snack stations along the route.

**PLANNING  Luján** Those who can't make the pilgrimage can visit on a day trip from Buenos Aires *(www.bue.gov.ar),* around 60 minutes away by bus or car; trains take more than twice as long.

After a 40-mile (65 km) walk from Buenos Aires, pilgrims are greeted by the neo-Gothic grand interior of the Cathedral of Luján.

A rainbow spans Iguazú Falls, which is actually a massive necklace of hundreds of falls.

BRAZIL/ARGENTINA/PARAGUAY

# IGUAZÚ FALLS

**Experience a close encounter with waterfalls so grand they are in three countries and dwarf Niagara's.**

Sacred to the South American Guarani Indians, for whom *iguazú* means "big water," Iguazú Falls is an incredible site. Several times larger than famed Niagara's grand display, the roar is incessant. Actually made of hundreds of individual falls and chosen as one of the new Seven Wonders of the World, the falls straddle the borders of three countries—Brazil, Argentina, and Paraguay—with the first two considered the best locations for viewing them.

October to December is ideal for taking it all in. The humidity drops, along with the crowds, and downpours disappear. Another bonus, says Leslie Shasha, who owns the Iguazu Grand Resort Spa and Casino in Puerto Iguazú, Argentina, near the falls, is that the water flow is lower. "All the catwalks are above water, and travelers can get as close as possible to the magnificent falls," she says. "There is also less mist, so the falls are easier to photograph."

Most visitors stay in Argentina's small Puerto Iguazú or the larger and more developed Foz do Iguaçu in Brazil. Paraguay's Ciudad del Este, famous for its shopping, is another access point. Tours from Brazil and Argentina take in walkways connecting jungle to the watery pulse of the falls. Or take a boat ride approaching the very edge of the falls, where massive sprays drench everyone aboard.

**PLANNING Iguazú Falls** Brazil, www.iguassu.com.br (use translation tools); Paraguay, www.senatur.gov.py; Argentina, www.iguazuargentina.com, www.argentina.travel.

Plan to dance the night away at the Shetland Islands' frenetic Accordion and Fiddle Festival.

## SCOTLAND

# SHETLAND ISLANDS

**Clink pints and sit fireside on these windswept islands for a Scottish music jam at fall's Shetland Accordion and Fiddle Festival.**

Set sail for the Shetland Islands, home to shaggy ponies and sheep as well as a thriving traditional Scottish music scene that reaches a crescendo in crisp and blustery fall. This archipelago is closer to Bergen, Norway, than to Edinburgh, and its windswept and treeless landscape has whiffs of Scandinavia. But the sounds of singsong Shetlandic dialect and homespun music are pure Scotland.

Fall is host to several festivals that offer a warm respite from the cold North Atlantic elements, including celebrations of Scottish food and even blues. For authentic eruptions of twangy, plucky music and merry folk dances, head to October's Shetland Accordion and Fiddle Festival, a five-day fall fete held at various venues around the islands.

These rugged, rocky islands themselves are often the muse of musicians. Lerwick is a bustling, picturesque port town, while Scalloway, the historic capital and marina, is lorded over by 16th-century Scalloway Castle. Bundle up for coastal walks: From Clickimin Broch to the Ness of Sound, you'll bypass Bronze and Iron Age structures on the way to cliffside World War II bunkers with spectacular views. Warm up inside the newly opened Mareel—with a live performance auditorium and home to the Mirrie Dancers—a vibrant public art and light installation that's just the antidote to autumn's increasingly long nights.

**PLANNING Shetland Islands** visit.shetland.org. **Shetland Accordion and Fiddle Festival** www.shetland accordionandfiddle.com.

### IN THE KNOW
*History of the Fiddle*

For a sound that conjures up the Old World, the fiddle is surprisingly new—from the tenth century to be precise. The instrument came to medieval Europe from Byzantium, where the *lira* was one of many bowed instruments of the Persian Islamic world. The lira's influence spread westward through Europe in the 11th century, and eventually the terms *fiddle* and *lira* were used interchangeably. The sounds of such instruments are still evocative of regions: A faster fiddle style dominates the British Isles and various parts of Eastern and Northern Europe, while the slower, plaintive style of violin became synonymous with Mediterranean culture.

# FRANCE
# BORDEAUX

**Join the harvest and feast with fellow grape pickers in the region's legendary vineyards.**

Inhale the sweet, fruity warmth of France's most famous vineyards during brilliant fall days when Bordeaux estates welcome all hands to join the harvest. Armed with a basket and shears, wind your way down rows of heavy-laden grapevines to capture the essence of the local viticulture during the annual *vendange* (harvest).

In mid-September, Martine Cazeneuve begins each day with a bite from a sweet Merlot grape. She invites visitors to do the same, learning the perfect moment for the harvest. "Winemaking is part of our culture," Cazeneuve says. Her Château Paloumey welcomes guests to clip fragrant bunches of Cabernet Sauvignon, Cabernet Franc, or Merlot to be blended into classic Bordeaux wine. "We want people all over the world to understand it."

After a morning bending and loading among the vineyard rows, take a seat with students earning money for the next term, Australian retirees, and other workers for a hearty pot-au-feu served with carafes brimming with the local specialty.

Return to the city center of Bordeaux, with its beautifully remade riverfront, and indulge in autumnal specialties: famed foie gras, roasted wood pigeon, and eel. Then toast to a job well done at a local wine bar like Bar à Vin, a sleek bistro offering dozens of regional wines by the glass.

**PLANNING  Harvest in Bordeaux** Mid- to late September is usually peak harvest season, though dates vary for each vineyard. Book harvesting trips through the Bordeaux Tourism Office *(www.bordeaux-tourisme .com)* or www.entredeuxmers.com. **Bar à Vin** baravin.bordeaux.com.

## FOR FOODIES
*Fall for Foie Gras*

Duck and goose are at the heart of southern Bordeaux's traditional gastronomy, and fall is when production of the region's foie gras—the birds' "fatty liver"—peaks. There has been well-publicized controversy about the feeding practices used to produce this specialty, but if you choose to indulge, local menus announce time-honored dishes like sautéed foie gras with a simple grape sauce, or fragrant stews simmered in the kettle. One local shrine to rustic "grandmother's cooking" is La Tupina ("The Kettle" in the Basque language; *www.latupina .com*), tucked into a storefront in the historic Quartier St.-Michel. The plaza outside the famous basilica hosts the neighborhood's colorful Sunday flea market, where you can browse for savory souvenirs.

The largest wine-growing region in France, Bordeaux's wine production began with the Romans in the first century.

# HARVEST FESTIVALS

**Reap the rewards of a bountiful season with wine, food, song, and fun.**

### NIAGARA WINE FESTIVAL

*St. Catharines, Ontario, Canada*

Join the jubilant Pied Piper Parade through St. Catharines' Montebello Park before sampling the cool-climate vintages at on-site tastings. The two-week (typically late September) grape harvest celebration also includes free concerts, culinary events, a closing weekend Grand Parade, and excursions to the region's 80-plus wineries.

*www.niagarawinefestival.com*

### SONOMA COUNTY HARVEST FAIR

*Santa Rosa, California*

With more than 250 wineries, Sonoma County, located 45 minutes north of San Francisco, is one of the world's premier winegrowing regions. At the county's annual October fair, all are welcome to mash their way into the World Championship Grape Stomp, sample wine from more than 150 wineries, and participate in hands-on farm activities.

*www.harvestfair.org*

### NATIONAL APPLE HARVEST FESTIVAL

*Arendtsville, Pennsylvania*

Rural Adams County, Pennsylvania's largest producer of apples, holds its National Apple Harvest Festival the first two weekends in October. Thousands flock to the event, enticed by the aromas of homemade apple dumplings, fresh-pressed cider, and piping hot apple pies.

*www.appleharvest.com*

### VENDIMIA FESTIVAL

*Jerez de la Frontera, Spain*

Throughout September, *vendimia* (harvest) fiestas are staged across Spain's winegrowing regions. Beginning on the weekend closest to September 8 (the Feast of the Nativity of Our Lady), head to Andalusia's sherry capital, Jerez de la Frontera, for one of the liveliest—a nonstop bullfighting/flamenco/dancing/grape-stomping fest.

*www.andalucia.com*

### CANNSTATTER VOLKSFEST

*Stuttgart, Germany*

Stuttgart's annual beer and harvest festival lasts three weeks, from late September through early October. Massive brewery tents surround a decorative, eight-story "fruit column." Between sips of pilsner, ride the world's tallest mobile Ferris wheel and try traditional dishes like *Käsespätzle* (Swabian noodles with cheese).

*www.cannstatter-volksfest.de*

### ALBA INTERNATIONAL WHITE TRUFFLE FAIR

*Alba, Italy*

Known as "white gold," the white truffles of northwest Italy's Piedmont region are prized for their near-garlic flavor and intoxicating aroma. Taste white-truffle-infused pasta, risotto, and sauces at Alba's annual fair, held every weekend from early October through mid-November. Festivities begin with traditional donkey races and a grand procession by more than 1,000 costumed locals.

*www.fieradeltartufo.org*

### ST. LEOPOLD'S FEAST DAY

*Klosterneuburg, Austria*

The monks of Klosterneuburg Abbey, where founder and Austrian patron St. Leopold is buried, have been making wine for 900 years. Visit the abbey in the Vienna Woods on Leopold's November 15 feast day and celebrate with a carnival, music, and good luck slides down a huge wooden wine cask.

*www.stift-klosterneuburg.at*

### MARUNADA FESTIVAL

*Lovran, Croatia*

Mid-October is sweet chestnut, or *maruni*, season along Croatia's Opatija Riviera. Historic, coastal resort Lovran kicks off the three-weekend festival before neighboring villages Liganj and Dobreć take a turn. Taste every imaginable chestnut-infused delight—from pancakes to sorbet—and then work off the calories in a bike race.

*www.tz-lovran.hr*

### SUKKOT

*Jerusalem, Israel*

Called the "time of our joy," Sukkot celebrates fall's bounty while remembering how the Israelites were protected as they wandered the Sinai. Families build ceremonial, open-roofed huts, or sukkah, to eat (or even sleep) in for a week. Visit the massive sukkah erected on Jerusalem's Safra Square for free concerts, food fairs, and other joyful events.

*www.gojerusalem.com*

### MOON FESTIVAL

*Hong Kong, China*

Held throughout Asia on the 15th day of the eighth month in the Chinese calendar (September or early October), the Hong Kong version of this harvest, family, and full-moon holiday is a high-voltage extravaganza with massive lantern sculptures and explosive fire dragon dances. See thousands of elaborate displays at Victoria Park's Lantern Wonderland.

*www.discoverhongkong.com*

It's all about the grapes at Jerez de la Frontera's September harvest festival in Andalusia, Spain—until the high-energy flamenco and bullfighting kick in.

# CHAMPAGNE

**Sip your way through Champagne, or pick the grapes that will be transformed into the effervescent Wine of Kings.**

In northern France, where turreted churches and medieval towns stand amid fields of waving grapevines, the process of making Champagne goes beyond simply producing a bottle of fine sparkling wine. It's rooted in a four-century history and codified as an art form—true Champagne can only be labeled as such if it's from Champagne. Champagne's connotation with luxury stretches back to its status as the celebratory drink of French royalty, a reputation painstakingly protected in regal, palacelike Champagne houses across the region today.

Early fall is the best time to experience the height of Champagne's excitement, as grapes are harvested and pressed in September and October. By timing your visit during the two- to three-week window of harvesting, your experience can bubble over from merely tasting to participating in the grape picking yourself. Many Champagne houses invite visitors to learn about the traditional process of hand-picking grapes and pressing during a daylong event called Les Journées Vendanges (The Harvest Days). Join volunteers and professional pickers alike and get your hands damp in the morning dew-covered vines. A typical harvest day includes detailed grape-picking instructions, a tour of the house or press, tastings, and a meal—accompanied by a glass or three of bubbly, of course!

**PLANNING  Champagne** www.champagne.fr/en/default.aspx. Reims and Epernay are central bases in the Champagne region, accessible by train, car, or bus from Paris.

An old Champenois locality dating from the seventh century, the village of Ville-Dommange nestles on the Montagne de Reims.

Hiking through Luxembourg's glacier-cut forests and hidden mossy trails is a magical fall excursion.

EUROPE
# LUXEMBOURG

**Explore the misty, moss-covered trails that make fall in "little Switzerland" a hiker's dream.**

Wedged between France and Germany, tiny Luxembourg is blessed with hundreds of miles of hiking trails. The most alluring of them thread through a lush, almost surreal region known as "little Switzerland." Its densely wooded forests and stunning rock formations are most romantic in the fall, when mists envelope the otherworldly landscape and leaves tumble through the waning sunlight into moss-covered gorges cut by Ice Age glaciers.

A good place to begin is Echternach, the country's oldest town, with a celebrated abbey, St. Willibrord. From the train station, follow signs to the E1, a 7-mile (11 km) stretch of the Müllerthal Trail, so named for the valley's many water mills.

The steep-walled Wolfsschlucht ("wolf's lair")—passable only single file in some places—leads you to the giant crag of Perekop, which affords a magnificent view over the forest canopy. "The trail is beautiful but strenuous, with steps and ladders hewn into the stone," says guide Hans-Georg Reimer. Following the creek, you come to Hohllay, a cave bearing traces of the millstones cut here in the Middle Ages. The well-marked route takes in rocky features with evocative names like Wëlkischkummer ("grain cave") and Geierslay ("vulture rock"). It is not difficult to imagine the historic battles fought for control of every slippery hill and vale.

**PLANNING** Hiking in Luxembourg www.mullerthal.lu, www.echternach-tourist.lu, www.ont.lu.

## IN THE KNOW
*The Wealthy Grand Duchy*

Luxembourg's history is as absorbing as its tangled web of hiking trails. The region's ruling dynasty bred several European sovereigns before coming under the cosh of the Austrians, Prussians, Spanish, and French, who all waged devastating wars to capture and defend it. Declared a grand duchy under Dutch control, the country finally won independence in 1839. Mining and steel brought newfound prosperity, but the cash really started to flow in the 1970s, when banking reforms turned Luxembourg into a busy tax haven. Smaller than Rhode Island, it now boasts a per-capita GDP among the highest in the world and, according to some wags, more liquid assets than Wall Street.

The colloquial name for Oktoberfest is "die Wiesn," the name of the fairgrounds where the festivities take place.

GERMANY

# MUNICH

**Indulge at the world's über-Oktoberfest and enjoy a hearty side of rich fall cultural offerings.**

By turns Old World and ultramodern, Germany's southeastern state of Bayern (Bavaria) is the storybook set for this historic city, founded by Benedictine monks in 1157, perched on the River Isar, and due north of the Bavarian Alps. A walk through its old-fashioned labyrinth of cobbled streets leads to hidden *passagen* (alleyways), lavish parks, and incredibly ornate palaces, ranging from the Gothic to the baroque. Spring here is pleasant and summer is nice, but Munich looks its best in crisp, cool fall when its crimson trees, orange church roofs, and clear skies make everything about the city pop.

Pack your lederhosen and dirndls: Munich's 16-day Oktoberfest—the world largest with more than 600,000 annual visitors—is as traditional as it is friendly. Every year, the onslaught comes to Bavaria during Oktoberfest in search of Old World Germany and friendly beer gardens. And every year, they find them in abundance . . . right in metropolitan Munich.

## RAISE A STEIN: BEER FOR ALL

The boozy pilgrimage is made up of tent beer halls. Big tents include the trendy Hippodrom, which seats 4,200 people and draws the occasional celebrity, and the Hofbräu-Festzelt,

*Munich looks its best in crisp, cool fall when its crimson trees, orange church roofs, and clear skies make everything about the city pop.*

Three staples of Munich's Oktoberfest: lederhosen, oversize beer steins, and men who aren't shy about showing a little leg.

More than six million people from around the world attend Munich's annual Oktoberfest, which has been held since 1810.

with room for more than 10,000 and popular with beer-swilling Americans, Aussies, and Kiwis. Smaller tents like the Wildmoser Hühnerbraterei, run by the Wildmoser family since 1981, seat a mere 320 and prove the go-to destinations for locals. The traditional costumes and folk-dancing Schlager music provide a welcoming *gemütlichkeit* ambiance that's distinctly German.

The beer itself is taken quite seriously and adheres to two important rules: It has to be brewed within Munich's city limits and should be at least 6 percent alcohol. Thus, only a handful of breweries qualify, including Löwenbräu and Spatenbräu.

## THE ULTIMATE INDULGENCE: BAVARIAN EATS

Oktoberfest's hearty food doesn't exactly play the supporting role. Often gargantuan-size dishes like whole roast knuckle of pork, known as *Hax'n,* served with fluffy potato *knödel* with thick brown beer gravy, tangy sauerkraut, chewy pumpkin-seeded breads, and a panoply of plump wursts dipped in spicy mustards are ideal hangover cures and rarely leave visitors hungry. *Weisswurst,* an herbed veal sausage in casing that must be peeled after being boiled, is the Munich specialty. The city's outdoor Viktualienmarkt is the center of culinary Bavaria and an ideal place to witness Münchners buying their fresh-pressed juices, local honeys, and mustards.

"Oktoberfest is not just an ordinary fair," says Dieter Reiter, governing member of the Munich City Council, which organizes the event. "It is the world's largest festival and a genuine Munich invention with a 200-year history. It is a Bavarian tradition and at the same time a big-city festival."

## ON THE FALL MENU: CULTURAL TREATS

But there's more to Munich than beer and food. The city's autumn cultural season is an excellent time to visit. When the Old World ambiance gets just plain old, check out Munich's modernist architecture, ranging from Bauhaus civic centers to contemporary projects (an arena, a shopping mall with gardens) by Herzog & de Meuron, of Beijing Olympic bird's-nest fame, to the Lenbachhaus, recently renovated and renowned for its collection of Blue Rider art. All of it is impressive, expanding, and vastly undersung.

The contemporary, art-filled Pinakotheken and the high-tech BMW Museum stage excellent exhibits. Ditto for the Opera House, one of Europe's best and in full swing in fall, when it stages award-winning productions like *Macbeth* and *Hansel and Gretel.* If that weren't enough, Christmas markets begin in November in Marienplatz, adding a bit of Teutonic holiday cheer to cap off the jolly, bustling season.

**PLANNING  Munich** www.muenchen.de.
**Oktoberfest** The tourism website is the place to go for specific information, from camping to beer tents. **Lenbachhaus** www.lenbachhaus.de.
**Bavarian Opera House** www.bayerische.staat
soper.de. Tickets can run into the hundreds, but watch the website for specials deals.

Augustiner Brewery's beer tent tempts passersby to stop in for a stein or two.

# OTHER OKTOBERFESTS

**Bavarian bashes brew worldwide, allowing stein-lovers to celebrate . . . wherever.**

### KITCHENER-WATERLOO, ONTARIO, CANADA

Expect an authentic taste of Germany from a city that was named Berlin until 1916. Be transported by the merriment pouring from Kitchener's festival halls and filling steins, plates, and dance floors. Family-friendly events include blunt-tipped archery showdowns, a fashion show, and art gallery romps downtown before the Canadian Thanksgiving parade.

*www.oktoberfest.ca*

### CINCINNATI AND COLUMBUS, OHIO

Lederhosen-clad locals, thirsty visitors, and even costumed racing dachshund pups raid six blocks of downtown "Zinzinnati" for one of America's most popular Oktoberfests—nearly 500,000 attendees strong. But the fairgrounds in Ohio's capital city of Columbus can't be overlooked, and you'll want to save room here for a half-pound cream puff from Schmidt's Restaurant und Sausage Haus.

*www.oktoberfestzinzinnati.com, www.columbusoktoberfest.com*

### LEAVENWORTH, WASHINGTON

A Bavarian-style village in the foothills of the northern Cascade mountains brings in millions of thirsty visitors during the first three weekends of October. Don't miss the traditional keg-tapping ceremony by the small town's mayor kicking off each weekend.

*leavenworthoktoberfest.com*

### COLONIA TOVAR, VENEZUELA

Called the "Germany of the Caribbean," this northern Venezuelan community an hour west of Caracas surprises with its unlikely Bavarian architecture and pride. The authentic culture lasts in the wake of immigrants from Germany's Black Forest who founded the town in 1843. Watch the trunk-sawing competition and enjoy a Tovar beer at one of the tables imported from Germany for the fest.

*www.venezuelatuya.com*

### BLUMENAU, BRAZIL

Why not southern Brazil for Oktoberfest? This city is as authentic as many—it was founded in the mid-19th century by a small band of German immigrants. Try beers from local craft breweries such as Das Bier at Latin America's largest Oktoberfest celebration. Cut straight for the *biergarten* among the pavilions of Blumenau's expansive German Village Park reminiscent of Munich's own 14-tent grounds, or snag a freebie from the *bierwagen* parading the town.

*www.oktoberfestblumenau.com.br*

### BANGALORE, INDIA

Leading Indian brewery Kingfisher throws an annual multi-stage music festival at the striking Jayamahal Palace in the heart of the southern Indian city. The musicians are bound to steal your attention, but the flea market is a highlight, too, complete with craft vendors and food stalls. More than 20,000 people attend the festivities each year.

*www.kingfisherworld.com/tgiof*

### HONG KONG, CHINA

Not to miss out, this bustling Chinese island is home to a rollicking, annual *bierfest* at the Marco Polo Hongkong Hotel. Listen to traditional oompah bands and sample the roasted pork knuckle from your open-air perch over Victoria Harbour at this German/Asian tradition that's been going strong for more than 20 years. Get there early for one of the 200 pints of the exclusive Löwenbräu Oktoberfestbier served each night.

*www.gbfhk.com/aj*

### DUBAI, UNITED ARAB EMIRATES

It's actually hard to miss Dubai's October salutes to old Bavaria with so many glittering venues around the city bedecked in German tinsel. A daylong bash is held in the Dubai Sports City complex, while area resorts such as the five-star Jumeirah Beach Hotel host their own. If you miss the October festivities, you can get a taste of Bavaria year-round at the Jumeira Rotana hotel's Brauhaus German Restaurant.

*www.definitelydubai.com*

### BRISBANE, AUSTRALIA

Aussies get a balmy Oktoberfest experience on Queensland's east coast, where temperatures average 70°F (21°C) for this dual-weekend salute to Bavaria. And boasting a spread of entertainment from a Bavarian Strongman Competition and cowbell ringing to music, dancing, and a yodeler named Heidi, the event deserves a *prost* for still being family organized. And don't forget the beer: The festival imports its handcrafted brews from the old Tucher Brewery in Bavaria.

*www.oktoberfestbrisbane.com.au*

### PORT ELIZABETH, SOUTH AFRICA

The German Club of Port Elizabeth might have a members-only beer garden, but it opens up its turf to the rest of Nelson Mandela Bay for one celebratory October weekend. The band Viva Bavaria plays classics from the Alps as well as classic rock and modern hits.

*germanclub.co.za*

Members of the Alpenrosen Dance Group raise their hats high as they twirl through some traditional moves at Brisbane, Australia's annual Oktoberfest.

Switzerland's orchards grow more than 600 varieties of apples, including Heimenhofer and Wildmuser.

EUROPE

# SWITZERLAND

**Pluck deliciously ripe apples among the autumn mists and picturesque orchards that dot the Swiss countryside.**

Clean, picturesque, and law abiding, Switzerland is not the kind of place where you casually jump the fence to pluck a low-hanging Jonagold or Golden Delicious. Fortunately, the countryside is dotted with orchards where you can legitimately pick your own. During fall's harvest season, it is a grand day out.

In Versoix, a sleepy agricultural town overlooking Lake Geneva, rows of trees bulging with ripe red and yellow apples melt into the delicate outline of the Jura Mountains. In late September, families wander the sprawling groves of farms like Verger de Saint-Loup or Domaine de l'Orcy, intoxicated by the autumn mists and overwhelming choice. Switzerland has more than 600 traditional, largely forgotten apple varieties all its own for everyday munching or turning into dainty *tartes* or cider. The small-fry dart among the boughs in pursuit of the biggest, juiciest Mairac or Junami, leaving their parents to schlep 20-pound (9 kg) bags to the till. "You'll smile at your children picking their own fruit," says Geneva travel writer Michela Mantani. "It lets them try new foods without making a fuss."

The season reaches a festive climax in early October. Verger de Saint-Loup organizes a *fête de la pomme* (apple festival), with an apple-peeling contest and samples of freshly pressed juice.

**PLANNING** **Apple-picking in Switzerland** www.opage.ch. The apple harvest runs from September to mid-October. **Geneva** www.geneve-tourisme.ch.

## BEST OF THE BEST
### Gardens for the Stomach

A short drive north of Versoix, the town of Nyon and surrounds host some of the country's most fastidiously kept gardens—for vegetables, that is. From the leafy terrace of Nyon Castle, onetime home to the Savoy family and later the Bernese administration, a path zigzags through the municipal gardens of La Duche down to Lake Geneva. Board a short ferry to Yvoire and putter around the sumptuous Garden of the Five Senses, a green labyrinth complete with fountains, aviaries, and obscure medicinal herbs. Back in Nyon, visit the historic vegetable patch of beautiful Château de Prangins, where you discover ancient tubers that helped royalty survive those long, hard winters. www.myswitzerland.com

POLAND

# MASURIAN LAKES

**Catch the fall foliage reflected in the crystalline waters of a vast Eastern European lake system.**

The secret has long been out on Poland's Masurian Lakes region in summer, but word is only starting to get around that the region makes a splendid autumn retreat as well. By late August, vacations have ended for summer revelers, and boat operators start to shutter. But a new season beckons with its open waters and changing shoreline scenery. Senses are heightened by the air's slight chill. The days—especially in September—are still warm enough for a comfortable afternoon out on the seemingly endless panorama of lakes—with some 2,000 to choose from. And by mid-month, the lakes' surrounding palette begins to turn fiery red and orange, shimmering in the crystal-clear reflection of the water's surface.

The Masurian chain of lakes, some interlinked by canal, begins 150 miles (240 km) northeast of Warsaw and stretches nearly to the Kaliningrad (Russia) and Lithuanian borders. The area once formed part of Germany's East Prussia and still retains a slight whiff of Teutonic sobriety.

In summer, ambitious kayakers set out on journeys that can last for weeks at a time and span several lakes, but in autumn, the tone is more subdued and the pleasures varied. Along with boating, get the blood flowing by hiking the leaf-strewn trails of the Masurian Landscape Park, a forest and biosphere that surrounds the waters.

**PLANNING  Masurian Lake District** www.masurianlakedistrict.com. **Poland** www.poland.travel.

With the summer tourists gone, the crisp fall days at Lake Harsz in Masuria, Poland, make for a perfect retreat.

# CYPRUS

**Enjoy fine wine at the island's autumn vineyard harvests and celebrate a tradition older than the Crusades.**

I t's a bit sweet to the palate, but who cares? Now you and Richard the Lion-Hearted have something in common: You have both quaffed Commandaria on Cyprus. The world's oldest named wine, Commandaria, a blend of several grapes, was first produced on the Mediterranean isle in 800 B.C. Thousands of years later, you can still enjoy Commandaria and a huge variety of other wines produced at vineyards perched along the rocky southern slopes of the Troodos Mountains.

During the September–October harvest season, the party kicks in. Koilani and many other highland villages host grape and harvest festivals that celebrate the year's bounty with music, food, and plenty of tastings from the island's 50-plus wineries. Another Cypriot tradition is under way at island monasteries, where Orthodox monks are said to make the best wine. Kykkos Monastery is surprisingly bright and modern, while Panagia Chrysorrogiatissa, perched on a 3,000-foot-high (915 m) ridge, is home to a dark, musty cellar founded by a hermit in 1152.

"We make so many different things from grapes," says Marios Hadjicharalampous, as he pours a shot of his own *zivania*, a 102-proof brandy. "*Yamus!*" he shouts invitingly. Cheers! And with a well-practiced flick of the wrist, the brandy slides down his gullet.

**PLANNING Cyprus** www.visitcyprus.com. The tourist bureau offers more information on Cyprus wines, including descriptions and e-brochures of half a dozen wine routes. The Cyprus Wine Museum (*www.cyprus winemuseum.com*) in Erimi is another good information source.

## FOR FOODIES
### *Cypriot Delights*

I n addition to fine wine, residents of the Troodos Mountains also create desserts made with local grapes. Chewy caramel-colored *palouzes* is a blend of grape must and flour flavored with rosewater or cinnamon and served warm like pudding. It also forms the base of another popular sweet called *soutzoukos*, 6-foot-long (1.8 m) dried-grape rolls that resemble sausages when hung in shop windows. Another favorite is *epsima*, grape juice boiled to the consistency and sweetness of honey. Although these desserts can be found throughout Cyprus, they are most delicious in the wine country villages such as Omodhos, Koilani, and Agros, where they are still made by hand.

Take the long view of Cyprus's 1,000-year-old winemaking tradition on a walk around one of the island's vineyards.

Take a relaxing break at the rooftop tearoom at Beirut's Albergo Hotel, an elegant way to refresh before exploring the city.

LEBANON

# BEIRUT AND THE BEKAA VALLEY

**Enjoy the "Paris of the Middle East" in autumn when crowds are gone and festive wine harvests are in full swing.**

Fall in Lebanon means the summer crowds that throng the country's beaches and the capital city Beirut's Mediterranean waterfront corniche have left, giving you space to see this tiny, sensual, and alluring country packed with striking contrasts. Sure, it's famous for its civil wars and militias, but you'll be surrounded by beaches, ruins spanning thousands of years, mountain resorts where you can hike through cedar forests, buildings of worship for 18 major religious groups, and, best of all, harvest season in the Bekaa Valley, one of the Middle East's most advanced wine-growing regions. There you will encounter both the historic, ancient Mediterranean love affair with viticulture and Lebanon's French-kissed colonial past. "Bekaa reflects Lebanon's wealth in agriculture, ecological, and historical treasures," says Bertho Makso, who runs LebTour, a gay travel and specialty market tour company.

In September, visitors can join the *vendange* (harvest) parties thrown by many vineyards. Along the way, notes Makso, you'll encounter archaeological sites dotted around the valley, including such jewels as the renowned Baalbek and Anjar. Many have been designated UNESCO World Heritage sites "due to their importance and beauty," he adds, a sign the world is noticing what Lebanon has to offer.

**PLANNING  Lebanon** www.lebanon-tourism.gov.lb. Individual and small group tours are available from LebTour (*www.lebtour.com*).

## FOR FOODIES
*Meze, the Middle Eastern Appetizer Tradition*

Calling them appetizers does not do justice to the dishes known as *meze*—an ancient Persian word for snack—that begin a Lebanese meal. Meze is more a meal in itself. Without even asking, whenever dining out, your waiter will immediately bring you hefty trays with some 10 to 20 Middle Eastern foods you probably already know, from hummus with pita, baba ghanoush (especially delicious during the fall eggplant season), olives, and dolma (stuffed peppers and grape leaves) to tabbouleh (made of bulgar wheat and parsley) and kibbe (spiced lamb meatballs). You might not have room for the main course!

Jerusalem's Old City encompasses some of the world's holiest sites, including the Western Wall, Dome of the Rock, and Temple Mount.

ISRAEL

# JERUSALEM

**Feel the pulse of the Holy City when fall beckons with perfect weather and spiritual uplift.**

Walking through Jerusalem, sacred to three faiths—Judaism, Islam, and Christianity—is a once-in-a-lifetime journey with a spiritual feeling even for those who have never before felt religious impulses. Believers flock here to see their holiest sites; tourists come to experience the ultimate intersection of history and faith.

Amid this amazing walled and honey-colored city, no season is more evocative than the fall. For Jews, autumn brims with special observances and celebrations. "Tens of thousands of Jews cross Israel to be with their rabbi," explains Rabbi Issamar Ginzberg, who lives in Jerusalem. "Like spokes in a wheel, Jerusalem is the wheel's center."

## BUSY STREETS, HOLY SITES

For visitors, the season brings instant immersion in this Holy City. One feels elevated spiritually and physically: The air high above the desert has a crisp snap, a marvelous change from the summer, when the hot streets teem with vacationers.

The season kicks off with the High Holy Days—September's celebratory Jewish New Year, Rosh Hashanah, followed by the holiest observance, the Day of Atonement or Yom

Kippur. Jews walk en masse, especially on Fridays during the High Holy Days, through the vast plaza in front of the Western Wall, the men with their heads covered in *kippahs,* or skullcaps, bobbing in prayer. Above, the Temple Mount and the gilded Dome of the Rock, where Muhammad is believed to have ascended to heaven, is crowded with devout Muslims. Against the edges, the curious watch the scene, many of them Christian pilgrims on their way from the Via Dolorosa, the route Jesus is said to have trod on his way to the Crucifixion. Thousands come every day to that path, placing their hands against stones that seem to speak.

## A SEASON OF CONTRASTS

It is a time full of contrasts. "The quietness on Yom Kippur is almost total," Rabbi Ginzberg says. But then comes Sukkoth, the Feast of Tabernacles, the seven-day harvest festival when crude *sukkahs,* or shelters, pop up over town. (They symbolize the wooden shacks made by farmers in their fields for the harvest, as well as the temporary desert dwellings of biblical Jews fleeing Egypt.) For Sukkoth, Ginzberg notes, "The city is full of banging and humming" of people building sukkahs. And where else but in Jerusalem would you find what's billed as the world's biggest sukkah? The structure fills Safra Square, where you can drop in on free concerts and children's events. And, come December, during Hanukkah's eight-day Festival of Lights, you'll see windows flicker with illuminated menorahs and hear the squeals of delighted children on a holiday scavenger hunt—the sounds of an ancient city still passionately alive.

**PLANNING  Jerusalem** www.gojerusalem.com. **Israel** www.goisrael.com. Fall weather can vary dramatically, from quite warm to as low as 40°F (4°C) or below into December. Expect limited transit on Shabbat—Friday sundown to Saturday sundown—when most parts of the city essentially shut down. **High Holy Days** www.jewfaq.org. Hotels fill up for the High Holy Days, so book early. Many places close. Conservative dress, including covered arms and legs for women, is essential in certain settings, especially religious buildings.

The traditional blowing of the shofar (ram's horn) takes place during the Jewish High Holy Days of Rosh Hashanah and Yom Kippur.

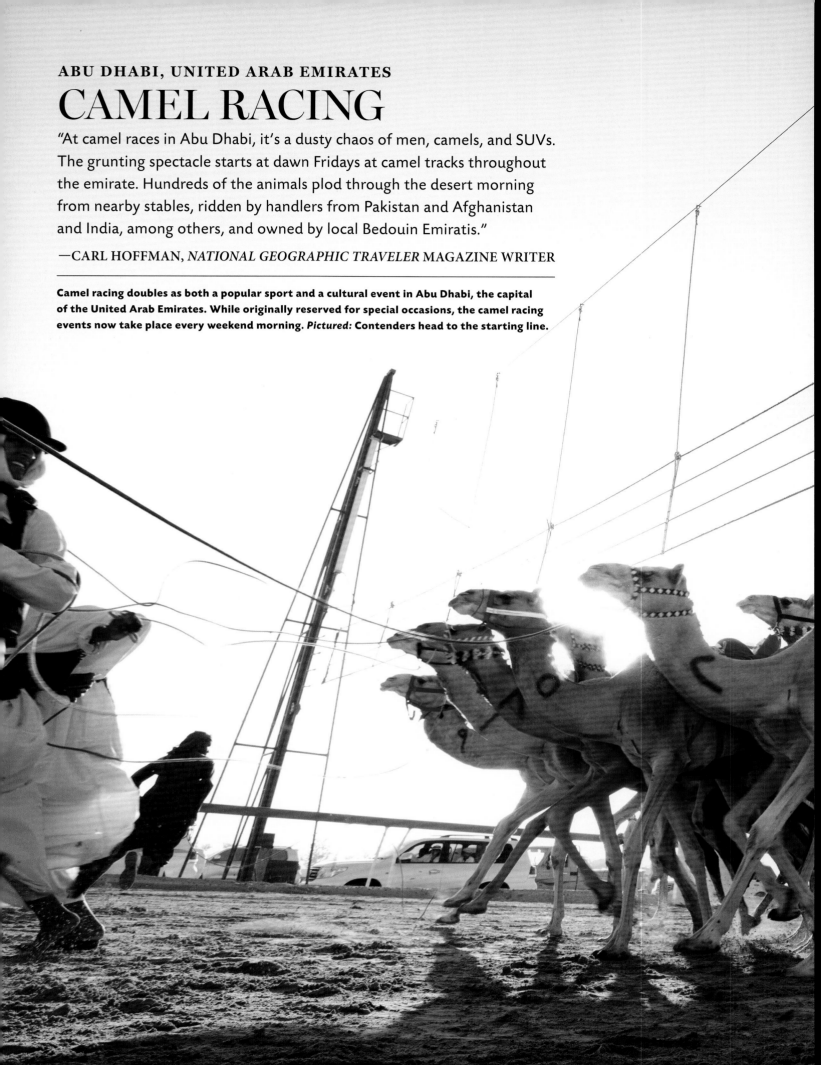

## ABU DHABI, UNITED ARAB EMIRATES
# CAMEL RACING

"At camel races in Abu Dhabi, it's a dusty chaos of men, camels, and SUVs. The grunting spectacle starts at dawn Fridays at camel tracks throughout the emirate. Hundreds of the animals plod through the desert morning from nearby stables, ridden by handlers from Pakistan and Afghanistan and India, among others, and owned by local Bedouin Emiratis."

—CARL HOFFMAN, *NATIONAL GEOGRAPHIC TRAVELER* MAGAZINE WRITER

Camel racing doubles as both a popular sport and a cultural event in Abu Dhabi, the capital of the United Arab Emirates. While originally reserved for special occasions, the camel racing events now take place every weekend morning. *Pictured:* Contenders head to the starting line.

Zambia's night sky fills with the sight—and sounds—of straw-colored fruit bats returning to roost along the Musola River.

ZAMBIA

# KASANKA NATIONAL PARK

**Witness a spectacle unlike any other when millions of bats fill the autumn skies in Africa's largest mammal migration.**

The Serengeti exodus may be more famous, but Africa's greatest annual mammal migration is the eight to ten million fruit bats that descend on Kasanka National Park between October and December. The specter of a bat-filled sky overwhelms the senses. "It's absolutely one of the most mind-blowing and mesmerizing things I have ever witnessed," says Kasanka park manager Frank Willems. And then there are the sounds: millions of flapping wings and countless cries echoing across the secluded savanna of north-central Zambia, one of Africa's least visited but most rewarding wildlife regions. The experience is especially potent at dawn, the primal scene set against a blood-red sky filled with the mulchy aroma of an early rainy-season shower.

Kasanka's bat migration is believed to be the world's highest density of mammalian biomass—an estimated 5.5 million pounds (2.5 million kg) of airborne animal. Or, as a safari guide put it: like 700 elephants flying overhead. At dusk, some 10,000 bats per second lift from the forest, almost covering the entire sky overhead. The following morning, gaze skyward to witness massive dark whirlpools of bats, circling the forest in a spectacle worthy of Alfred Hitchcock. "It just goes on, and on, and on," Willems says.

**PLANNING** **Kasanka National Park** kasanka.com. **Zambia** zambiatourism.com. Robin Pope Safaris *(www.robinpopesafaris.net)* offers guided adventures to Kasanka National Park to witness the annual fruit bat migration.

## BEST OF THE BEST
### *Zambia's Wildlife Strip*

Kasanka National Park lies in the heart of a wildlife corridor that stretches across north-central Zambia and into parts of neighboring Malawi and the Congo. The strip includes more than a dozen national parks and game reserves. The lush Luangwa River Valley boasts three of these preserves, including the world-renowned South Luangwa National Park with its large elephant herds and healthy populations of buffalo and hippos. The region's Bengweula Swamps are one of Africa's greatest wetlands, home to copious birdlife and antelope. www.zambiatourism.com

# THE WESTERN AND NORTHERN CAPES

**Set out on a leisurely wildlife safari of a different sort: to see wildflowers.**

It's springtime in South Africa—fall in the U.S.—and before the sun dries out the earth of its west coast, it puts the last of the winter moisture to work. Colors that only nature could conjure up appear. No, this isn't the place to go to see Africa's famous "big five" game animals, but make the trip and your senses will be overwhelmed by one of Nature's great shows: the Western Cape's spring wildflowers. (You might see a few of the "little five," too: Look down for elephant shrews.)

Drive—or take a tour—from Cape Town up to Springbok in Namaqualand (the Northern Cape). This is not the time to rush: The 349-mile (561 km) route features, first, Cape Town's Kirstenbosch National Botanical Garden (consider it your flower immersion course) and, then, a mind-boggling number of fields and mountains newly blanketed with flowers—purplish-blue African flaxes, hot pink daisies, spiky pincushions, and more. You'll fill camera memory cards and vow to take up painting. But nothing can do this beauty justice. Lay down amid the flowers so that, forever, you can feel this place on your skin. And press a few blooms into the pages of your journal: They'll turn any season back to spring.

**PLANNING** **Kirstenbosch National Botanical Garden** www.sanbi.org/gardens/kirstenbosch. Kirstenbosch scientist John Manning's *Field Guide to Wild Flowers of South Africa* is an essential guide.

## FOR FOODIES
### A Meat-Lover's Ultimate Snack: Biltong

Road trips require good snacks. South Africa's roadside stands are stacked with sleeves of bright oranges and packets of dried mango, but (unless you're a vegetarian) the one snack you must not miss is biltong. It's a far cry from the dried-out gas station jerky U.S. road trippers often depend on. Biltong comes with or without fat, moist to dry, and the range of meats available will send the most carnivorous of eaters into a full-on froth. Try some ostrich or a taste of game, from springbok to kudu. One of the best biltong stops in Cape Town: Gogo's Deli. gogosdeli.wozaonline.co.za

Before Namaqualand goes dry under a scorching summer sun, the land shows off with one of nature's greatest flower shows.

# Top 10

# CELEBRATED SPORTS VENUES

**Share the thrill of the world's greatest fall face-offs.**

---

## ICE HOCKEY: THE MONTREAL CANADIENS AT THE BELL CENTRE

*Montreal, Quebec, Canada*

A trip to the home of the Montreal Canadiens is a pilgrimage to Quebec's sporting mecca. The "Habs" (short for Canada's oldest hockey "inhabitants") are the National Hockey League's winningest team, with 24 Stanley Cups.

*canadiens.nhl.com*

## BASEBALL: THE BOSTON RED SOX AT FENWAY PARK

*Boston, Massachusetts*

"America's Most Beloved Ballpark," proclaims the sign outside Boston's Fenway Park. Red Sox fans endured an 86-year "Curse of the Bambino" before the hex was finally lifted when their team won the 2004 World Series.

*boston.redsox.mlb.com*

## BASKETBALL: THE NEW YORK KNICKS AT MADISON SQUARE GARDEN

*New York, New York*

Stroll past Times Square down to Madison Square Garden to find drama and glamour on the marquee at Manhattan's crucible of sporting competition. When the Garden comes alive with the amped-up attitude of 18,000-odd New Yorkers, you'll know you're in one of the great temples of basketball. During time-outs, you can play "spot the celebrity."

*www.nba.com/knicks*

## COLLEGE FOOTBALL: ARMY VS. NAVY

*Philadelphia, Pennsylvania, or other venues*

Salute the ultimate college football rivalry, as the U.S. Military Academy takes on the U.S. Naval Academy, usually in Philadelphia. The Army Black Knights and the Navy Midshipmen are roared on by masses of uniformed supporters as they battle for sporting supremacy.

*www.phillylovesarmynavy.com*

## POLO: THE ARGENTINE POLO OPEN IN "LA CATEDRAL DEL POLO"

*Buenos Aires, Argentina*

If you love polo, go to the world's premier club championship, the Argentine Open. The Open is played in the Campo Argentina de Polo, the so-called Cathedral of Polo, in the city's chic Palermo neighborhood.

*www.aapolo.com*

## EUROPEAN SOCCER: MANCHESTER UNITED AT OLD TRAFFORD

*Manchester, England*

Walk down Sir Matt Busby Way by the statues of United's two knighted coaches. Pay your respects to the ill-fated "Busby Babes" at the Munich Clock, its hands stalled at the minute of their 1958 plane crash. Then spend a heart-racing 90 minutes inside soccer's "Theatre of Dreams."

*www.manutd.com*

## GAELIC GAMES: ALL-IRELAND HURLING AND GAELIC FOOTBALL FINALS AT CROKE PARK

*Dublin, Ireland*

These hurling and football finals are sporting must-sees. Thrill to the speed and dexterous skill of hurlers as they zing a hard, small ball with flat-faced sticks. Then revel in the spirited tribal rivalry engendered by Gaelic football, as counties compete to become Ireland's champs.

*www.gaa.ie*

## RUGBY: SPRINGBOKS VS. ALL BLACKS

*Various venues in South Africa and New Zealand*

Each fall in the Southern Hemisphere, the Rugby Championship climaxes, and the Freedom Cup is contested between the Springboks of South Africa and New Zealand's All Blacks. The venues vary, but if possible, catch this clash in Johannesburg's historic Ellis Park Stadium: It was here in 1995 that Nelson Mandela presented the World Cup to Springboks.

*www.sanzarrugby.com/therugbychampionship*

## WORLD SOCCER: FIFA CLUB WORLD CUP

*Morocco (for the 2013 and 2014 tournaments)*

Enjoy the best club teams from every continent (except Antarctica) at the FIFA World Club Championship, a ten-day festival of world-class soccer.

*www.fifa.com/clubworldcup*

## HORSERACING: MELBOURNE CUP

*Melbourne, Australia*

Dress up down under and get yourself to the Melbourne Cup. This "race that stops a nation" is run at the Flemington Racecourse on the first Tuesday in November. The public holiday in Melbourne ensures that Victoria's society—both high and low—is on hand along with the thoroughbreds.

*melbournecup.com*

Though the United States is keen enough on hockey, fans who really want to watch a game with the truly devout should head to Montreal's Bell Centre.

INDIA

# RAJASTHAN

**Rejuvenate your sense of romance and feast amid the glittering guests during the region's opulent fall wedding season.**

When summer temperatures finally sink in India's rusty, dusty, royal province, wedding season kicks into high gear. Hotels swell with grooms, brides, and their thousands of guests, who include everyone from statesmen to stars, both Bollywood and Hollywood, not to mention the occasional 2-ton (1.8 tonne) elephant. Wedding season starts in September, peaks in October, and runs through February. And amazingly, many are open occasions where any and all, especially foreigners, are welcome.

Rajasthan's magnificent medieval temple- and fort-crowned cities are prime backdrops for these lavish nuptial celebrations. Udaipur, Jaipur, and Jodhpur, long known for their extravagant Mughal architecture, are adorned with lacy *jali* screens and *jharokha* arches originally built for kings. The streets swell with glimmering color, palaces fill with the scent of luxurious curries, and skies light up with fireworks.

"The women's gorgeous and fashionable saris and jewelry, the men's rich and colorful outfits or *sherwanis,* the elaborate decor, and the array of food have to be seen to be believed," says Averil Haidar Ali, India guest relations manager for Micato Safaris tours. "The experience will make one understand the meaning of the big fat Indian wedding."

**PLANNING**  Though you may luck out and be able to stroll into a wedding, a few tour operators like Micato Safaris *(www.micato.com/india)* can arrange invites, complete with customized fittings of saris.

## IN THE KNOW
### *Customs of Indian Weddings*

Nuptial customs and practices vary throughout India. At some weddings, men and women are separate for much of the time. Women might gather for ornate henna bodywork in one tent, while men talk business over whiskey in another. Weddings typically take several days, and food is often homemade and served potluck style. Be sure to experience the Kanyadaan, when the groom promises the bride's parents to be just, to support her, and to love her; the Byaha Haath, when the bride and groom purify their minds by slathering themselves in *uptan,* a sandalwood, turmeric, and rosewater mixture; and the flower bed ceremony, when the marriage bed is decorated with flowers.

At a wedding in Rajasthan, women's saris mimic a field thick with vibrant wildflowers.

Traditional thatched houseboats ply the backwaters of Kerala, India.

INDIA

# KERALA

**Slow life down with a ride among elephants and temples in the magical backwaters of southern India.**

Time slows in Kerala. This narrow region of southern India, between the Arabian Sea and the Western Ghats, is one of the country's most diverse, crammed with colonial history, wildlife, and changing landscapes, from cool, verdant tea plantations to golden tropical beaches.

In the fall, the monsoon rains have passed, tourists are fewer, and prices drop. Autumn's cooler days allow visitors the perfect chance to take in Kerala like many locals do: by bike.

Peter Bluck, a Kerala cycling guide with Exodus, notes that most roads are paved, making it possible to wind through timeless villages, visit centuries-old forts or Hindu temples, spot elephants, watch the thatched *kettuvallam* houseboats drift downriver, or just enjoy a perfect cup of tea. "It's likely someone will invite you into their home," says Bluck, who calls Kerala the "friendliest state in India." He adds, "You can't get a better experience than home cooking and Keralan hospitality."

Kerala's famous spices and abundant coconuts give the region a reputation for one of India's most exciting cuisines, especially vegetarian food and spicy Chettinad curries—perfect for refueling after a tough, or even a very gentle, day's ride.

**PLANNING Kerala** www.incredibleindia.org, www.keralatourism.org. **Cycling tours** www.exodus.co.uk.

Though the world's giant panda population hovers around 1,000, panda cubs are thriving at the Chengdu Research Base of Giant Panda Breeding.

CHINA

# CHENGDU

**Watch China's much beloved giant pandas frolic and gambol in sprawling outdoor enclosures.**

China's ancient city of Chengdu is known for many things: as the capital of Sichuan Province, as the epicenter of spicy Sichuanese cuisine, and for its tender, loving care of the famed giant panda. The Chengdu Research Base of Giant Panda Breeding is a world-class center devoted to studying and saving China's endangered national treasure.

For visitors, fall is the time to alight on this special place. Come autumn, subtropical humidity and rains have abated, temperatures are mild, and you can enjoy impressive displays of fall foliage in and around Chengdu.

Visit the panda base around 9 a.m. when the pandas are being fed—you'll catch them at their most animated. Andrew Evans, National Geographic's Digital Nomad, had the opportunity to hold a panda cub here and called it the "experience of a lifetime." It had a "woody, musky smell: like forest soil and green tea," he observed; it was so absorbed in lapping honey off its paw that it scarcely blinked at the human arm thrown over its shoulder. For a considerable fee, you can hold a panda cub, too, but even the experience of watching the bears romp in their enclosures—meticulously designed to mirror their natural habitat—will make your visit a memorable one.

**PLANNING  Chengdu Research Base of Giant Panda Breeding** www.panda.org.cn/english. The base is in the Chengdu suburbs, accessible by bus or, easier, by taxi.

CHINA

# SHANGHAI

**Crack into a meaty claw during Shanghai's famed hairy crab culinary season.**

Once a year, Shanghainese gear up for the annual autumnal hairy crab season. Everyone from small street vendors to Michelin-starred chefs offers up a smorgasbord of the fuzzy, mud-dwelling crustaceans in a variety of sauces, dishes, hot pots, and plates. Private dining rooms, exceptionally popular in China, swell with diners digging in with their hands. The crabs have long been and remain popular business gifts and, like many food and drink customs in China, they grease the wheels of Chinese business.

To foreigners, it might seem odd to go this crazy for an animal that has a third the amount of meat of a Maine lobster, but in Shanghai the crab's subtle and fragrant taste is considered sublime. The most prized are the crabs from Yangcheng Lake, just outside the city, which once graced the dinner table of the Chinese emperor. Male and female crabs taste very different, so don't be afraid to swap. Females have roe, while male crabs have reproductive fluid; both are embedded in the frothy mess of meat. Cracking one open yourself is the ultimate treat, but meat from the furry crabs is not easy to shell out, so waitstaff stand by with several surgical instruments ready to help.

**PLANNING  Hairy crab season** The season is short-lived, from October to November. Chinese crack their own during the messy urban fete, but elegant restaurants like Shàng-Xí at the Four Seasons Pudong (*four seasons.com*) and Jin Xuan (*ritzcarlton.com*) offer more refined options.

---

**FOR FOODIES**
*Shanghai Street Foods*

Shanghai's most ubiquitous street food is the fermented (and practically rotting) "stinky tofu." Foreigners hold their noses, but locals go crazy for this Shanghai specialty. Just follow your nose. Tofu flower soup—made with curdled soy milk, dried prawns, seaweed, soy sauce, pickled radish, and scallion—is much easier on the olfactory system and makes a tasty lunch. Tea eggs, boiled in green tea and soy sauce, are found on every corner and are the quintessential Shanghai snack. The most popular street food, however, is the savory and juicy *xiaolongbao* (soup dumplings) sold at snack stalls and five-star restaurants alike.

Don't let the name—or their fuzz—put you off: With your first taste of hairy crab, you'll understand why locals consider it a delicacy.

Volcanoes and hot springs hide among Daisetsuzan National Park's fall foliage.

JAPAN

# HOKKAIDO

**Think Vermont with an Asian flair: leaves exploding with fall colors, surrounded by volcanoes and hot springs.**

Spangled with raw nature and wide open spaces, Hokkaido is the perfect antidote to the gleaming towers of Tokyo. And come fall, the huge, undeveloped island becomes Japan's own New England, its exploding palette changing from green to spectacular splashes of oranges and reds.

Stake out Daisetsuzan National Park for the best show. The trails in and around the park transport hikers through fall landscapes resembling intricate Japanese paintings. "The most colorful alpine plant is Aleutian avens, what we call *chinguruma* in Japanese," says local tourist office manager Kanako Wilcock of the ubiquitous tiny flower.

One of the most chromatic routes runs through Tenninkyo Gorge. Striking out from the *onsen* (hot springs), the terrain explodes in both sight and sound, changing from silent forests to brilliant autumn colors on either side of Hagoromo ("angel's robe") Falls.

The color spreads to other national parks—Shiretoko, Akan, Shikotsu-Toya—reaching the island's southern tip around mid-October. Between admiring the red, gold, and ginger leaves, you can soak in Hokkaido's many onsen, snap photos of the brown bears before they go into hibernation, or count the soon-to-be-snowcapped volcanoes. With daytime temperatures hovering above 60°F (16°C), the autumn weather is also spectacular.

**PLANNING** **Hokkaido** en.visit-hokkaido.jp. **National parks** hokkaidonationalparks.com/en.

## FOR FOODIES
*Hokkaido's Regional Cuisine*

Tucked in Japan's far north, it's not surprising that Hokkaido's regional cuisine runs heavy on dishes that keep you warm. After a brisk day of leaf-peeping, try *Ishikari nabe,* a hot pot that blends fresh salmon with vegetables, tofu, miso, and *sansho* peppers; Kindaitei, a neighborhood eatery in Ishikari City that opened in 1880, serves one of the best. A delicious barbecued lamb and vegetable dish called *jingisukan* is often cooked right at your table. The delicacy in Hakodate, near the island's southern tip, is *ika somen,* thinly sliced raw squid dipped in sauce. Those with a sweet tooth should try Sapporo's *shiroi koibito,* melt-in-your-mouth cookies made with white chocolate.

# THAILAND

**Experience Loi Krathong, the mystical, magical celebration that unfurls each year in cities and villages throughout Thailand.**

On the full-moon night of the 12th lunar month (usually in November), Thais dressed in traditional regalia approach the country's rivers and canals. They carry in their hands a *krathong*, a little boat made of banana or lotus leaves and decorated with a burning candle, incense stick, coins, and flowers. Silently making a wish and releasing the boat onto the ink-black waters, they ask forgiveness from Pra Mae Khongkha, goddess of water, and request good luck in the future. The waterway soon glows as the candle-lit boats make their way downstream—to flow, it is hoped, into larger rivers and finally the sea, symbolizing the drifting away of bad luck and misfortune. If the candle flame remains burning, one's wishes will be fulfilled and longevity is inevitable.

This enchanting tradition, called Loi Krathong, roughly meaning "floating lantern," may have evolved from a holiday that originated in the ancient kingdom of Sukhothai in the 13th century, when people paid their respects to three different gods: Shiva, Vishnu, and Brahma. These days, cities and villages alike make a full day of it (or even several), with krathong-making contests, beauty pageants, parades, entertainment, and fireworks.

**PLANNING Thailand** www.thailand.com, thailandforvisitors.com. **Loi Krathong** www.loikrathong.net. This website has features on the history of Loi Krathong, the various festivals held in different provinces, accommodation options, and how to make your own krathongs.

## BEST OF THE BEST
### *Loi Krathong Celebrations*

● **BANGKOK:** At Santi Chai Prakan Park, watch colorful illuminated boats and cultural shows, and learn how to make traditional Thai cuisine. Some riverside hotels have special celebrations for guests.

● **CHIANG MAI:** A four-day festival, called Chiang Mai Yi Peng, includes crowd-filled celebrations, fireworks, and a parade of floats decorated as illuminated krathongs; thousands of balloon-like lanterns are released into the sky as well.

● **SUKHOTHAI:** As the place where Loi Krathong originated, Sukhothai puts on an especially spectacular show, with a sound-and-light performance illuminating the town's ancient ruins; a special *khantoke* dinner of northern dishes is served in small gilded bowls set on a large bamboo-woven tray.

Thais in Chiang Mai hope to launch away life's misfortunes by floating lanterns into the night sky in the northern Thai style of celebrating Loi Krathong.

# A KALEIDOSCOPE OF AUTUMN LEAVES

**Discover fabulous fall foliage the world over.**

### SONOMA COUNTY, CALIFORNIA

With leaves on both tree and vine, fall foliage is doubly intense in Sonoma County. Drive through Sonoma Valley along Arnold Drive, lined with multicolored canopies of oak and maple. Continue through the Russian River Valley, where vineyards paint the ground with sun-fire hues and wines are paired with the October squash harvests.

*inside-sonoma.com*

### NORTHERN NEW MEXICO

In a state mischaracterized as a one-season desert, New Mexico's northern tip—which brushes the foot of the Rocky Mountains—beats to a seasonal rhythm. Drive the 83-mile (134 km) Enchanted Circle stretching from Taos to Red River, a diverse and scenic landscape of verdant valleys, cottonwood forests, and aspen-rimmed mountain lakes that turn to gold in late September and October.

*www.enchantedcircle.org*

### HOLMES COUNTY, OHIO

In the heart of central Ohio's Amish Country, maple, oak, and the iconic state tree, the buckeye, hang over narrow roads that meander through wavy fields of corn. Drive under the boughs of bright reds and yellows, sharing the road with horse-drawn carriages of the Old Order Amish and stopping at roadside farm stands along the way.

*fallinamishcountry.com*

### GASPÉ PENINSULA, QUEBEC, CANADA

Along coastal Quebec, maple leaves turn reds reminiscent of the leaf on Canada's flag. On the Gaspé Peninsula, the trees have the blue waters of the St. Lawrence Gulf as a backdrop. Hike the mountains of Parc National de la Gaspésie, or leaf-peep while whale-watching in Forillon National Park, where seven types of whales visit through October.

*www.tourisme-gaspesie.com*

### DOURO VALLEY, PORTUGAL

Autumn transforms the Douro River Valley, which slices across northern Portugal, into a sea of red, orange, and yellow as the terraced vineyards that slope along the riverbanks prepare for winter. Take a cruise along the 125-mile (200 km) waterway, fortifying yourself against the autumn chill with a glass of the region's famed local port.

*www.dourovalley.eu/en/*

### BAVARIA, GERMANY

Southern Germany is saturated with Alpine forests that pop with color against snow-dusted mountains. Meander along the 224-mile (360 km) Romantic Road, beginning in the Franconia wine region—where local wine festivals punctuate the autumn calendar—and heading south through centuries-old towns such as medieval Rothenburg ob der Tauber and Dinkelsbühl. Crowded with tourists in summer, fall offers more relaxed tempos for leaf-peeping.

*www.romanticroad.com*

### TRANSYLVANIA, ROMANIA

Autumn breaks Count Dracula's spell in Transylvania, a place steeped in legend and imagery of sepia-toned medieval castles and hazy moonlight. Challenge yourself on the Transfăgărășan, a 56-mile (90 km) drive through the Fagaras Mountains full of 90-degree turns, hairpin curves, and spectacular vistas of autumn's finest foliage.

*www.romaniatourism.com*

### MOSCOW, RUSSIA

Moscow is defying its stereotype as a forbidding gray, Soviet-era metropolis and converting the estates of former tsars into public parks that paint the city with autumn hues. Try Kolomenskoye, where whitewashed palaces and blue, onion-shaped church domes punctuate a forest and rows of apple orchards.

*mgomz.com*

### JIUZHAIGOU VALLEY, SICHUAN PROVINCE, CHINA

The Jiuzhaigou Valley hosts some of the most diverse flora and fauna in China. Autumn whips up a colorful competition between the dramatic red-orange leaves, rainbow-hued prayer flags of Tibetan villages, and emerald-tinged lakes that dot the landscape.

*whc.unesco.org/en/list/637*

### KYOTO, JAPAN

In Japan, the leaf-viewing tradition—called *koyo*—mirrors its spring cherry blossom customs. One of the best spots for koyo is Kyoto on the island of Honshu, where vivid leaves frame sloping temple roofs, remnants of the city's many centuries of imperial history. Nighttime illuminations pierce the translucent, heavy branches at their colorful height from mid-November through December.

*www.japan-guide.com*

Hundreds of maples at Kyoto's Kitano Temmangu Shrine peak during autumn leaf season between November and mid-December.

VIETNAM

# MID-AUTUMN FESTIVAL

"It was like Halloween and Christmas combined . . . Downtown Hội An at night was loud and spectacular: There were dragons and lions and earth gods moved along by the kids inside . . . I walked down to the waterfront. Following everyone's example, I bought paper lanterns and boarded a small boat. I did what my fellow passengers did, lighting candles in these floatable lanterns and setting them free."

—JOSEPH HOBBS, DIRECTOR OF THE UNIVERSITY OF MISSOURI'S VIETNAM INSTITUTE

Tet Thrung Thu, the Mid-Autumn Festival, is celebrated across Vietnam. On the 15th day of the eighth lunar month, families and friends reconnect after the harvest. *Pictured:* Festivalgoers set paper lanterns aglow.

# PHNOM PENH

**Join the friendly exuberance that engulfs the streets and waterways of the city's fall festival.**

A visitor to this exotic Asian capital channels the merging pulses of the city's troubled past and vibrant present. Once yearly, its heady scents and sights kick into overdrive for Bon Om Touk, the three-day Water and Moon Festival. It's a crowded, chaotic, but always—as is characteristic for Cambodia— incredibly friendly celebration, with fairground rides, fireworks, drinking, pop music, and traditional Khmer dancing. The occasion? "To give thanks to the holy spirits that helped us in agriculture and ask for enough rain in the next year for crops," explains Aki Pich, a guide with Cambodia Trails.

In darker times, the Khmer Rouge banned Bon Om Touk; today, the friendly exuberance that infuses the festivities is contagious. Be sure to bring your appetite—and adventurous spirit—as you sample local delicacies from sizzling food stands: refreshing sticky rice with mango and, for the really game, fried tarantulas. Then, along with two and a half million revelers, make your way to the waterfront at the Royal Palace to cheer on local boat racing teams.

Bon Om Touk also honors the changing direction of the Tonlé Sap River and the start of fishing season. You'll understand why after you've tasted some fish amok, Cambodia's rich, coconutty national dish.

**PLANNING** **Cambodia** www.tourismcambodia.com, www.cambodiatrails.com. **Bon Om Touk** The festival takes place in October or November, at the full moon. Covered VIP seats for tourists provide shade from sun or rain, or join spectators on the banks.

## IN THE KNOW
### *Khmer Rouge*

The bloody mission of Pol Pot and the Khmer Rouge to create a Communist utopia in the 1970s saw widespread detention, torture, and the deaths of two million people. The Tuol Sleng Genocide Museum is housed at S-21, a former school building in Phnom Penh that was one of hundreds of sites around the country used for interrogation and killing. Photos convey the horrors inflicted on prisoners. Just outside the city is the Choeung Ek Genocidal Center, with mass graves across the "killing fields" and a memorial temple filled with victims' skulls. Visiting these sites is a harrowing but important part of understanding modern Cambodia. tuolslengmuseum.com

Team spirit—and unity—takes a colorful turn at the longboat races during Phnom Penh's Water Festival.

Breathe deep when these speckled beauties are in view—the vanilla orchid received its name for a well-scented reason.

FRENCH POLYNESIA

# TAHITI

**Quaff the thick fragrant air of the gloriously remote and pristine islands during vanilla orchid blossom season.**

A visit during fall harvest is an excellent way to get a hands-on experience with a sensitive and gentle botanical, vanilla. Often playing second fiddle to chocolate and coffee, this undersung bean is actually an orchid that derives from Mexico. But the vanilla in French Polynesia's Society Islands is purported to be exceptionally fragrant and considered by many to be the world's best. It's no wonder, considering the idyllic beauty of these balmy, paradisiacal Polynesian islands, studded by palm trees and surrounded by gin-clear waters and open blue skies interrupted only by a wayward pink cloud.

More than 80 percent of Tahiti's vanilla plantations are on fertile and flower-shaped Taha'a, earning it the nickname "Vanilla Island" (though watermelon and coconut farms also abound). Several plantations invite visitors to walk among the rows of climbing vine orchids, experience a hand-pollination of the orchid, or learn about the curing process. The intoxicating butter-colored flowers need to be pollinated by hand since the *Melipona* bee, native to Mexico, is the only insect capable of pollinating the delicate flower. That's lucky for you, though, since the experience is bound to provide an unforgettable sensory memory.

**PLANNING Taha'a** www.tahiti-tourisme.com. Several vanilla plantations are open to visitors.

# WIN

HOLIDAY LIGHTS, AURORA
NIGHTS, COLD-WEATHER SPORTS,
AND GETAWAYS SOUTH

An Iditarod team of Siberian huskies begins the 1,049-mile (1,688 km) race, which follows one of two routes from Anchorage to Nome.

ALASKA

# ANCHORAGE

**Bundle up for a thrilling, adrenaline-fueled kickoff to the Iditarod, the "last great race on Earth."**

Brave a visit to Alaska at the tail end of its winter for both bragging rights and the chance to watch a start like none other of one of the world's greatest sports events, the Iditarod Trail Sled Dog Race.

Of course, most of the Iditarod's 1,049 miles (1,688 km) traverse unsparing, remote terrain where the mushers and their dogs race alone. But the rip-roaring ceremonial start takes off right from downtown Anchorage. There, nearly 70 teams of what Iditarod musher vet Lynda Plettner calls the "best-bred mutts in the world"—endurance athletes with skill sets that most professional human athletes would covet—take off one by one on streets lined with restaurants and shops.

The ceremonial beginning of the race, on the first Saturday in March, is more show than sport. But the dogs don't know that. Stand near the start. When the next musher up yells "Hike!" and the dog handlers let the pups go, the barking creatures go quiet, all of their energy funneled into the task ahead.

Visitors who need a mid-event warm-up (two hot chocolates, please) don't have to worry about missing anything: The staggered start goes on for hours.

**PLANNING Alaska** www.travelalaska.com. **Iditarod Trail Sled Dog Race** iditarod.com. To watch the (more serious) restart at Willow Lake, rent a car for the nearly 70-mile (113 km) drive or sign on with a tour company like Alaska Tours *(alaskatours.com)*.

---

**IN THE KNOW**
*Iditarod Air Force*

With a course that stretches more than 1,000 miles (1,610 km) from Anchorage up to Nome, the Iditarod could be a logistical nightmare. But the all-volunteer Iditarod Air Force, one of the event's great traditions, is integral to the race's existence. The IAF's 30 or so pilots help move race staff around, pick up extra dogs, transport supplies—125,000 pounds (56,700 kg) of dog food and 391 bales of hay alone—and, when necessary, rescue mushers. The pilots fly their own planes, the wheels hooked into skis that allow the aircraft to land on ice or snow. www.dogflying.com

# WHISTLER

**Schuss down some of the best slopes in North America on trails of endless, fresh powder.**

At the foot of the mountain, Whistler's narrow village streets are lined with boutiques and restaurants that manage to combine refinement with catering to people who like to pack in the calories before hitting the slopes again—because those slopes are why people come. The powder can be eyeball high on runs that cut deep through pristine forest; odds are, you're skiing over a hibernating bear or two. And every Sunday night from December into March, there are the lights of the Fire and Ice Show. How do you beat fireworks and skiing through flaming hoops in falling snow? Well, maybe with January's TELUS Winter Classic, which throws team races, dances, and live music into the mix. Whistlerite Elizabeth Kovics explains the town's appeal: "Imagine a place where the people you meet in the lift lines will become your best friends. Imagine a place where every night is a Friday night."

From the bunny slope to the black diamond trails that wiped out some of the best skiers in the world at the 2010 Winter Olympics, Whistler's peaks scratch away at the sky. In the early twilight, the last run of the day is just like all those that came before it—those flying dreams come true.

**PLANNING  Whistler** www.whistler.com. **Ski conditions and lift and gondola reservations** www.whistler blackcomb.com. **TELUS Winter Classic** www.whistlerblackcombfoundation.com. Whistler is about a two-hour drive north of Vancouver along the Sea to Sky Highway.

## BEST OF THE BEST
### Over the Mountains

When the knees get a little too shaky for one more run, Whistler has a different way to experience the mountain—the Peak 2 Peak Alpine Experience, the world's longest free-span gondola ride. It travels as high as 1,430 feet (436 m) above the valley floor and crosses an unsupported span nearly 3 miles (4.8 km) long. Below, the village looks like a prop for a model train set. Ahead is nothing but jagged peaks and snow. Go to Whistler for Canada's best powder, and then linger for the toddies on either end of the gondola ride. www.whistlerblackcomb.com/p2pg

Easing off the slopes is easy at Whistler's Village Stroll, a panoply of picturesque shops, fine restaurants, and bars amid ever-present mountain views.

# BEYOND SKIING:
# SINGULAR WINTER SPORTS

**Expand your cold-weather repertoire with these exciting activities (if you dare).**

## LUGE

*Canada Olympic Park, Calgary, Canada*

Suspended only by a fiberglass sling and two razor-sharp steel blades, zip feet-first down the icy run constructed for the 1988 Winter Olympics. Canadian Luge Association athletes coach you in the sport's basics (such as, no brakes), before you careen through five turns reaching speeds up to 37 mph (60 kph).

*www.winsportcanada.ca*

## SNOWMOBILING

*Palmer, Alaska*

In Alaska's Mat-Su (Matanuska-Susitna) Valley 45 miles (72 km) north of Anchorage, take a guided "snow machine" tour over frozen lakes, through frosted meadows, or along a stretch of the legendary Iditarod Trail. Small group and custom itineraries can include ice fishing, wildlife photography, and viewing the northern lights. No snowmobiling experience required.

*www.youralaskavacation.com, www.snowmobile-alaska.com*

## SKIJORING AND DOGSLEDDING

*New England Dogsledding and Telemark Inn,*
*Mason Township, Maine*

Paw power fuels the winter games at this White Mountain National Forest inn. Resident big dogs pull sleds on the multi-day "Learn to Mush" excursions and Nordic skiers (intermediate and above) on exhilarating skijoring runs.

*www.newenglanddogsledding.com*

## BIATHLON

*Whiteface Mountain, Lake Placid, New York*

Of all the Olympic experiences available at the 1932 and 1980 Winter Games' host venue, Lake Placid, "Be a Biathlete" is arguably the most unusual. Offered from late December through early March, the ski-and-shoot session begins with an hour-long cross-country ski lesson and ends with supervised target practice at the biathlon shooting range.

*www.whiteface.com*

## CURLING

*The Royal Caledonian Curling Club, various locations, Scotland*

If every Winter Olympics leaves you wondering what's so tough about sliding and sweeping polished rocks across a sheet of ice, find out at a free "Try Curling" session. Sponsored by the Royal Caledonian Curling Club, the two-hour workshops are held at rinks throughout Scotland. Wear sneakers and dress warmly.

*royalcaledoniancurlingclub.org*

## BOBSLED AND SKELETON

*Lillehammer Olympic Bobsleigh and Luge Track,*
*Hunderfossen, Norway*

Scandinavia's only bobsled and luge track is located 9 miles (15 km) north of central Lillehammer. Hop into a piloted four-person bobsled or six-person rubber bobraft to hit speeds up to 74 mph (120 kph), or slide solo—and face-first—half an inch (1 cm) off the ice on a skeleton.

*www.olympiaparken.no/index.php/en*

## SKI JUMPING

*Rennsteig Outdoor Center, Steinach, Germany*

Rennsteig's "Skiflyer" delivers the thrill of soaring off a 492-foot (150 m) ski jump while ensuring a pain- and crash-free landing. A harness-rope contraption keeps jumpers on course down the ramp and safely suspended over the Thuringian Forest for an 8- to 10-second flight. Single jumps and multi-jumps as well as lessons are available year-round.

*www.thuringia-tourism.com*

## NIGHT SLEDDING

*Preda to Bergün, Switzerland*

In winter, the Albula Pass road between Preda to Bergün is closed, creating Europe's longest floodlit toboggan run at 3.7 miles (6 km). Wear a ski helmet and rent a sled at the Preda train station (about 30 minutes from St. Moritz via rail) to rumble down the icy path past forests, farms, and villages.

*www.myswitzerland.com/en/toboggan-run-preda-berguen.html*

## SNOW KITING

*Obertauern, Austria*

The big-air, big-rush sport of snow kiting is a paragliding-snowboarding hybrid requiring wind, snow, and a heavy dose of courage. Spend the morning at the aptly named Hang on! Snow Kite School at Obertauern resort to rent equipment and take a lesson, before attempting takeoff from the high plateau.

*www.obertauern.com*

## SPEED SKATING

*Nagano Olympic Memorial Arena, Nagano, Japan*

From October through March, public skating and lessons are offered under the Olympic Memorial Arena's iconic ridgeline roof. Known as M-Wave, the world-class speed skating venue has hosted numerous Olympic events. Learn speed skating basics on the oval or ride a lap on the ice resurfacing machine.

*www.nagano-mwave.co.jp*

Nobody expects a midair jump out of first-time winter kiteboarders, but it's definitely a good reason to keep going back for more lessons.

El Capitan and Three Brothers Rock radiate in an alpine-glow sunset, one of the highlights of Yosemite in winter.

CALIFORNIA

# YOSEMITE NATIONAL PARK

**Ditch the crowds and plunge into the many adventures this great wilderness offers during snow-laden winter months.**

Most of the four million people who visit Yosemite National Park each year call during the warmer months. But in many ways, winter is most enchanting, when snow and ice blanket California's High Sierra wilderness. "Not to 'hole up' or sleep the white months away," naturalist John Muir wrote, "I was out every day . . . wading, climbing, sauntering among the blessed storms and calms, rejoicing in almost everything." And, on one occasion, riding an avalanche down a canyon.

Admittedly, it is easy to curl up with a good book in front of a fireplace at the Ahwahnee Hotel. But Muir had the right idea: You won't be sorry when you're headed out for adventures only winter can deliver in America's third oldest national park.

## THE WILDERNESS ON SNOWSHOES

The pioneers who homesteaded Yosemite before the valley became a national park were normally snowed in for the winter. "You could get in and out," says former park historian Jim Snyder, "but you needed a good pair of snowshoes." In the intervening years, snowshoes have morphed from a utilitarian object into one of the park's best means of winter recreation.

*Between December and March, Yosemite Valley transforms into a warren of snowy paths across frozen meadows and through frosty forests.*

Nothing but the swish of skis across groomed trails—more than 350 miles' (560 km) worth starting from Yosemite's Badger Pass Ski Area—breaks the silence of a snowy woodland.

Famed for its wildflowers during the warmer months, Tuolumne Meadows morphs into a favorite Sierra high-country snowboarding spot come winter.

Get a quick introduction—how to strap them on, trek through heavy powder, and upright yourself after tumbling sideways—by taking one of the free ranger-guided snowshoe walks offered daily by the National Park Service in the winter. More intense snowshoe adventures range from a hearty six-hour trek to Dewey Point to a romantic full-moon walk at Badger Pass. Or rent your own snowshoes and go off-road in the snow-mantled Tuolumne Grove of giant sequoias.

## NIGHTFALL'S WINTER MAGIC

Between December and March, Yosemite Valley transforms into a warren of snowy paths across frozen meadows and through frosty forests. Winter is an excellent time to spot and photograph wildlife, including the park's celebrated bears—which hibernate only some of the time—mule deer, coyotes, and bobcats, often by following their tracks through fresh snow.

As magic as the days might be, the valley is even more charming after dark. Skate to the rhythm of big-band tunes at the Curry Village ice rink and then cozy up around the rink's fire pit with a warm drink and blanket as you gaze up at the star-spangled sky above Half Dome. Or hike to the base of Upper Yosemite Falls to see the massive "snow cone" that forms when the cascade's mist freezes and falls to the ground as snow. Or try a picture-perfect, family-friendly sleigh ride offered by the Tenaya Lodge. A jingle-belled sleigh dashes through the snow for 45 minutes most winter weekends to a camp complete with hot cider and a roaring fire ready to toast a marshmallow or two.

## COUNTRY SNOW SPORTS

Developed in the early 1930s when Yosemite bid (unsuccessfully) to host the Winter Olympics, Badger Pass Ski Area is one of America's oldest winter sports resorts. Charlie Chaplin and Walt Disney are among those who have skied Badger in the past. With gentle slopes, short runs, and a beginner-level terrain park, it's an ideal place for kids (or anyone else) to learn how to ski or snowboard. The Badger Pups program takes children as young as four onto the slopes. Kids can also glide down on rubber snow tubes.

Those seeking more of a physical and mental challenge can set off on cross-country skiing adventures into the Yosemite backcountry. The classic run is the 21-mile (34 km) round-trip to Glacier Point with an overnight at a historic ski hut overlooking Yosemite Valley. Hard-core skiers can join six-day snow treks to Tuolumne Meadows—with overnights in tents or ski huts—in the company of guides from the Yosemite Mountaineering School. All told, the park offers almost 350 miles (565 km) of skiable trails and roads in winter.

PLANNING **Yosemite National Park** www.nps.gov/yose. **Lodging reservations** www.yosemitepark.com. **Badger Pass** www .yosemitepark.com/BadgerPass.aspx. **Curry Village ice skating rink** www.yosemitepark .com/ice-skating.aspx. For a schedule of winter ranger-guided hikes in the valley, check out the winter version of the *Yosemite Guide* available at www.nps.gov/yose/planyourvisit/guide.htm. **Tenaya Lodge sleigh rides** www.tenayalodge.com.

A pair of coyotes lazes about on a winter's day, resting up for their next hunt.

## SCOTTSDALE, ARIZONA
# NATIVE TRAILS FESTIVAL

"Native Trails is a collaboration of performing artists from Southwestern tribes in which we take the audience on a sensory journey, sharing our traditional and contemporary ways with instruments, regalia, food, song, and dance. While imparting our culture, we unite our energy, thereby encouraging a healthy outlook for future generations."

—DERRICK SUWAIMA DAVIS (HOPI/CHOCTAW),
NATIVE TRAILS ARTISTIC DIRECTOR

Scottsdale's Native Trails Festival runs from noon to 1 p.m. on most Thursdays and Saturdays between late January and early April at the Scottsdale Civic Center Park. *Pictured:* A traditional hoop dance

# QUEBEC CITY

**Bundle up and put your hearty on for the annual citywide—and outdoor— Winter Carnival.**

**M**on pays ce n'est pas un pays, c'est l'hiver, goes the famous song by Québécois chansonnier Gilles Vigneault. Translation: My country is not a country, it's winter. It's an anthem to a place as inhospitable in climate—temperatures can drop to –40°F (–40°C)—as it is welcoming in culture. When it comes to winter, the city just deals. Everyone dresses warmly, of course. But more than that, locals make the best of it. They create amazing snow sculptures that decorate the squares (Google the pictures if you think we're exaggerating). And they throw a huge party.

Festivities blanket the city in a storm of activities during Quebec's Winter Carnival—billed as the world's largest. Take a dogsled ride on the Plains of Abraham, the city's answer to New York's Central Park. Check out the yearly Canoe Race on the St. Lawrence River, where more than 50 teams hailing from Canada, France, and the U.S. take to the icy waters (the race begins at Bassin Louise). Even though you didn't partake in the competition, enjoy the oxymoron that is Carnival's Village Arctic Spas. Here, brave bathers take to outdoor hot tubs, hot swimming pools, and saunas scattered amid snow-dressed pines. And why not? Heck, even the churches, where icicles bejewel the steeples, get into the winter spirit.

**A** snowball's throw from all Carnival activities, Auberge Saint-Antoine—historic, snug, and stylish—is as close as you're going to get to a sleepover at the Louvre. The city's finest hostelry is a romantic cross between a European museum and a Manhattan boutique hotel: 750 archaeological artifacts exhibited throughout the hotel belie its past lives as a wharf, cannon battery, and warehouse. The fully renovated inn boasts 95 elegant rooms and suites. Its superb Panache restaurant is the coziest reservation in town, with flagstone walls, a coiling wrought-iron staircase, pillow-heaped banquettes, and sumptuous, seasonal food. www.saint-antoine.com

**PLANNING  Quebec Winter Carnival** www.carnaval.qc.ca. Events kick off sometime between late January and mid-February. (The pre-Lent merrymaking typically lasts until Mardi Gras.) Accommodations near party HQ (downtown Quebec City) abound.

The Bonhomme Ice Palace, rebuilt each year in a slightly different style, is an enchanting highlight of the Quebec Winter Carnival.

The Boston Public Library gussies itself up for First Night, New Year's Eve.

MASSACHUSETTS

# BOSTON

**Ring in the New Year by reveling in the arts at North America's oldest First Night fete.**

On Boston Common, pastoral heart of New England's cultural capital, the calm stillness of a new-fallen snow inspires quiet contemplation of what has been and what is yet to be. Here in the nation's oldest public park—purchased by local colonists in 1634—colonial militia mustered for the Revolution, John Adams celebrated a fledgling independence, and Bostonians rallied against slavery, segregation, and the Vietnam War.

On December 31, the nearly 50-acre (20 ha) common is the midpoint of Boston's First Night, a progressive cultural smorgasbord packed with more than 200 performances, from dance to film, techno music to tango. From 1 p.m. until a midnight fireworks finale, about a million revelers—most cloaked in some manner of festive fleece—scurry between venues from the waterfront westward, past Copley Square, where colossal ice sculptures rise in the shadows of Romanesque-style Trinity Church.

"My favorite First Night tradition is the Grand Procession, and it's little known, so that everyone can join in," says First Night organizer Joyce Linehan. "Pick up a handcrafted giant puppet at the Hynes Convention Center and march down Boylston Street as thousands of Bostonians cheer you on. It's a great way to celebrate a new beginning."

**PLANNING First Night Boston** www.firstnight.org. Admission buttons permitting entry to all indoor events (those outdoors are free) can be purchased online.

## IN THE KNOW
*Boston Common 101*

As Boston evolved from Puritan colony to Commonwealth capital, so did the role of its center-city common. The green was originally established as a livestock grazing area, though proper Bostonians permanently banned cows in 1830. Public hangings—first by tree and then by gallows—ended in 1817. John and Frederick Olmsted, Jr., orchestrated the common's total transformation to restorative green space in 1913. And some 80 years after on-site Civil War recruitment drives claimed New Englanders for Union Army service, World War II scrap metal drives collected most of the park's iron fencing to help build tanks, planes, and weapons.

There's no better—or sparklier—window-shopping to be found than New York City department stores done up for the holidays.

NEW YORK

# NEW YORK CITY

**Take to the streets, holiday markets, and the ice when the Big Apple dolls up for the holidays.**

Nobody would fault you for heading to New York City in the spring when Central Park blooms big or, really, in any of the seasons—but to see the city in a full-on glittery frenzy, winter can't be beat. The city's usual go-go-go energy (there are places to go and people to see, people!) swings into overdrive once you add holiday shopping, lights, the shop windows along Fifth Avenue, and a world's worth of visitors into the mix.

Hop right into the swirl, but when you need a breather, choose a spot to sit and enjoy the people-watching. As artist Jason Polan, a columnist and the pen behind the drawing project "Every Person in New York," puts it: "I love getting hot chocolate with a friend and about eight million other people." Really, one of the great joys of New York is the mix of moments large and small all winter long.

## GIFTED EXCURSIONS

The city's normal abundance of flea and farmers' markets gets holiday company every year: gift and craft markets. Some are outdoors, so you'll want to bundle up. Take a deep breath and hop into the traffic streams that crawl through the aisles of the Union Square

*The city's usual go-go-go energy . . . swings into overdrive once you add holiday shopping, lights, the shop windows along Fifth Avenue, and a world's worth of visitors into the mix.*

From first-time skaters to serious jumpers, New York's outdoor rinks—including this one in Central Park—offer ice fun for everyone.

Rockefeller Center's glittering year-round resident, Prometheus, welcomes his holiday company: the Christmas tree and two rows of horn-tooting angels.

Holiday Market or its midtown cousin, the Columbus Circle Holiday Market. The booths stock everything from artisanal chocolate to delicate jewelry. Or, for crafts from some up-and-coming artists, head to Brooklyn Flea's Gifted, a weekends-only event in the month or so leading up to Christmas.

Get a four-for-one experience with a visit to the Holiday Market in Grand Central Terminal's Vanderbilt Hall. Stop for gifts that range from trinket to pricey before tackling the mall's worth of shops set up underground. Then give your eyes and ears a treat by taking in the sights and sounds of the main concourse before gifting the rest of your senses with a meal at the legendary Oyster Bar.

## LIGHT IT UP

Holiday lights aplenty shine all over Manhattan—the Empire State Building sparkles in green and red—but it's off to Brooklyn you go for some of the city's most dramatic lights. Forget "Go big or go home"; when it comes to the holidays in New York, it's "Go big and say shalom!" Standing an impressive 32 feet high (10 m), the menorah at the entrance to Prospect Park has to be lit from the basket of a cherry picker. The celebration—held each of the eight nights of Hanukkah—features dancing and plenty of latkes for all. Then head to the borough's Dyker Heights neighborhood for a house-by-house tour of its over-the-top holiday decorations. (No, we can't imagine their electric bills, either.)

If you're in the mood for a good old-fashioned tree lighting, the Rockefeller Center tree is notable, but it's not the only spruce (or fir) in town. The New York Botanical Garden in the Bronx lights up its trees in late November, and Manhattan's Metropolitan Museum of Art goes for multiple lighting ceremonies.

## HIT THE ICE

Hans Brinker may be the world's most famous skater, but the Rink at Rockefeller Center is easily the best known spot to twirl (or fall) in front of a crowd of onlookers. Under the legendary Christmas tree at 30 Rock and the watchful eye of the golden Prometheus statue, lace up and then hit the ice (gracefully). The rink is also a *very* popular spot for marriage proposals, so keep an eye out; part of your day may include wishing well to a newly engaged pair.

For another classic NYC skating experience, head into Central Park. The park sports two rinks: the Trump (though locals will always call it by its former name, Wollman) and Lasker rinks.

PLANNING  **New York City** nycgo.com. **Shopping** Union Square and Columbus Circle Holiday Markets, urbanspacenyc.com; Brooklyn Flea's Gifted, www.brooklynflea.com; Grand Central Terminal, www.grandcentralterminal .com. **Holiday lights** Prospect Park menorah, www.worldslargestmenorah.com; bus tour of Dyker Heights' holiday lights, www.asliceof brooklyn.com; Botanical Garden, www.nybg .org; Metropolitan Museum of Art, www.met museum.org. **Ice skating** Rockefeller Center, www.rockefellercenter.com; Central Park rinks, www.wollmanskatingrink.com, www.lasker rink.com.

The Empire State Building is reimagined in lollipops and candy canes for a sweet New York window display.

# HOLIDAY LIGHTS

**Light up your winter amid these dazzling displays.**

### NEW YORK CITY, NEW YORK

Whether you're a twirl-around-the-rink pro or a stumble-in-place novice, take to the Rockefeller Center ice rink to immerse yourself in New York–style holiday sparkle. Above, a grand evergreen—a tradition since the 1930s—towers against the plaza's iconic skyscraper. Gaze up at the tree's very top and a Swarovski star winks back. And there's more once you've had your hot chocolate—the elaborate holiday windows of the famed stores of Fifth Avenue beckon right around the corner.

*www.rockefellercenter.com*

### WASHINGTON, D.C.

Both Hanukkah and Christmas light up the Ellipse, a public park near the White House, every holiday season. Whether you're savoring potato pancakes as rabbis ride bucket lifts to light the 30-foot (9 m) menorah each of Hanukkah's eight nights or singing along to "Jingle Bells" and other Christmas favorites while admiring the towering, star-topped national evergreen tree, the south portico of the President's home always glows softly in the background.

*www.thenationaltree.org, www.afldc.org/ellipse*

### MEDELLÍN, COLOMBIA

Holiday radiance stretches for miles as whimsical lights flood the Medellín River and the city's streets, parks, and landmarks are draped in illumination. Displays, which might be inspired by artisan weavings or the local mountains, won't dazzle just the eyes; one year, a coffee scent was piped through one area, while recordings of birds chirped in another. It's a multimedia, multisensory celebration.

*www.medellin.travel/en*

### BRUSSELS, BELGIUM

With choreographed music and lighting, the baroque- and Renaissance-style facades surrounding Brussels's Grand Place become dancing architectural confections every December. The city's annual Winter Wonders event also includes large-scale installations by artists, who, in previous years, have woven a ceiling of illuminated ribbons above the Belgian capital city's fashion and design center.

*www.brussels.be*

### GUBBIO, ITALY

A nearly half-mile-tall (650 m) silhouette of a Christmas tree is strung in lights on the slope of Mount Ingino every year. Dwarfing the central Italian medieval town of Gubbio at the foot of the mountain, the "tree" requires more than 700 giant lights, takes nearly 2,000 person-hours to complete, and has been a tradition since 1981.

*www.alberodigubbio.com*

### BUDAPEST, HUNGARY

A twinkling tram coated in 39,200 lights transports commuters across Budapest every Christmas season. It runs regular routes, adding some holiday cheer to routine, and could even deliver you to the city's Christmas Fair, where a candle lit with a flame from Bethlehem glows.

*www.budapestinfo.hu*

### JERUSALEM, ISRAEL

Soft flames flicker across the Jewish Quarter of Jerusalem's Old City throughout Hanukkah, but on the eighth night—when families light the full complement of candles or oil lamps on menorahs displayed outside their homes—you'll feel most surrounded by the holiday's warmth. Stroll among the stone dwellings at sunset and you might hear songs and blessings as the flames are lit.

*www.jewish-quarter.org.il*

### KOBE, JAPAN

After an earthquake shook Kobe in 1995, Italy sent raw materials for an intricate display of remembrance and resilience: thousands of small, hand-painted bulbs. Now, every December you can stroll among them, as the city laces the lights into cathedral-like arches, gateways, and pavilions.

*www.feel-kobe.jp*

### SAN FERNANDO, THE PHILIPPINES

Brightly colored lanterns inspired by the Star of Bethlehem adorn Filipino homes every Christmas. While the original *parols* of the Giant Lantern Festival, begun in 1931, were simple star-shaped affairs of rice paper on bamboo frames, today artists in the northern Philippine city of San Fernando create massive, dizzying designs and parade them down the street.

*cityofsanfernando.gov.ph*

### SYDNEY, AUSTRALIA

Some of Sydney's major landmarks become canvasses during Christmas light shows. Bring a picnic dinner and pick a spot outside. You'll find all kinds of displays, from images of Renaissance art bathing the ornate sandstone facade of St. Mary's Cathedral to Sydney Town Hall glowing in an array of kaleidoscopic colors.

*www.sydneychristmas.com.au*

Established as a way to boost
the spirits of locals devastated
by an earthquake in 1995,
Japan's Kobe Luminarie has
become an annual light delight.

Literature lovers will want to sit tight in George Vanderbilt's library, but there's no time—the tour must go on.

## NORTH CAROLINA
# ASHEVILLE

**Indulge in the opulence of a Gilded Age Christmas in an enchanted mountain château.**

At first breathtaking glimpse, George Vanderbilt's Biltmore Estate mesmerizes, a lavish Gilded Age vision rising from the Pisgah National Forest. Spread across four acres (1.6 ha), the 175,000-square-foot (16,260 sq m), 250-room French Renaissance château was once one of America's largest homes, yet it's the site, not the size, that captivates. "No one expects to encounter a European castle in the middle of the North Carolina mountains," says Biltmore spokesperson LeeAnn Donnelly. "No matter how many times you see it, you can't believe it's here."

Vanderbilt first welcomed guests to his family's home on Christmas Eve 1895. The tradition continues from November though New Year's Day during "Christmas at Biltmore." All halls are decked in elaborate period decor: 300 hand-lit luminaries, nearly 500 wreaths, and 68 Christmas trees. The signature three-story-tall Fraser fir, decorated per Vanderbilt tradition with 1,500 gift boxes, ornaments, and electric lights, dwarfs the estate's cavernous Banquet Hall.

The event's reservation-only Candlelight Christmas Evenings most closely re-create the family's first holiday. "The ambience at night changes completely," Donnelly explains. "When people walk through the door, they start speaking in hushed tones. The lighting is dimmed, the massive Banquet Hall fireplace warms the house, and the aroma of the Fraser firs spark memories of Christmas morning. It's an enchanted experience."

**PLANNING Biltmore** www.biltmore.com. When purchasing Candlelight Christmas Evening tickets online, reserve a table in the estate's historic Stable Café for a pretour, candlelit dinner.

### GREAT STAYS
*The Grove Park Inn Resort and Spa*

With millions made from his Grove's Tasteless Chill Tonic (an 1890s antimalaria potion), Edwin Wiley Grove chiseled a mountain slope into an iconic Blue Ridge retreat. Opened in 1913, the 512-room Grove Park Inn is furnished with the world's largest collection of Arts and Crafts—style furniture. The legendary guest list includes ten U.S. presidents and countless glitterati (F. Scott Fitzgerald flamboyantly flirted with female guests while wife Zelda convalesced at a nearby psychiatric facility). The Great Hall's bookend, 14-foot-tall (4.3 m) fireplaces conceal hand-operated elevators. Luxury upgrades include a $50 million, 43,000-square-foot (4,000 sq m) subterranean spa. www.grove parkinn.com

# BLUE SPRING STATE PARK

**Spot rare, gentle manatees at play on their annual winter vacation.**

I f Florida's manatees could name their favorite winter resort, it might just be Blue Spring State Park. When their home waters get too chilly, hundreds of the 1,000-plus-pound (more than 450 kg) creatures journey down the St. Johns River to the central Florida spring, where temperatures stay warm and fairly even year-round.

From afar, it can look as though Blue Spring has been filled with oblong gray boulders. But peer into the water, and you'll see that these slow-moving aquatic mammals really do seem to treat their time here as a well-deserved vacation. When they're not lounging, watch them turn logs into toys, gnaw on palm fronds, and spin through the water doing barrel rolls. Pat Rose, executive director of the Save the Manatee Club, says he's even seen a curious manatee approach an alligator (don't worry—the manatee wasn't harmed). "With that many manatees there, the odds of some really cute thing happening is quite high," he says.

Rose insists you'll fall in love. But you might also have your heart broken. While manatee numbers are improving in Florida, it's not hard to spot propeller scars on some of their backs.

**PLANNING  Blue Spring State Park** www.floridastateparks.org/bluespring. The official manatee season starts in November, but January—when Blue Spring's manatee population is the highest—is best for viewing. Check with the park before you travel.

## FOR FOODIES
*The Old Spanish Sugar Mill*

J ust 30 minutes from Blue Spring State Park, you can take a dip in a spring yourself and have an unusual breakfast to boot. At De Leon Springs State Park, the Old Spanish Sugar Mill restaurant is true to its name, with some of the old gears still in place and a small exhibit on how sugar was once milled here. The restaurant specializes in pour-your-own—pancakes, that is. Servers deliver pitchers of batter that diners cook themselves on built-in griddles at the tables. www.florida stateparks.org/deleonsprings

West Indian manatees cluster around warm-water sources in winter, such as those found at Blue Spring State Park.

## THE BAHAMAS
# JUNKANOO

"Junkanoo is the ultimate Bahamian street party, celebrated throughout the islands on Boxing Day and New Year's Day. In Nassau, thousands of dancers don elaborate, brilliantly colored headdresses and costumes and parade down Bay Street to the music of cowbells and goatskin drums. It's a wild, joyful, utterly Caribbean festival."

—KAREN CARMICHAEL, NATIONAL GEOGRAPHIC WRITER

Junkanoo honors the freedom of African slaves. Starting at 2 a.m. on both December 26 and January 1, the festivities last until sunrise and include music, dance, and parades. *Pictured:* The

# R. A. Dickey

## Eleuthera, Bahamas

I n my line of work, you don't get much alone time. You pitch in front of tens of thousands of fans. Your every move is scrutinized, not only by the people in the ballpark, but by hundreds of thousands more watching on TV.

There's no place to hide on a big-league mound, and that's one reason why I love the Bahamian island of Eleuthera. Because in Eleuthera, along with pinkish sand and turquoise water, there is an abundance of places to hide.

*Eleuthera* is the Greek word for freedom. It is aptly named.

There are many Caribbean islands bigger than Eleuthera, 110 miles (177 km) of crescent-shaped splendor, and plenty that probably have more breathtaking scenery. I wouldn't trade Eleuthera for any of them. It's more built up now than when my wife Anne and I first went there together, but the places we go are not written up in travel guides. There's a beach where I've never seen another footprint besides our own. The first time I looked at the expanse of sand and water that is almost a make-believe color, I thought, "This must be how Robinson Crusoe felt." I also thought: "This must be what heaven looks like."

One of my favorite spots is Lighthouse Point, on the island's southern tip. There are three rock outcroppings where we go, with idyllic little coves in between. There are often sharks there, but I always swim from one side to the other anyway. (What can I say? I've always been into adrenaline rushes.) Then there's "Sam's Reef" that we named after Anne's father. We snorkel in and out of the coral, amid the Technicolor fish. I sometimes take a spear with me, in the hope of landing a lobster for dinner.

So much of what I cherish about Eleuthera is the sweet, simple rhythm of our days there. We stop at the home of people we know and have conch fritters. We swing by a little bakery for key lime pie. I run on the beach and listen to the waves and let the tranquility fill me up. I love being a major league pitcher, but when I am looking for a winter refuge, a place to recharge my knuckleballing soul, I know just where to go.

*R. A. Dickey, the 2012 National League Cy Young Award winner, is a husband, father, adventurer, and pitcher for the Toronto Blue Jays. He is the author of a best-selling memoir,* Wherever I Wind Up: My Quest for Truth, Authenticity, and the Perfect Knuckleball.

*"I love being a major league pitcher, but when I am looking for a winter refuge, a place to recharge my knuckleballing soul, I know just where to go."*

Doing nothing at all is a vital skill for those looking to recharge on Eleuthera's beaches.

# DOMINICAN REPUBLIC

**Catch some winter baseball fever where potential future major league stars are only part of the action.**

"¿*Habla béisbol?*" asks a taxi driver as he picks you up outside the thatched-roof Punta Cana airport. Seeing you cock your head in confusion, he continues, "Manny Ramirez! Vladi Guerrero!" Suddenly you understand: Dominicans would rather talk—and play—baseball than anything else. This Caribbean nation has supplied more U.S. major league players—well over 200—than any other foreign country. Your chances of spotting the next Albert Pujols at its highly competitive Winter League, where most of the star players cut their teeth, are pretty high.

Leave the island's perfect white-sand strands behind for a while and watch a couple of the league's six teams play between mid-October and January. The hottest action is at Estadio Quisqueya in Santo Domingo and Estadio Tetelo Vargas in San Pedro de Macoris. But be prepared for a whole new game—in the stands, that is, not on the field. Dominican baseball is more carnival than sporting event, a cacophony of drums, whistles, clowns, and cheerleaders dancing atop the dugouts. Of course, you'll feel right at home when you nab a roasted corncob and a *chatica* full of local rum from one of the ever-shouting vendors. Don't be surprised if you find yourself dancing in the aisles from first pitch to last out.

PLANNING **Dominican Republic** www.godominicanrepublic.com. **DR Winter League scores, statistics, and schedules** www.mlb.com/mlb/events/winterleagues. Tickets are available at the stadium box offices on mornings before the games.

See Major League Baseball's future stars hit one out of the park during a Winter League game in the Dominican Republic.

A royal residence dating from 250 to 800, the Mayan Palace of Palenque rises dramatically in the northernmost hills of the Chiapas highlands.

MEXICO

# CHIAPAS

**Explore ancient civilizations and encounter current descendants amid the exotic wildlife of the rain forest.**

Boasting some of Latin America's most significant Maya sites and an astounding array of exotic wildlife, the vast, rain-forest-covered state of Chiapas in the south of Mexico offers travelers the opportunity to explore Indiana Jones style.

Chiapas's many charms captivate most during winter, with its soft, warm breezes and unique celebrations. The terraced ancient city of Palenque, dotted with temples, crypts, and sculptures, is the area's most famous. But many more adventures await. Remote expeditions up rivers (Yaxchilán is reachable only by boat) or treks through dense rain forest bring visitors deep into a brave natural world sound tracked by the rumbling groans of howler monkeys.

"Chiapas is much more than the unique archaeological sites," says Rebeca del Rosal, who runs local tours. "Traveling off the beaten path is a once-in-a-lifetime opportunity to see the world through the eyes of living Mayas." Del Rosal adds that "these friendly people are eager to share" their homes, food, and customs.

The dry season has fewer mosquitoes and more chances of seeing wildlife, forced out of the jungle to rivers in search of water. Enthralled visitors should not forget to look up: Many migratory birds also pass through Chiapas in winter. Christmastime in particular brings out the best, as Maya meets Catholicism and celebrations abound.

**PLANNING Chiapas** www.visitmexico.com. Local guides such as the Muddy Boot *(www.themuddyboot.org)* are good sources on the state's ancient sites, traditions, nature, and wildlife.

## IN THE KNOW
### *The Maya Empire*

The mighty empire of the Maya civilization, which reached its peak around the sixth century A.D., stretched across Guatemala, Mexico, El Salvador, and Honduras, leaving its mark with the famous sites of Chichén Itzá on the Yucatán Peninsula, Tikal in Guatemala, and Palenque in Chiapas. The Maya's knowledge of astronomy, mathematics, the arts, architecture, and agriculture was advanced. Though many of their cities were mysteriously abandoned and they later suffered at the hands of the colonial Spanish forces, Maya descendants and their language survive today. The known archaeological sites of Chiapas are just a tantalizing taste of what's out there, with much more still to discover about this region's early residents.

MEXICO

# MONARCH BUTTERFLY BIOSPHERE RESERVE

"The monarchs are everywhere. Hanging on the pines like flat Christmas ornaments and clumping like swollen beehives on the ends of branches. Some evergreens are so covered with butterflies that they resemble maples in the fall."

—MELINA GEROSA BELLOWS, *NATIONAL GEOGRAPHIC TRAVELER* MAGAZINE, NOVEMBER/DECEMBER, 2009

Falling temperatures trigger the beginning of the monarch butterflies' migration from the northern United States and Canada to their winter habitat at the Monarch Butterfly Biosphere Reserve near Mexico City. In the wintertime, millions of butterflies can be found in this UNESCO World Heritage site covering more than 138,000 acres (56,000 ha).

A male resplendent quetzal shows off the magnificent tail feathers it grows during mating season.

CENTRAL AMERICA

# COSTA RICA

**Trek through misty jungles and around active volcanoes in search of a brilliant, feathered Aztec god.**

An unimaginable array of flora and fauna can be found in Costa Rica's jungles amid the purr of jaguars, mist of clouds, and sputter of active volcanoes. But one creature is so vaunted that it was the inspiration for the Aztec and Maya feathered snake god: the aptly named resplendent quetzal. Famed ornithologist Roger Tory Peterson called it the most spectacular bird in the New World. From December to April, during the dry season, its swooping, elegant tail is the giveaway to spotting it in the thick canopy. Sadly, it has become threatened, making it more elusive, and sightings of it rare. Encountering this graceful creature, even if just for a moment, offers a glimpse of living color you won't find elsewhere.

Locals refer to the dry season as *verano* (summer), when road mud dries and rivers and foliage recede, making passage and spotting easier. The bird can be found in Costa Rica's necklace of national parks, which includes Arenal and Poás Volcano. The quest brings you past crushed-seashell beaches, mountainous cloud forests, deep lakes, streams, and waterfalls. It is a sublime and transformative natural experience that will stay with you long after the quetzal's striking plumage disappears into the mist.

**PLANNING** **Bird-watching** costaricanbirdroute.com. Costa Rica's Bird Route, Central America's first, is a string of 18 sites where resplendent quetzals are reported regularly. **Costa Rica's national park system** www.costarica-nationalparks.com.

## BEST OF THE BEST
### Outstanding National Parks

Winter is Costa's Rica's drier season and the ideal time to visit the country's vast and varied park system. The eco-rich Arenal Volcano National Park features two volcanoes, Chato Volcano and Mount Arena. Monteverde Cloud Forest Reserve is a privately managed rain forest and home to 2,500 plant and 400 bird species, many still being discovered. The 12,350-acre (5,000 ha) Los Quetzales National Park is covered in clouds and mist. Experts claim it's the easiest place to spot the quetzal; other bird species, like colibri, trogons, tanagers, and hummingbirds, also share the habitat, along with sloths, coyotes, and pumas. www.costarica-national parks.com, www.arenal.net

COLOMBIA

# CARTAGENA

**Flowers, the season's clear skies, and literary and musical events create an eclectic allure in this coastal resort city.**

The calendar might say winter, but Cartagena de Indias, just a few degrees north of the Equator, is warm year-round. One of South America's oldest colonial cities, Cartagena was founded in 1533, its wealth built on slavery, sugar, and gold. More than seven miles (11 km) of walls and ramparts attesting to its strategic prominence surround the Old City, now a charming UNESCO World Heritage site. Walking through it is a step back in time, especially in this season when the balconies, windows, and gardens are alive with tropical flowers. Music fills the streets, a mix of cumbia and other Afro-Caribbean sounds, giving an islandlike sensibility.

Rich with history and alive with cultural attractions, the coastal city makes for a sunny and cerebral winter vacation spot. New Yorker Barbara Kolber spends her winters in Cartagena—ideal, she says, because "it is a hot, dry season," perfect for boating and wandering the cobblestone streets with little fear of rain. "Cartagena is en route to the Panama Canal, so yachties from all over the world stop off there before transiting the canal, which makes for a very lively international boat scene," she explains. 'Tis also Cartagena's season of celebrations, from January's Hay Literary Festival and International Music Festival to February's International Film Fest.

**PLANNING** **Cartagena** www.colombia.travel, www.cartagenadeindias.travel. **Music, film, and literary festivals** www.cartagenamusicfestival.com, ficcifestival.com, www.hayfestival.com/cartagena/en-index.aspx.

Historic Cartagena abounds with color and energy.

Rio's many neighborhoods offer a nightly show of the city at sunset.

BRAZIL

# RIO DE JANEIRO

**Celebrate the famed Carnival or the New Year amid miles of glittering beaches, flower-lined streets, and parties, parties, parties.**

R io is one of the world's most sensual cities, its urban landscape set between wave-kissed, sandy beaches and unusual, forest-covered granite mountains lorded over by Christ the Redeemer's open embrace, the largest art deco sculpture in the world. Winter in the Northern Hemisphere is a summer blessing in Rio de Janeiro, with its steamy Christmas and New Year's, known as Réveillon, and the world's most famous celebration, Carnival. The city's beauty—man-made and natural—is most striking during these warm months, from its lush urban rain forest, Tijuca National Park, which rises up the cliffs of Corcovado Mountain, to the splendid miniature gardens edging the sidewalks all over town.

## PLAY AT THE BEACH PARTY RIO

Rio is a city of beach lovers, especially this time of year, from the urban paradise of crowded Copacabana to upscale, bossa-inflected Ipanema. It is during the holiday season that samba beats heat up the swirly beachside Avenida Atlantica sidewalks and *caipirinhas,* the drink made from sugarcane-fermented *cachaça,* cool down the sun-worshippers as night falls. Less famous beaches offer something, too, like Praia Vermelha

*Winter in the Northern Hemisphere is a summer blessing in Rio de Janeiro, with its steamy Christmas and New Year's, known as Réveillon, and the world's most famous celebration, Carnival.*

Once the annual Carnival celebration kicks off, Rio transforms into a giant nonstop party, complete with music, frenetic dancing, and plenty of food.

A season of spectacle, Carnival's showiest celebration unfurls at Rio's Sambadrome.

("red beach"), with its military base, allowing beachgoers to watch the surf-side daily drills. Or head to the suburbs' very wealthy enclave Barra da Tijuca, with its unspoiled beaches and lakes.

## CELEBRATE THE HOLIDAYS UNDER THE SUN AND FIREWORKS

Though it generally has a progressive take on religion, Brazil is the world's largest Catholic country. Christmas here is about family, and many folks head home. Still, there is plenty of spectacle for the visitor. On Christmas Eve, fireworks ignite over Lagoa Rodrigo de Freitas in southern Rio, illuminating the lake's neon, 28-story Christmas tree. Then, head to one of the city's many churches, including some of the oldest colonial ones downtown, for midnight and Christmas Mass; a special treat is visiting the gilded chapel of the Monastery of São Bento, dating from the late 1600s. And don't forget to stop by a bakery for a fresh Christmas *bolo rei,* Portuguese "king cake."

Beaches become the playgrounds of Rio's New Year's celebration, Réveillon. Millions of Brazilians and visitors alike, dressed in white for peace, line the sandy shores, tossing flowers into the sea at midnight to honor Yemanjá, the African sea goddess, in the hopes she will grant them their wish for the New Year. On her holiday, February 2, tens of thousands return to the water, lighting candles in ships made of coconuts, gourds, and other seaworthy candleholders as offerings.

## JOIN THE BIGGEST PARTY OF ALL

Nothing matches Carnival, though, the biggest party of all. Related to Easter and Lent, events begin the weekend before Ash Wednesday, with samba schools competing in the Sambadromo, a huge, open-air stadium with seating options from VIP to nosebleeders. Watch or be a part of the parades, with schools renting out costumes to visitors who trail their multistory floats, some toting supermodels like Naomi Campbell or native-born Gisele Bündchen.

For the full flavor of the festival, hit Carnival's ubiquitous street parties, suggests Alexandra de Vries, a Rio resident and author of two travel books on Brazil. *Blocos,* or street bands, "parade around as followers tag along pied-piper style, singing, dancing, and partying," she explains. Free, informal, and fun with tons of dancing, "blocos are everything that is fabulous about Rio," de Vries says. Each is unique, "from small, cute neighborhood parties" with a few hundred people to humongous throngs with hundreds of thousands in Ipanema or Leblon. And each has a theme: drag queens, polka dots, the Beatles, pets.

From music to beaches to nightlife, the city flaunts its Brazilian flair in this season like none other. With the World Cup in 2014 and the Olympics in 2016, soon everyone will know the joys of Rio.

**PLANNING** Rio de Janeiro www.rcvb.com .br. **Beaches** www.ipanema.com. **Carnival** www.rio-carnival.net.

The world-famous Copacabana beach earned its claim to fame with rock-till-you-drop nightclubs, glitzy hotels, and a bossa nova vibe.

# MARDI GRAS CELEBRATIONS

**Kiss pleasures of the flesh goodbye at the planet's most exuberant carnivals.**

### NEW ORLEANS, LOUISIANA

Napoleon may have sold Louisiana to the Americans, but French traditions endured, most notably Mardi Gras (Fat, or Shrove, Tuesday), the raucous carnival that really defines New Orleans. Beginning with a masked ball on the Feast of the Epiphany on January 6, celebrations build to fever pitch during five days of pre-Lenten parties.

*www.mardigrasneworleans.com*

### VERACRUZ, MEXICO

Eight days before Lent, Carnival kicks off in this eastern port city with the *quema del mal humor*—the "burning of ill humor" in the form of an effigy of Satan or (more likely) an unpopular political figure. Days of joyous parades and Latin revelry include the crowning of children as the Carnival Queen and the King of Joy and culminate in a mock burial for Carnival Juan, the symbol of the festivities.

*www.visitmexico.com*

### PORT OF SPAIN, TRINIDAD AND TOBAGO

With headdresses, hot pants, and painted bodies swinging to infectious soca, Port of Spain hosts one of the largest and most elaborate Caribbean carnivals. Brace yourself for all-night parties and raucous steel-pan music. Two days before Ash Wednesday, paint, oil, and melted chocolate fly during the *mas* (masquerade) parades.

*www.gotrinidadandtobago.com*

### OLINDA, BRAZIL

Unlike its flashy Rio cousin, this historic coastal town celebrates Carnival with small bands playing *frevo* (from the Portuguese word for "boiling") and giant papier-mâché puppets lurching through the cobbled quarter. Every street boasts its own *bloco,* or Carnival band, driving throngs of gyrating dancers in audacious costumes. The wildest getups are worn by transvestite groups on Carnival Friday.

*www.carnivalbookers.com*

### ORURO, BOLIVIA

Nestled high in the Andes, this quiet mining town comes alive during a four-day pre-Lenten procession featuring dancing *diabladas,* or devils. Indian miners feared their underworld deity, Supay, would be jealous of the Virgin of the Mineshaft, patron saint of Carnival, so appeasing residents don devilish costumes—and chuck water balloons at each other. The town recently unveiled a 150-foot (48 m) statue of the Virgin Mary, taller even than Rio's "Christ the Redeemer."

*www.boliviaturismo.com.bo*

### COLOGNE, GERMANY

Stereotypically serious Germans throw a communal silly fit during Karneval, also known as Fasching in some parts of Germany. Festivities begin November 11 and flow all the way through winter. In Cologne, the hundreds of festive events include parades, balls, concerts, and traditional variety shows. On the Monday before Ash Wednesday, a rowdy pageant of fools is followed by an all-night ball.

*www.koelnerkarneval.de*

### VENICE, ITALY

The mother of all Mardis Gras celebrations, the flamboyant Venetian Carnevale was invented in the 13th century, marrying the Latin *carne* (flesh) to *vale* (farewell). Although rooted in Catholicism, this has always been a secular extravaganza and an excuse for Venetians to act out their fantasies behind the anonymity of disguise. Visit about two weeks before Lent to see locals in authentic costume.

*www.carnivalofvenice.com*

### PATRAS, GREECE

A meeting of myth and reality, Patras's Carnival draws its inspiration from ancient Greece—in particular, Dionysus, the god of wine. St. Anthony's Day (January 17) marks the official start of a carnival season that stretches all the way into early March, finishing with a lavish parade and a kite-flying competition.

*www.visitgreece.gr*

### MINDELO, CAPE VERDE

Just off the coast of Senegal, the lush Cape Verde islands host a curious mix of Carnival traditions in the run-up to the fast. In the handsome town of Mindelo, jerry-built floats and curvy dancers sway to Creole *coladeira* punctuated by ululating African shrieks. Competitions are held for best outfit, prettiest girl, and the finest oil-smeared, drum-beating group of Mandingo warriors.

*www.capeverde.com*

### GOA, INDIA

Unique to India, the Goa Carnival still exudes the free, harmonious spirit that made this former Portuguese colony a hippie legend. On Fat Saturday, King Momo reads a decree entitling him to rule for three days and ordering everyone to party. Gorgeous floats and graceful dancers wend their way through the streets of Panjim to traditional folk songs and strumming of guitars.

*www.goatourism.gov.in*

Carnival in Bavaria has a distinct sound: bells. They're hung off costumes and rung by hand, in the hopes of chasing winter away.

PERU

# PUNO

**Watch thousands dance in the streets—for miles—at the colorful Fiesta de la Virgen de la Candelaria.**

T he sun, the earth, the bounty. During the pre-Hispanic period of the place we now call Peru, February was harvest time. Couple that with a desire to celebrate the city of Puno's patron, the Virgin of Candelaria, and it's time to dance in the streets—literally.

Every February in Puno, the country's folklore capital, about 200 teams of dancers and musicians—totaling 50,000 dancers and 15,000 musicians—compete at the 18-day Fiesta de la Virgen de la Candelaria. Each team chooses one of seven traditional dances, from the devilishly playful *diablada* to the *waka waka,* a bullfighting dance.

Backed by brass horns and drum lines, the vibrantly costumed competitors dance for miles in a seemingly never-ending parade through Puno's streets—the sidewalks lined with spectators packed onto temporary bleachers or folding chairs. It's a mashup of a holy procession, the Macy's Thanksgiving Day Parade, and Rio's Carnival—all in a city that sits more than 12,500 feet (3,830 m) above sea level, a place where just walking uphill leaves some out-of-towners moving ever so slowly.

Long after the last dancers have gone home, visitors may find themselves humming the folklore tunes, anxious to return for more of the beautiful madness.

**PLANNING  Fiesta de la Virgen de la Candelaria** www.visitperu.com.

## FOR FOODIES
### *Peruvian Street Snacks*

Y ou'll never go hungry on the streets of Puno. While watching Candelaria's dancers prance by on the street, small, easy-to-eat treats are a must. Put your hand up to summon vendors with trays hanging from straps around their necks. For a few *nuevos soles* (Peru's currency), they offer up everything from *choclo* (ears of corn served with small slabs of cheese) to sliced roast pork sandwiches. Buy several cellophane sleeves of salty fried fava beans and crunchy corn kernels. You will get thirsty, but not to worry—another vendor will be along soon with ice-cold Coca-Colas for sale.

Candelaria dancers put on a colorful display as they twirl through the streets.

Argentine gauchos race across a lake near Beron de Astrada in an endurance test—for both rider and horse—that stretches back centuries.

ARGENTINA/CHILE/URUGUAY

# THE PAMPAS

**Watch legendary gauchos compete, then join them for a barbecue under vast lowland skies.**

Cowboys may be rare in the American West, but gauchos still populate vast *estancias,* or ranches, of the grassy pampas at the bottom end of South America. Come summer (winter in North America), the best of them compete in *jineteadas* (rodeos) that are an integral part of life in rural Argentina, Chile, and Uruguay.

Most of these are small-town affairs. You'll find yourself among a handful of spectators crowded against a wooden fence as each rider enters the dirt arena on a bucking bronco. The gauchos put on a fierce display of horsemanship, complete with *rebenques* (leather whips) whirling overhead and sporting red berets, green scarves, and sashes around their waists. "It's kind of like a black belt in karate," laughs veteran cowpoke Patricio Varcaza. "A gaucho must earn these by being a good rider. And a woman must give you these three things after watching you ride."

After every jineteada, it's a party on the pampas. Everyone gathers with the gauchos beneath an endless blue sky for a barbecue. The best riders aspire to national rodeos, like January's huge Doma (Rodeo) and Folklore Festival near Córdoba, Argentina. But you don't get to have a cookout with the victors afterward.

**PLANNING  Rodeos of the Pampas** www.turismo.gov.ar. **Doma and Folklore Festival** www.festival.org.ar. Ask your estancia owner or concierge about attending smaller, local rodeos.

The Andes Mountains provide a scenic backdrop to many of Mendoza's vineyards.

ARGENTINA

# MENDOZA

**Taste the region's rich seasonal offerings in the shadows of the Andes when wine harvest festivals are in full swing.**

Mendoza lies in the heart of Argentina's wine country, a vast, lush land of grapevines stretching into the shadows of the majestic Andes. December through March coincides with the harvest season, when the fields and the celebrations of horticultural bounty are at their most glorious.

This western Argentine city is the country's second most visited, because of what surrounds it: the vineyards that make it one of the world's leading wine regions. The rich purple-black grape Malbec rules, but other varieties abound. Spend your days touring wineries, tasting as many of them as possible.

Still, Mendoza at this time of year is more than just vineyards. It is an effervescent city of music-filled plazas lined with flowering trees and fine restaurants surrounded by intense natural beauty.

## VINEYARD TOURS AND MOUNTAIN BACKDROPS

Coming at this time also allows you to experience wine country at its best. Harvest season "is the best time to visit because the weather is perfect: dry, hot days and cool nights," says Argentine Sandra Borello of Borello Travel & Tours. "The grapevines are all dressed with

*Mendoza lies in the heart of Argentina's wine country, a vast, lush land of grapevines stretching into the shadows of the majestic Andes.*

The wine country of Mendoza, stretching like endless green vines against the snowcapped Andes, is dotted with restaurants like the one at the Lagarde Winery.

Open-air, farm-to-glass breaks, like this one at the Postales Hotel Boutique in Valle de Uco, are a common pleasure in Mendoza wine country.

green leaves and adorned with the colorful and tastiest grapes, all with the magnificent white-capped Andes as a backdrop."

Reserve a few days to fully experience the region and tour wineries, from the bottle-green Maipú Valley and Luján de Cuyo, closer to the city, to the desert where vines emerge like leafy phoenixes from vast, earthy stretches. Some of the best include the small, family-owned Mendel Winery, the welcoming Familia Zuccardi, and Bodegas Salentein, with its modern art gallery inside. Most excursions take in three or four wineries in a day and break for an open-air luncheon of *asado*—Argentina's famed grilled meat—amid the rows of grape-laden vines. You'll while away a few hours in sated splendor.

Borello also takes visitors to see olive oil farms, like Pasrai, which, she says, "makes olive oil the old fashioned way," using stones to crush the olives into paste. And for genuine foodies, many wineries and restaurants hold cooking classes where you can truly immerse yourself in this culinary capital and the ingredients that are at their peak of tasty ripeness in this season.

## VENDIMIA, MENDOZA'S GLAMOROUS HARVEST FESTIVAL

A fun, kitschy experience in Mendoza is the Fiesta de la Vendimia, the annual harvest festival, usually held in late February or early March, that's been a tradition for nearly eight decades. One highlight is the Friday night parade of harvest queens, called Via Blanca, along Avenida San Martín and Avenida General Las Heras through the city's center. Young women, each representing a neighborhood or suburb of Mendoza, are decked out in all their finery on lighted floats as they cast bunches of grapes, melons, and even bottles of wine to the crowds lining the route. The next day, the city abounds in open-air dance and gaucho festivals, many visited by Argentine stars and politicians. Then, that Saturday evening, tens of thousands come to the musical spectacular in Parque San Martín. It is literally the crowning event, when one of the harvest queens is named National Vendimia Queen, representing Argentina's agricultural bounty and heritage to the world.

## SPORTY ADVENTURES BEYOND WINE CULTURE

This season also offers adventure. Raft on the Río Mendoza as it roars down from the Andean valleys. "Class IV rapids thrill visitors, and the river is a particularly epic ride during full-moon excursions," says Irishman Charlie O'Malley, who runs Mendoza-based Trout & Wine tours and edits the city's English-language wine magazine, *Wine Republic*. Or choose horseback riding, kayaking, hiking, or some of the world's best fly-fishing.

**PLANNING Mendoza** www.turismo.mendoza.gov.ar, www.argentina.travel. Borello Travel (*www.borellotravel.com*) offers custom luxury tours. Trout & Wine (*www.troutandwine .com*) is great for winery day trips and adventure.

Pours can be straight from the barrel at the Familia Zuccardi Winery.

# EASTER ISLAND
# TAPATI RAPA NUI

"Decades ago the word 'compete' was defined as striving together, and the Rapa Nui festival on Easter Island embodies this concept wholeheartedly. With unique traditions such as racing down a 330-yard (300 m) hill on nothing more than a banana tree trunk, this old-school competition in the middle of the Pacific needs to be on your bucket list."

—YOGI ROTH, TV HOST, ACTOR, PRODUCER, AUTHOR, AND TRAVELER

Easter Island celebrates its Polynesian heritage with Tapati Rapa Nui, a two-week bash in February that blends traditional food, music, dress, and outdoor endurance events. The festival is inspired by and honors the heritage of the island. *Pictured:* A contestant in the banana tree slide

# Andrew McCarthy
## Patagonia

I t used to be just sheep and gauchos. Now they come to El Calafate (population 7,000) from all over. Julia, who makes my smoothie at Viva La Pepa, moved down from Buenos Aires because she was "tired from the city." Jorge, who runs a bed-and-breakfast, came so he could "feel the sky." Even the old man with the gray mutt, who wears a black *boina* and sits all day on the bench on Avenida del Libertador, isn't local.

The January summer sun hovers in a sprawling sky. Then clouds roll in; rain pours down. Then the sun shines. Then it's raining again. Now the sun is out—all in 15 minutes. Sometimes the wind here blows so hard picnic tables roll like tumbleweeds. Small gray and white horses graze on long yellow grass while pink flamingos haul themselves up and fly off from glacier-milk lakes.

The gaunt lady who moved down from Rosario 11 years ago because "enough was enough" stares out at me from beneath long, dark bangs. She rents me a car and reminds me to park against the wind: "I don't need to have another door ripped off the hinges."

Down near the bottom of the world, the roads are narrow and empty, the vistas vast. Over a rise, the mammoth Perito Moreno glacier appears and glows, refracting light like a spaceship. When I step out onto the undulating, soaring, jagged ice, it crunches under the metal teeth of my crampons. Once I head back to town, I eat the largest and best steak of my life in a small and ugly restaurant.

A few hours up a deserted road, outside the village of El Chaltén, climbers from around the world appear like ants, clinging high up to the side of Mount Fitz Roy's sheer face. I hike the mountain's lower slopes. From a thorny bush, I pluck and nibble the blue-black calafate berry. Legend says that if a visitor eats one, he is sure to return—I grab another handful.

*Andrew McCarthy is an actor, director, and editor at large for* National Geographic Traveler *magazine. He is the author of the* New York Times *best-selling memoir* The Longest Way Home.

The spires, jagged peaks, and namesake glaciers of Los Glaciares National Park provide a dramatic frame around Lake Torre.

*"Over a rise, the mammoth . . . glacier appears and glows, refracting light like a spaceship."*

A curbstone's mystical carvings include the triple-spiral design that's become a symbol of Newgrange.

IRELAND

# NEWGRANGE

**Renew your spirit when this prehistoric burial chamber fills with light on the winter solstice.**

Step back in time to an ancient dawn at Newgrange, the dome-shaped stone tomb constructed on the rich lands of Ireland's Boyne Valley more than 5,000 years ago—before Stonehenge and the Great Pyramid of Giza. Your journey truly begins once you step inside, and a 62-foot-long (19 m) inner passage leads you into a chamber in the shape of a cross.

But time your visit to December's winter solstice, and a single, golden ray of light will illuminate your sense of awe. At dawn on several days around the solstice, December 21 or 22, a narrow beam of sunlight penetrates the opening just above the entrance. It reaches the floor, gradually crawling toward the rear of the chamber. As the sun rises, the beam expands, filling the tomb with the first light of the year's shortest days. The Neolithic light show, encapsulating the natural cycle of life and rebirth, lasts for 17 minutes.

"Archaeologists have classified Newgrange as a passage tomb," writes local expert Michael Fox, "but it is more than that. 'Ancient temple' is a more fitting label: a place of astronomical, spiritual, and ceremonial importance." Ancient carvings can be seen on many of the massive, kidney-shaped mound's curbstones, including the triple-spiral design synonymous with Newgrange.

**PLANNING** Newgrange www.newgrange.com. Access is only by guided tour from Brú na Bóinne Visitor Centre (*www.heritageireland.ie*). Area tours are available from Boyne Valley Tours (*www.boynevalleytours.com*).

### IN THE KNOW
*How to See the Newgrange Winter Solstice*

Admission to the chamber is limited to 20 people a day during the winter solstice and is decided annually by lottery. Application forms are available at the Brú na Bóinne Visitor Centre, or you can email your name, address, telephone number (including international code), and email address to brunaboinne@opw.ie. At the end of September, 50 names are drawn by local schoolchildren. But even without a place inside, many gather for sunrise on the mornings between December 18 and 23 at the entrance to the mound.

# EXMOOR NATIONAL PARK

**Watch stars glitter and meteors blaze against the black canvas of Europe's first dark-sky preserve.**

The remote, rolling hills of Exmoor National Park, tucked away in England's shy and overlooked southwest corner, are home to Europe's first dark-sky preserve, established in 2011. In winter, the park becomes an ideal stargazing destination, when clear, long-lasting skies sparkle with natural light shows and hotel rates plummet.

By day, this is jolly old England, a popular place to hill-climb over the prehistoric mounds dotted with sheep and ribbed with ancient stone walls overlooking ocean and village vistas. But come night, another kind of drama unfurls. A theatrical orange sunset yields way to glittering Cassiopeia, the Plough (the British name for the Big Dipper), Polaris, and thousands of other stars that can be seen with the naked eye while meteor showers blaze across the crisp, cold, chimney-smoke-scented air.

"Winters used to be long and dull around here," says Lucy Naylor from husband-and-wife-run Exmoor Stargazers. "But now we chase the brilliant stars in the sky all night and couldn't be happier." There are ways to get in on the stargazing action in this coastal park, where organized bog night walks and constellation-centric pub meets have become increasingly common. On chilly winter nights, spend a few evening hours watching the shimmering Milky Way and then warm up with a fireside pint in a cozy pub afterward.

**PLANNING** Exmoor National Park's International Dark Sky Preserve www.exmoor-nationalpark.gov.uk.

---

## BEST OF THE BEST
*Inns and Pubs Ideal for Stargazing*

● **BLUE BALL INN:** The spacious, 13th-century Blue Ball Inn in Countisbury is a spacious inn and pub overlooking the moors of the Doone Valley and a popular meeting spot of Exmoor Stargazers. www.exmoorsandpiper.com

● **EXMOOR WHITE HORSE INN:** This River Exe–perched, 16th-century inn and pub drips with Virginia creeper and charm. It also offers safaris and is an ideal spot for stargazing. www.exmoor-whitehorse.co.uk

● **YARN MARKET HOTEL:** In the tiny village of Dunster, the Yarn Market is a cozy getaway with stargazing packages, including guided tours by astronomers. Its jolly proprietor Antony is happy to suggest hill climbs, walkabouts, and stargazing sites. www.yarnmarkethotel.co.uk

Long, dark nights create a glittering ceiling above Exmoor National Park.

Twilight along the Thames's South Bank offers a serene evening view of the Palace of Westminster.

ENGLAND

# LONDON

**Embrace winter's chill with seasonal activities that use the royal city as a sparkling, historic backdrop.**

Some cities close their doors when winter strikes and the weather makes sightseeing a frigid ordeal. Not London. Though skies can be gray, you'll also get plenty of crisp, clear days. The museums, shows, restaurants, and quaint pubs are as tempting as ever and—Christmas week aside, when visitors arrive in force—largely the preserve of Londoners.

If anything, London adds *more* in the way of temptations, creating the sort of attractions only a proper winter can provide. Thus, Hyde Park puts on Winter Wonderland, a vast seasonal make-believe that embraces a wide range of shows, markets, and other attractions, while elsewhere the city creates outdoor ice rinks that allow you to skate in the shadow of some of the capital's finest historic buildings.

## A COLORFUL WINTER FAIR IN THE HEART OF LONDON

The sun sets on a frosty central London. Black cabs and red buses run up and down Park Lane, past Speakers' Corner and the venerable Dorchester Hotel, marking the eastern edge of Hyde Park, once a private hunting ground for Henry VIII and now a much-loved public space.

As dusk falls, walk to Winter Wonderland, a magical mixture of attractions that takes over much of the park starting in late November. Ride the giant Ferris wheel for views over the park and the twinkling lights and city skyline beyond. Then wander the German-style

### GREAT STAYS
*The Dorchester*

The Dorchester opened in 1931, some years after the Ritz, the Savoy, and Claridge's, London's other historic and classic five-star hotels. But the Dorchester immediately became a favorite of the great and the good. Gen. Dwight D. Eisenhower, for one, took a suite here when he arrived in Britain in 1942. With its heritage, fine rooms, service, and lovely art deco exterior, it's an exceptional place to stay, especially in winter, when its position opposite Hyde Park makes it the ideal base for exploring Winter Wonderland and beyond. www.thedorchester.com

Christmas Market, with more than 1,000 stalls selling seasonal crafts and food. Take children to Santa Land or hold tight on one of the adrenaline-boosting fair rides. Skate on the country's largest ice rink and finish with a visit to Zippos Circus.

## CAPITAL SKATING

"The Thames used to freeze regularly," says Maggie O'Sullivan, a travel writer and editor with London's *Telegraph* newspaper. "They held frost fairs on the ice. In some ways, the city's ice rinks are their modern-day equivalents."

There's no shortage of impressive venues for you to strap on your blades. At Hampton Court, you can skate in front of the breathtaking Tudor palace begun for Cardinal Thomas Wolsey around 1514. Another majestic frontage, the neo-Gothic Natural History Museum, provides the backdrop for a skating session that you can follow with a visit to this or the nearby Science and Victoria and Albert Museums. The neoclassical courtyard of the 18th-century Somerset House provides another sublime setting, this time on the Strand at the city's heart, meaning that theaters, galleries, and restaurants are just a snowball's throw away.

**PLANNING Winter Wonderland** www.hydeparkwinterwonderland.co.uk, www.royalparks.org.uk. Open from the last week of November to the first week of January. Entry is free, but tickets, available online, are required for rides and attractions. **Ice rinks** Hampton Court Palace *(Dec.–mid-Jan.)*, www.hamptoncourt icerink.com, www.hrp.org.uk; Natural History Museum *(Nov.–early Jan.)*, www.nhm.ac.uk; Somerset House *(mid-Nov.–early Jan.)*, www.somersethouse.org.uk.

### FOR FOODIES
*Afternoon Tea With a Twist*

Warming up after a day's winter sightseeing with afternoon tea is a quintessential London ritual. Claridge's hotel *(www.claridges.co.uk)* offers the classic genteel experience—a choice of 40 teas, dainty finger sandwiches, pastries, scones, cream, jam, and more—but be sure to reserve ahead. Brown's Hotel *(www.brownshotel.com)* offers a rejuvenating, healthy "Tea Tox" alongside its traditional afternoon tea, or tip the scales in the other direction at Sanctum in Soho *(www.sanctum soho.com)* with its belt-busting Gentleman's Tea rounded off with a cigar.

Somerset House's grand 18th-century facade provides one of several dramatic backdrops for winter skating in England's capital city.

# *Alec Baldwin*
## Christmas in London

London's famed Palace Theatre presents a stately visage for West End productions.

**M**y first trip overseas was to London. It was 1988. I was 30 years old. Having never traveled west of L.A. or east of St. Croix and being older than one normally might be for such a maiden voyage, I arrived at the Dorchester Hotel both wide-eyed and -eared. London meant the Tate, Turnbull & Asser, and Covent Garden—but London also meant, foremost, that inimitable sound: the British treatment of our nearly common language. And where better to hear that than in the temples built to celebrate the language in, perhaps, its highest form? So it was on to the theater to see Vanessa Redgrave in *A Touch of the Poet* and *Cat on a Hot Tin Roof* with Ian Charleson and Lindsay Duncan.

Londoners claim to have almost no relationship with sunshine, so winter is most familiar. Bundled up and uncomplaining, fireplaces and alcohol seem to replace zinc lozenges as protection from the effects of the cold. Eventually, Christmas in London became a nearly biannual tradition. Londoners adorn their city modestly for the occasion, so there were no giant plastic reindeer bobbing their heads, no unlicensed Santas marauding the airwaves to sell you credit card travel rewards (wink). And where that holiday summons images of cathedrals and choruses, the churches I tilted toward had names like the Olivier, the Royal Court, and Donmar Warehouse.

For Christmas 2007, my friend Jessica de Rothschild took me on a "tour" like no other of the London theater scene: *The Entertainer* at the Old Vic, Maggie Smith in *The Lady from Dubuque, Equus* with Daniel Radcliffe, and *Warhorse* at the National. We visited theater producers for lunch, ate dinner at J Sheekey or the Wolseley on Piccadilly. In between, I drifted off alone to the Garrick Club for Stilton cheese, Sautters on Mount Street for cigars, and Harrods to read the paper at the sushi bar.

London became an addiction, and thus fitting in those trips became more urgent. The Concorde, which once seemed foolish, became indispensable. And London at Christmastime, with its mix of solemnity, sarcasm, and the spoken word as an art form, became another home to me.

*Alec Baldwin is a Golden Globe– and Emmy Award–winning actor and philanthropist.*

*"Londoners adorn their city modestly for the occasion, so there were no giant plastic reindeer ... no unlicensed Santas marauding the airwaves to sell you credit card travel rewards (wink)."*

# LAPLAND

**Whiz through the spectacular snowscapes of the Arctic wild behind a team of charging huskies.**

Above the Arctic Circle, Sweden's Lapland region unfolds with snowcapped mountains, deep forests, and vast stretches of untamed wilderness. Forget about snowmobiles: The hands-on, eco-friendly, and far more rewarding way to tour is by dogsled. Under the watchful eyes of expert guides, you drive your own team of huskies from one wilderness lodge to the next, unwinding at the end of each day in wood-heated saunas and under a mantle of starry spring skies.

The most exciting time to visit is March and April, when sunny promises of a thaw are broken by the occasional sharp blizzard. The exhilarating journey through the Arctic wild allows you to get thrillingly close to moose, lynx, and other wildlife. Drink from crystalline lakes in Padjelanta and Sarek National Parks and witness the ancient reindeer-herding culture of the Sami people. Happily spent by evening, you and your fellow mushers dig into local fish and game dishes around a roaring fire.

"It's good medicine for stressed minds," says Catrine Anderback, who runs Silent Ways Dogsledding Adventures from the hamlet of Umnäs. "When you are out for many days, you get really close to your team of dogs."

And when the sun sets, don't forget to look skyward: The world's most magical light show, the aurora borealis, often makes a special guest appearance in March and April.

**PLANNING** **Lapland regional tourist office** hemavantarnaby.se. **Silent Way Dogsledding Adventures** www.dogsledding-adventures.com. NextJet *(www.nextjet.se)* flies to Hemavan Tärnaby (near Umnäs).

## GREAT STAYS
### The Treehotel

Remember how you wanted to sleep in a tree house, but your parents wouldn't hear of it? Now's your chance. About 40 miles (64 km) south of the Arctic Circle, outside the village of Harads, the brilliant Treehotel is an assembly of unique and zany quarters suspended in conifers high above the forest floor, a carpet of wildflowers in bloom come spring. Thatch and branches camouflage the Bird's Nest, the Mirrorcube is virtually invisible, and the UFO is shaped like the perfect 1950s flying saucer. As the winter snows melt, an eight-person Tree Sauna fitted with hot tub and lounge area provides a perfect Nordic retreat. www.treehotel.se

A team of huskies drives its musher through the quiet, deep winter snows of Lapland's Arctic woodlands.

Part of the total Finnish sauna experience is a chilly dunk before racing back to the Zen-like heat.

# FINLAND

**Wake up with a polar bear plunge into fresh snow after relaxing in a steamy Finnish sauna.**

Upon entering the dim, wood-paneled room of a Finnish sauna, where hot, heavy air muffles sound and slows time to a delicious crawl, any prior associations of saunas with affluence, luxury, or sensuality are dispelled. In a Finnish sauna, you're meant to sweat. Sauna time is spent alternating between extreme heat and cold. The experience is enhanced in winter when, rather than cooling off with a cold shower, it's tradition to roll in a pile of powdery snow or dive into a frozen lake, the icy surface prickling the skin and stimulating circulation with thousands of frosty needles.

Saunas are rooted in Finnish history and entwined in Finns' daily hygiene. Knowledge of their health benefits reaches back centuries, when they were used for sweat baths and as sterile spaces for women to give birth. Modern science quantifies what ancestral saunagoers intuited. Heat relaxes muscles, soothes joints, and possibly lowers blood pressure. "From olden times, children were taught to behave in the sauna as if in a church," writes Pirkko Valtakari, a former Finnish Sauna Society official. Today, visitors, too, can appreciate the saunas' transcendent atmosphere.

**PLANNING Finland saunas** www.visitsauna.fi/en, www.sauna.fi. Though many saunas are in private homes, there are plenty of opportunities to use public saunas or saunas in your hotel.

## IN THE KNOW
*How to Take a Finnish Sauna*

Full-body exposure to the sauna's extreme heat is taken seriously. Bathing suits are typically not worn. Begin with a shower to clean off. Enter the hot room, whose temperatures hover between 175°F and 200°F (80°–93°C). When you feel warmed, cool off by swimming, taking a cold shower, or sitting outside. Repeat the process as long as you feel comfortable. Begin the final cooldown process by washing, and then enter the hot room at a lower temperature. Take a final cold shower or swim. Finish with a drink or snack, relaxing until you stop sweating.

# VALENTINE'S DAY RETREATS

**Find cozy seclusion, starry views, ancient gardens—whatever your romantic heart desires.**

### POST RANCH INN

*Big Sur, California*

Perched on the Big Sur coastline, between the majestic Santa Lucia Mountains and the endless Pacific Ocean horizon, everything but the romance of the present moment is sure to fade away at the Post Ranch Inn. Choose from an array of ocean- or mountain-view accommodations, suites, or private houses, complete with outdoor hiking activities and relaxing spa amenities.

*www.postranchinn.com*

### SEDONA

*Arizona*

Famous for its breathtaking red-rock landscape, Sedona is a prime spot for a secluded, romantic getaway. Take a sunset hike or horseback ride, or experience Sedona's rich viticulture with a tour of wine country in Verde Valley. Private canyon cabins, bed-and-breakfasts, and luxurious resorts are sprinkled throughout the area.

*www.visitsedona.com*

### COVERED BRIDGES

*Vermont*

Known as "kissing bridges" back in the days of horse-and-buggy courtship, covered bridges provided a coveted moment of romantic privacy. A century later, these structures remain historic emblems of craftsmanship and are now a hallmark of picturesque New England. With more than 100 covered bridges, Vermont's scenic drives are the perfect reason for a bed-and-breakfast getaway.

*www.visit-vermont.com/romantic-getaways*

### BRITISH PULLMAN TRAIN

*United Kingdom*

Step aboard British Pullman and transport back in time to the golden age travel of the 1920s. The sister train to the *Venice Simplon-Orient-Express,* the British Pullman celebrates the most romantic day of the year with a Valentine's Day tour through the British countryside. Featuring an elegant, locally sourced lunch or dinner, passengers enjoy cocktails and Champagne in luxury vintage carriages.

*www.orient-express.com*

### HOTEL KAKSLAUTTANEN

*Saariselkä, Finland*

From the comfort of the Hotel Kakslauttanen's heated glass igloos, visitors sleep under a million-star canopy and the glowing northern lights. During the day, book a reindeer safari, sample from one of four restaurants, and relax in the world's largest smoke sauna.

*www.kakslauttanen.fi/en*

### EIFFEL TOWER

*Paris, France*

Forgo the clichés and scale the Eiffel Tower to view fully the expanse of the most romantic city in the world. Stop on the second level for a cup of Parisian coffee and search the horizon for all the city monuments alongside your sweetheart.

*www.eiffel-tower.com*

### THE LOVER'S WALK (VIA DELL'AMORE)

*Cinque Terre, Italy*

On the eastern shore of the Ligurian Sea lies one of Italy's most enchanting venues, Cinque Terre, comprising five villages etched into the salt-stained cliffs and connected by coastline paths. The pathway between Riomaggiore and Manarola, dubbed Via dell'Amore, provides breathtaking views of the turquoise sea and niches perfect for a romantic stroll.

*www.cinqueterreriomaggiore.com*

### ISTRIAN PENINSULA

*Croatia*

Called the "Croatian Tuscany," the Istrian landscape abounds with rolling hills and valleys, hilltop villages, and patchwork expanses of wheat fields, vineyards, and olive groves. On February 14, couples will find a backdrop of snowcapped alpine mountains. View it all from above on a hot-air balloon ride.

*en.gral-putovanja.eu*

### CLASSICAL GARDENS OF SUZHOU

*China*

Choose from dozens of exquisitely designed gardens dating from the 11th to 19th centuries—including the UNESCO World Heritage list–inscribed Lingering Garden and Couple's Garden Retreat—and wander arm-in-arm along winding paths and across elegant bridges.

*www.china.org.cn*

### HA LONG BAY

*Vietnam*

Containing more than 1,600 islands, Ha Long Bay is a vision of astonishing beauty. Book an overnight cruise to watch the islands' limestone pillars, caves, and arches become steeped in rich oranges and purples at sunset and veiled in an ethereal morning mist at sunrise.

*www.emeraude-cruises.com*

The snowbound isolation of a log cabin at Inari, Finland's Hotel Kakslauttanen resort provides a very private Valentine's Day getaway.

A northern lights show sends dazzling waves of green pulsating over Tromsdalen, Norway.

EUROPE

# NORWAY

**Chase the fluorescent northern lights that illuminate Norway's Arctic evening skies.**

Weathered stave churches line the lush fjords of Norway's majestic west coast, unrivaled for its natural beauty, cascading waterfalls, and wildlife such as whales and puffins. But come wintertime, snow covers the emerald shore, and the wild green of the cliffs ascends to the sky. Norway's northern lights—best seen from December to March when they are most vivid—offer a unique fireworks show visible only in proximity to the Earth's poles. By turns explosive and elusive, the northern lights, also known as the aurora borealis, inspired countless Vikings and Sami, and they continue to draw photographers today who seek out their neon celestial beauty as it streams and morphs in the crisp winter sky like giant alien will-o'-the-wisps.

Norway's Hurtigruten fleet now offers astronomy-centric cruises on which guests can chase the lights, best seen from the Lofoten Islands to the Arctic Circle towns of the North Cape like Tromsø, Øksfjord, and Honningsvåg. They're also visible at sea, best during easterly winds. "This is not your typical cruise," says Judy Brass, an Omaha, Nebraska–based cruise travel agent, recalling a northern lights voyage. "We could program our phone for a wake-up call anytime the lights appeared, which we saw on three successive nights. The colors were amazing."

**PLANNING Northern lights** www.visitnorway.com/us. Sip hot chocolate from the on-deck Jacuzzi while chasing the northern lights aboard a Hurtigruten cruise *(www.hurtigruten.com).*

## IN THE KNOW
*The Animals of the Arctic*

Beneath the blazing northern lights, the Arctic is home to wildlife rarely seen anywhere else. Mighty polar bears live only in the Arctic, where they spend most of their time on ice floes. They are amazing swimmers and sometimes can be spotted 50 miles (80 km) away from any ice or land. Narwhals are mysterious ocean ghosts that travel in pods of up to 100, at times using their long, swordlike tusks against one another. The Arctic's snowy owls can sometimes be spotted swooping against the winter sky. Arctic foxes, brown all summer, turn fluffy white with snowfall.

# LAKE BAIKAL

**Take to the ice when winter transforms the world's deepest lake into a vast, frosty getaway.**

Lake Baikal is so big it makes its own horizon, one not always visible in winter when the snow and clouds can blend with the lake's ice, eliminating all perspective from the landscape. But what hope is there for proportion on a lake that holds 20 percent of the world's freshwater supply? Never mind how hard it is to see anything through all the layers of clothes needed for winter temperatures that regularly hit 15°F (-9°C)—and well below!

But winter is when you can travel Lake Baikal's ice on a horse-drawn sleigh, hooves sure-footed and mouths steaming like trains, and best enjoy the mineral hot springs that dot parts of the lakeshore. Or you could take a hovercraft over the ice or drive out in an ice truck, with the heater on high. Dinner comes out of holes drilled deep through ice—often as clear as a magnifying glass—as fishermen pull up some of the lake's grayling or *omul*, a kind of salmon. And this is Russia, so the vodka flows easily, a useful medicine against the cold.

Dark comes early to the winter lake—reason enough to wear those ten layers of clothes. Or do as the locals do—have a couple more drinks and a long stay in a traditional *banya* steam house.

**PLANNING Lake Baikal** baikal.ru/en. **Tours** www.lakebaikaltravel.net. The lake is easily reached by flying into Ulan-Ude, or take the Trans-Siberian Railway.

In winter, horse-drawn sleighs turn Russia's icy Lake Baikal into a vast open highway.

# MENTON

**Enjoy the carnival-like festivities celebrating the lemon—the beloved local fruit—when delightful citrus sculptures adorn this French Riviera resort.**

The exclusive coastal resort of Menton is said be the warmest on the French Riviera. That means lemon trees love it here, and visitors can enjoy its late winter Fête du Citron, when temperatures average in the comfortable 50s°F (10°–15°C).

It's the festival saluting the yellow citrus fruit, not the weather or even the beautiful, hill-edged setting, that brought Menton its fame and fortune. From February to early March, the normally sedate parks and squares become a carnival of citrus, filled with outlandish sculptures made almost entirely of oranges and lemons—enormous *amuse yeux,* if you will. Some 145 tons (132 tonnes) of the fruits are carted in and attached to wire frames with half a million rubber bands. You might see a tart, three-story Eiffel Tower, a mock Taj Mahal, or a juicy, giant Buddha; the theme varies from year to year.

"It's more local and less touristy than the Nice Carnival," says Jeanne Oliver, a travel author and blogger who lives on the Riviera. Among the events, the most spectacular is the Corsi des Fruits d'Or (Procession of Golden Fruit Floats). This series of Rio-style parade floats trundles along the seaside Promenade du Soleil, complete with thumping music, acrobats, folk groups, and lots of confetti. When it's all over, the produce that can be salvaged is turned into marmalade and limoncello, the wonderfully tart lemon liqueur.

**PLANNING Menton** www.tourisme-menton.fr. **Fête du Citron** www.fete-du-citron.com.

The winter months, when roads are quiet, are the wisest time to brave the nail-biting 17-mile (30 km) route between Menton and Nice. The winding stretch among the pine-forested Alps that drop vertiginously into the sea is among the world's most spectacular coastal drives. The Grande Corniche—the highest and most dangerous of the three parallel roads, built during Napoleon's reign—climbs to 1,800 feet (550 m) above the Mediterranean. Scenes of Alfred Hitchcock's legendary *To Catch a Thief* were filmed here. Princess Grace of Monaco—costar of the film with Cary Grant—died in a car crash here in 1982, while Princess Stephanie survived. Flowers are laid at the spot.

During the annual festival, Menton delivers a citrus blast of kitsch with lemon-studded sculptures all over town.

Swine supervise one of the secretive outings in southwest France in search of French gold: the truffle.

FRANCE
# PÉRIGORD

**Search alongside experts, both human and animal, for precious, perfumed truffles in France's earthy, secretive southwest corner.**

All summer long, France is the playground for Europe's *grandes vacances*. But come winter, visitors dwindle, and *les trufficulteurs* take to the rocky woods and sun-dappled pastures of Périgord, some 50 miles (80 km) east of Bordeaux, for truffle-hunting season.

Truffle-loving tourists fill the cozy medieval village markets and restaurants to buy and eat the subterranean fungi, but few actually come to harvest these little aromatic nuggets. Hunts are open to visitors, guided by some of the world's leading truffle experts. Join an expedition and be privy to their truffle-finding secrets. Venture through secretive, musky territories in chilly forests thick with oak and hazelnut trees. Alongside, specially trained pigs and dogs help unearth the magic mushrooms. It's the ultimate earthy scavenger hunt. The most memorable prizes: heady, perfumed black Périgord truffles worth their weight in gold.

Of course, diners here are rewarded with the finds of the harvest, too. Area bistros plate up truffle dishes of all sorts, often at remarkably low prices, from classic truffled foie gras, gamey pâtés, and savory egg dishes to more innovative takes on the tuber, such as truffled ice cream, crème brûlée, and a most heady truffled vodka.

**PLANNING** **Truffle hunting in France** uk.rendezvousenfrance.com/en/special/dordogne. The season runs from November to April. Visitors can hunt, distill, and cook at truffle workshops. Local expert Edouard Aynaud teaches courses on truffle gathering and cooking; for information, email pechalifour@gmail.com.

## VENICE, ITALY
# CARNEVALE

"All the world repair to Venice to see the folly and madness of the Carnevale; the women, men, and persons of all conditions disguising themselves in antiq dresses, with extravagant musiq and a thousand gambols, traversing the streets from house to house, all places being then accessible and free to enter."

—JOHN EVELYN, ENGLISH DIARIST, 1646

**In the 12 days leading up to Ash Wednesday, locals and visitors alike dress in brilliantly colored costumes and masks throughout Venice for Carnevale.** *Pictured:* **The city center, Piazza di San Marco, is home to many of Carnevale's main events.**

Mallorca's almond trees bloom like spring clouds in shades of pink, purple, and white from January to early March.

SPAIN

# MALLORCA

**The Mediterranean island's almond blossom season brings a trembling carpet of pink, purple, and white.**

The Serra de Tramuntana, a dramatic mountain range soaring nearly 5,000 feet (1,445 m), limns Mallorca's northwest coast. Every year, long before the snowcapped peaks mull the thaw, a blanket of almond blossoms rolls across the great plateau to the east—the "snow of Mallorca," as poetic locals put it. Almond trees grow all over the island, but from January to early March this is the jaw-dropping region to visit.

On sunny days, the delicate hues of pink, purple, and white melt into the sugarcoated backdrop of the mountainous tableau. The spectacle has inspired countless painters and photographers and turns a simple walk into a wildly romantic experience.

Where to go? Fiona McLean, owner of Mallorca Hiking, recommends a 5.5-mile (9 km), roughly three-hour walk from the pretty village of Es Capdella through the publicly held Galatzó estate. "The density of the almond trees is the best I know on the island," she says. "There are lots of double blossoms, so it's a very showy show." This sleepy, rural corner of the island affords a stupendous view of the conical Puig Galatzó.

If you're wondering where all those juicy nuts go, try *gató de almendra*, an almond cake often served with toasted almond ice cream.

**PLANNING  Mallorca** www.infomallorca.net, www.seemallorca.com. **Bus transport** www.caib.es *(see Horaris Transports).* **Hiking** www.mallorcahiking.com.

## FOR FOODIES
*Restaurante Es Verger*

From the town of Alaró, 18.5 miles (30 km) northeast of Palma de Mallorca, the island's main city, a brisk four-hour hike runs through groves of almond and olive trees to the rustic Es Verger farmhouse, a delight for roving gastronomes. This place is no longer a secret, but popularity hasn't diminished its rural charm. Fluffy sheep roam the forecourt, while Grandma's recipes seem as eternal as the nearby Roman vineyards. The big draw is her legendary roast lamb, marinated in beer for 24 hours and roasted to tender perfection in a wood-fired oven. Wash it down with a tasty house red bottled on the premises. www.esvergeret.com

# PRAGUE

**Celebrate St. Nicholas Day with costumed devils and angels in the medieval heart of the city.**

As winter descends and crowds diminish, the ancient Czech capital sparkles. "At heart, it is a cold-weather city," says writer Katerina Pavlitova, a Prague native. "In December, it gets dark at 4 p.m., but that makes the illuminated windows and street lamps all the more appealing." Celebrate the traditions of St. Nicholas Eve on December 5 in high baroque with classical music at St. Nicholas Church. Across the Charles Bridge are more revelers, this time outside in Staroměstské náměstí, the Old Town Square.

In Czech folklore, St. Nicholas arrives in a white robe and bishop's miter for his feast day, always accompanied by comic angels and devils. You'll see the trios roaming the pedestrians-only square beneath the 15th-century Astronomical Clock, where the Apostles parade on the hour. A bit of souvenir shopping is de rigueur at the outdoor Christmas market, where trinkets include a favorite Bohemian tradition: gaudy blown-glass ornaments. "They come in all shapes and sizes and are still made by hand by Czech artisans," says Pavlitova, who fondly recalls them from childhood. It may be wiser to go home with some less breakable options that also populate her childhood memories: clip-on birds, pinecones, and little houses "with roofs sparkling with snow."

**PLANNING  Prague** www.visitprague.cz. This music-loving city hosts dozens of wintertime performances, from classical to jazz, each evening; flyers distributed on street corners will point you to excellent choices.

## BEST OF THE BEST
*Photographing the Charles Bridge*

The 600-year-old pedestrian bridge that spans the Vltava River bristles with artists, street musicians, and tourists by day. The religious statues standing sentinel along the route, their hands frozen in prayer, testify to the powerful Catholic religious orders that flourished here. To capture the serenity of the saints and the river, arrive at dawn, when shifting patterns of fog and sun offer a kaleidoscopic view of the city spires. Or set up your tripod at night to capture spotlit baroque facades along the shore.

A seemingly endless display of lights, angels, trees, and decorations dress up Prague's already beautiful Old Town Square.

# HOT WINTER DRINKS

**Warm up your chilly bones with the locals and experience culture in a cup with these classic drinks, perfect for cold weather.**

## CRAFT COFFEE
*Seattle, Washington*

Starbucks served its first cup in 1971 from a quaint Pike Place Market café, spawning a Seattle coffee culture of artisan roasters and cafés. The Capitol Hill neighborhood offers the town's best brews, such as the two-story Caffè Vita, the flagship of an 18-year-old Seattle institution.

*www.caffevita.com*

## YERBA MATE
*Argentina*

Argentines embrace this mainstay steeped beverage as a way to gather, slurping the earth-noted elixir from colorful, carved gourds through the same *bombilla,* or metal straw. Travelers can set out across the mate-producing regions on the Route of Yerba Mate to learn about the production process—from tree to gourd.

*www.rutadelayerbamate.org.ar*

## WASSAIL
*Somerset, England*

Wassailing was originally a ritualistic English toast to healthy orchards marked by a January ceremony. The tradition continues in communities like those in the county of Somerset, where you can partake by dousing tree roots with cider and adorning limbs with bread—but save a cup of the wassail (hot cider) for yourself.

*www.visitsomerset.co.uk*

## GRZANE PIWO
*Krakow, Poland*

Polish traditions rarely disappoint the taste buds, and *grzane piwo,* a seasonal mulled beer, is no exception. Just like wines or ciders in other places, the ale is heated, infused, and served. Plenty of pubs offer the hot brew, which complements a chilly day; try the patio at Glonojad Vegetarian Bar, flanking Matejki Square.

*www.glonojad.com*

## GLOGG
*Norway*

Something heated, spiced, and/or spiked belongs on every winter menu, and for Scandinavians, glogg is a regionwide favorite. Usually it's made with hot red wine and zingy citrus and cinnamon, then spiked with spirit-soaked raisins. It can be mixed with hot (but never boiling) water or served as a straight shot.

## ESPRESSO
*Florence, Italy*

Experiencing Italian café culture is as important as people-watching in the piazzas or admiring Renaissance masterpieces. The motherland of espresso has bragging rights to the potent little cup. Savor a buzzworthy shot at Caffè Scudieri's bustling espresso bar on Piazza San Giovanni.

*www.scudieri.eu*

## HOT CHOCOLATE
*Vienna, Austria*

Wellsprings of culture, Vienna's ubiquitous coffeehouses create an aperture into everyday Viennese life. Hot chocolate is a sweet departure from the classic *kaffae,* especially when served the Austrian way: *mit schlag,* with whipped cream. The luxe Demel chocolatier offers its *schokolade* laced with ginger or cardamom, while Vienna's oldest coffeehouse, Cafe Frauenhuber, sticks to the chocolatey classic—mit schlag, of course.

*www.demel.at, www.cafe-frauenhuber.at*

## MASALA CHAI
*Kolkata, India*

Shards of red clay cups linger around the bases of roadside stalls, and chai wallahs, or tea vendors, beckon passersby to add to the piles. This sweet-spiced milky comfort, also known as *chai karak,* steeps across India. In Kolkata, throwing empty cups against a wall or the ground is a tradition.

## COFFEE CEREMONY
*Addis Ababa, Ethiopia*

An invitation to a traditional household coffee ceremony proves a sure sign of Ethiopian hospitality. The occasion includes green coffee bean roasting, hand-grinding, and steady refills. Savor the experience at Habesha Restaurant in the heart of Addis Ababa, or trek southwest to Jimma to see the quirky *jebena* coffeepot statue, oversized and overlooked by locals.

*addisababaonline.com*

## PU-ERH TEA
*Yunnan Province, China*

Chinese tea porters used to traverse the 1,400-mile (2,250 km) Tea Horse Road swapping tea for horses in Tibet, and this dark, fermented tea got its name from a small trading post along the route. The most common kind, Pu-erh, develops a bitter flavor during the storage-fermentation process that soothes effects from oily foods.

Mexico bumps hot chocolate up a flavor notch by mixing in some heat with the sweet—and a side of dunk-worthy churros at the ready.

TANZANIA

# ZANZIBAR

**Rock to sounds from all over the continent during a music festival on an idyllic East African island.**

As sunset descends on Stone Town in Zanzibar, the fabled island off the East African coast, you buy samosas and seafood kebabs from vendors in Forodhani Park and amble over to the ancient Old Fort. Inside, you stake your claim to a grassy patch near the main stage. But before you can finish your impromptu meal, you are dancing to the wildly varied sounds of the African mainland and Indian Ocean islands: desert soul from Mali, *marrabenta* from Mozambique, kora guitar virtuosos from Guinea.

It's one of the hottest times of year in equatorial Africa, but that doesn't stop people from moving to the rhythms at Sauti Za Busara, a February festival launched in 2004 that brings together dozens of established genres and fusion blends from all around the continent and beyond. The audience is equally eclectic. "It's quite something to be listening to a soul singer from Malawi, with a Maasai in full gear swaying next to you," says Zanzibar guidebook author Elizabeth Wollen.

Music is only part of the spectacle. Festivalgoers can watch dhow (sailboat) races, join a parade through the streets, browse handicrafts at the festival market, or even entertain the crowd at open-mic sessions where anyone is invited to sing.

**PLANNING** **Zanzibar** www.zanzibartourism.net. **Sauti Za Busara** www.busaramusic.org.

### IN THE KNOW
*The Irresistible Sounds of Taarab*

Freddie Mercury may be the best known singer from Zanzibar; the former Queen front man was born there in 1946. But the island's favorite music is *taarab*. Reflecting Zanzibar's multicultural heritage, taarab is a heady blend of Middle Eastern, European, and Indian influences. The name comes from the word *tariba*, which means to be "moved" or "agitated" in Swahili. And that's exactly what taarab does— moves you to get off your bum and dance. Although it can be performed solo, taarab is best with a full orchestra of Western instruments like accordions, keyboards, and violins mixed with traditional African ouds and *qanuns*.

Hundreds of musicians and dancers from all over Africa and beyond inject Zanzibar's annual Sauti Za Busara festival with an infectious, genre-busting energy.

Mozambique's endless expanses of empty coastline and clear waters create a rare, beachy respite.

MOZAMBIQUE

# BENGUERRA ISLAND

**Lose yourself in endless stretches of empty beaches along emerald waters when tropical skies are clear and dry.**

On Benguerra, an island in the Bazaruto Archipelago off Mozambique's southern coast, the horizon dissolves between translucent turquoise waters and an aquamarine sky. Silence characterizes the coastline, where cars are a rarity. And best, even in its high season (winter in the Northern Hemisphere), when the tropical weather is optimum—dry and not too hot—other people are largely absent, too.

Walking is the main mode of transportation on Benguerra—an activity best enjoyed in the evenings, after characteristic afternoon rains soften the seasonal humidity. The slow pace gives the senses time to process the vast expanse of undulating beach. "All you focus on is the amazing blue sea," says longtime traveler Christine Laciak. "The water is just beautiful and serene."

Fishing, of course, is big here. Try casting for deep-sea catches like marlin and tuna, common in the summer waters, or spend the afternoon alongside local fishermen who navigate dhows, their nonmotorized wooden sailboats. "There's nothing industrial about it," Laciak says. "Just 30 people out there, hand-hauling nets."

Watching for Benguerra's 140-plus bird species and diving are also popular, eco-oriented activities. The good news for the island's roughly 1,000 residents: The World Wildlife Fund recently designated it a "gift to the Earth" to help preserve its Indian Ocean waters and the community that depends on them.

**PLANNING  Benguerra Island** www.mozambique.co.za. The island is accessible by boat from the mainland town of Vilanculos. Vilanculos International Airport services flights, most of which connect from Johannesburg and Maputo.

## GREAT STAYS
*Luxurious and Eco-Friendly Resorts*

These resorts help you leave a relatively small footprint, even during Benguerra's "busier" December-to-March high season.

● **AZURA RESORT:** Private beach villas dot Benguerra's first resort, community-minded since inception, from employing island-based construction workers to hiring local staff. azura-retreats .com/benguerra

● **BENGUERRA LODGE:** Gorgeous villas with thatched roofs and beachside views. The lodge collaborates with members of the island community to initiate environmental conservation projects and donates part of its revenue to an island trust. www.benguerra.co.za

It's not all "big five" game in Tanzania's Serengeti National Park—meet a petite lilac-breasted roller.

KENYA/TANZANIA

# THE SERENGETI

**Witness herds of wildebeests, lions, and other animals thunder across the untouched Serengeti during their spectacular annual procession.**

The Serengeti is a gargantuan, 12,000-square-mile (31,800 sq km) game ecosystem in the heart of African bush country, crossing the border of Kenya and Tanzania, inscribed on UNESCO's list of World Heritage sites, and still hunted on and inhabited by Maasai warriors. This is the Africa of *Out of Africa* and the very birthplace of the safari. If you're coming to Africa for animals, it doesn't get any better than this. Calving season, when the grasses are ripest, lasts from January to March and is the ideal time to visit.

## A SPECTACLE OF GREAT GAME, BIG . . .

The Serengeti is arguably the continent's best spot to witness "big five" game—lion, leopard, elephant, rhino, and buffalo—although hippos, crocodiles, cheetahs, bush babies, and hundreds of others animals abound, too. Watching the cavalcade peel down dirt paths worn by animals of generations past is one of Earth's grandest parades and most mysterious natural wonders.

The rainstorm-scattered season is the best to see this mass migration, when more than 400,000 wildebeest calves are born in a two- to three-week, naturally synchronized period. The voyage kicks off in the Ngorongoro Crater area of Tanzania's southern

Serengeti and bucks, charges, and grunts its way to the Maasai Mara reserve in lower Kenya. The journey is longer than 500 miles (800 km)—and not all the animals survive. A great way to guarantee seeing the sights and sounds of the Great Migration "is to stay at the private game reserves closest to the river crossing points," suggests Lewela Mwawaza, guide for Micato Safaris. "Taking a hot-air balloon or helicopter is even better."

## . . . AND SMALLER

The awesome spectacle also includes the migration of two million other herbivores, everything from gazelles to zebras, that graze on Serengeti spring buds and young grasses and perch on rocky kopjes, pausing at watering holes and windswept plains, at times just a few arms' lengths away from you. The big game is the most obvious lure, of course, but many visitors return for up close photo encounters with Africa's gentler and lesser known species, like colorful lilac-breasted rollers, herds of shy giraffes, and umbrella thorn acacia trees that dot the landscape and have inspired visitors (and sundowner sippers—see sidebar) for generations.

Even for safari vets, watching the mass movement of Serengeti wildlife is thrilling. "Every year I show guests the annual migration," says Tom Lithgow, founder of Firelight Expeditions and Tanzania's Lupita Island resort, "I always look upon this saga with awe. No year is the same."

**PLANNING  Serengeti migration tours** Many consider Micato Safaris *(www.micato.com)* the best tour operator. &Beyond *(www.andbeyondafrica.com)* also has a portfolio of incredibly located properties and is lauded for its warm, local guides, each equipped with an extraordinary knowledge of natural history.

### FOR FOODIES
*History of the Sundowner*

Unlike most cocktails, the sundowner—a colloquial British term—is more about the where and when than the what. It can be any number of cocktails taken after completing a day's work—or, in the case of tourists, a day's game drive through the bush. But the drink must be experienced at sundown in Africa. It offers safarigoers not only a chance to unwind but also a moment to reflect on the greatness of this wild, vast landscape. Its name originates from the early 20th century and was popularized by such safarigoing imbibers as Ernest Hemingway, Karen Blixen (of *Out of Africa* fame), and Teddy Roosevelt.

Hundreds of thousands of wildebeest, joined by zebras and other animals great and small, make their annual pilgrimage across the Serengeti.

CHINA

# HARBIN

**Wander among glittering castles and pagodas in a fairyland of ice and snow.**

Winters are harsh in Heilongjiang, China's most northeastern province, bordering Siberian Russia. The residents of Harbin, its capital, brighten the long, frigid months by carving fantastical frozen sculptures for the International Ice and Snow Festival that takes place in January and February.

Bundle up and pull on your sturdy boots to explore. Pale winter sunlight sparkles on immense, life-size re-creations of famous landmarks. Hard-packed snow crunches underfoot as you hike to the top of the Athens Acropolis or peer inside the gates of the Forbidden City. Warm up with an exhilarating ride down a giant ice slide on the frozen Songhua River, then watch the island become an otherworldly land of shimmering ice and brilliant colors. As darkness falls, shades of crimson, sapphire, and lime green blaze forth from the translucent ice blocks.

"It's quite surreal, due to both the scale and all the lighting—like being in a fantasy movie," says Christian Stanley of the China Travel Company, which offers tours of Harbin and the festival. "You feel very small and can't help wondering how they manage to build all of this so quickly. It's also hard to believe that within a matter of weeks it is all gone—melted away."

**PLANNING International Ice and Snow Festival** en.cnta.gov.cn. The China Travel Company's (www.thechinatravelcompany.com) Ice Festival tour visits Harbin as well as Beijing and Shanghai.

## BEST OF THE BEST
### *Siberian Tiger Park*

Rumble with Siberian tigers at the Siberian Tiger Park, an easy day trip from Harbin. Located northwest of the city on the Songhua River, the park was established to help protect these magnificent animals, the largest felines in the world. Hundreds of purebred tigers—accustomed to the winter cold—freely roam the 355-acre (144 ha) park, along with lynx, leopards, and black pumas. Visitors must ride in buses encircled by wire mesh, which the curious tigers will occasionally investigate. Those with strong stomachs can buy live animals such as ducks, chickens, or even cows to feed the tigers—and watch the master hunters stalk their prey. www.thechinatravelcompany.com

Come nightfall, the colorful sculptures of ice artists, crafted from frozen water, lights, and imaginations, illuminate China's northeastern city of Harbin.

Serene moments abound along Ko Chang's Hat Sai Khao beach, with its views of both river and sea.

THAILAND

# KO CHANG ISLAND

**Choose between river and sea, rain forest and waterfall—or just relax on white sand beaches.**

Until about ten years ago, the only foreigners to reach the beaches of Ko Chang were curious backpackers ready to explore the island's mystique in the warm sunshine of the dry, temperate winter months. Despite the fact that Ko Chang and its satellite islands have recently become major tourist destinations, the archipelago maintains its allure. *National Geographic Adventure* magazine writer Christian DeBenedetti recommends it for an "excellent gulf adventure, with mist-wrapped mountain peaks and offshore reefs." Head to the western coast of the island for paradisiacal beaches of fine, ivory sand, while dense rain forest, mangroves, and most of the island's elegant waterfalls lure visitors to the east.

The island's longest and most popular beach is Hat Sai Khao (White Sand Beach). Farther south, and with a greater degree of solace, lies Hat Klong Prao. The beach is divided into three sections by two converging rivers. A glassy estuary in the center provides magnificent views of both the river and the sea. Rent a kayak or canoe and paddle down into the estuary past the fishermen's houses or out to the nearby islands of Ko Yuak and Ko Pli, both of which offer exceptional snorkeling.

PLANNING  Ko Chang www.tourismthailand.org. Ferries regularly leave the mainland pier at Laem Ngop and stop at various beaches; Ao Sapparot, on Ko Chang's northern tip, is the most convenient destination.

Singapore's Orchard Road, the main entertainment district, turns into a swirl of lights for the Christmas season.

ASIA

# SINGAPORE

**The Asian island stakes its claim to the world's most flamboyant Christmas with extravagant decorations and light displays.**

Giant M&Ms dance across the porch of a three-story-high gingerbread house. Reindeer prance through a snow-mantled forest. An animated snowman croons familiar carols beside fully flocked trees with glimmering golden bulbs. And everywhere you look there are lights—crawling up the side of skyscrapers, smothering the front of department stores, and strung as far as you can see down the avenue.

Though less than 15 percent of the population is Christian, the holiday dazzle this city mounts might blind a visitor into thinking this is Manhattan . . . if not for the sticky tropical heat. Rather, this is December in Singapore, the little Asian island with a think-big attitude, including a quest to create the world's most flamboyant Christmas decorations and displays.

"We don't have snow, we don't have pine trees, we don't have reindeer, we don't have chimneys, and we definitely don't have silent nights," says author and social commentator Adrian Tan. "But Christmas is certainly a Singaporean festival. We have two consuming passions—shopping and eating. Combine those with a holiday that comes at the end of the year when Singaporeans get their bonuses, and what you've got is a perfect storm."

**PLANNING  Singapore tourism** www.yoursingapore.com. **Christmas in Singapore** celebratechristmasin singapore.org.

## IN THE KNOW
*Deepavali: Singapore's Other Light Show*

The holiday season in Singapore kicks off with the colorful Deepavali, the Hindu festival of lights, a national holiday and weeklong celebration that culminates with flamboyant arches and light displays along Serangoon Road in Little India. At home, Hindus light oil lamps to celebrate the victory of light over darkness and good over evil, as personified by the ancient tale of Lord Krishna defeating the evil King Narakasura. Other Deepavali traditions include henna hand tattoos, fireworks, special holiday cakes and candies, and wearing your best new sari to the local Hindu temple or outdoor performances of Indian song and dance. www.lisha.org.sg/Little_India_Celebrations.aspx

AUSTRALIA

# THE GOLD COAST

**Hang ten on curling combers at Australia's surfing mecca.**

With more than 40 miles (64 km) of beaches, Queensland's Gold Coast, just south of Brisbane, offers some of the best, most reliable waves in Australia. From December to April, easterly swells rolling in from the Pacific produce regular one- to two-foot (30–60 cm) waves around the aptly named epicenter of the action, Surfer's Paradise, drawing hordes of surfers eager to test their skills.

Practice your moves at one of the many surf schools scattered along the coast. Board in hand, pad along golden sands glowing pink at sunrise. At this early hour, only serious surfers roam the beach. But perfect summer temperatures beckon at any hour. Strike into the sun-warmed waters at famed sites like the Spit, Rainbow Bay, or Burleigh Heads, whose right-hand point break produces long, tubular waves.

Paddle furiously to catch an incoming breaker. As it roars toward shore, shift onto your knees, then finally, shakily at first, stand up. For a brief moment, you're surfing like the pros, suspended between dazzling Aussie sunshine above and shimmering aquamarine waters below. The next second, you've wiped out with a spectacular tumble as the wave crashes about you. No matter: The instant you resurface and grab your board, you're charging offshore again, ready to catch the next perfect crest.

**PLANNING  Australia's Gold Coast** www.goldcoast.com.au. The Surf in Paradise surfing school *(www.surf inparadise.com.au)* holds lessons for beginners at the Spit.

The waves continuously churn and often challenge along Australia's Gold Coast.

# Top 10

# NEW YEAR'S EVE CELEBRATIONS

**Chime in the New Year with festivities both large and small around the world on this intercontinental journey.**

### NEW YORK CITY, NEW YORK

New Year's Eve in New York's Times Square defines the evening for hundreds of millions around the globe who watch on television, wishing they were there. A million revelers squeeze into the city's neon epicenter where Broadway and Seventh Avenue come together, waiting for the Waterford crystal LED ball to drop from the former New York Times Building, for which the iconic square is named. It's an American tradition more than 100 years old.

*www.nycgo.com*

### LAS VEGAS, NEVADA

Ring in the New Year casino style in kitschy Las Vegas, where fireworks blast over Paris Las Vegas, the MGM Grand, the Bellagio, and the array of other casino hotels on the famous Strip. The city buzzes with tens of thousands who come in for special concerts and performances with the biggest stars, until the sun comes up over the surrounding desert.

*www.lvcva.com*

### RIO DE JANEIRO, BRAZIL

Réveillon, Rio's New Year's celebration, is one of the world's largest. Dressed in white like Candomblé priestesses, millions of locals and visitors line the city's miles of beaches, throwing flowers into the waves at midnight for the African sea goddess Yemanjá, whose traditions have become mixed with the Virgin Mary. Afterward, the streets, bars, and restaurants fill with parties, dancing, and music.

*www.rcvb.com.br*

### LONDON, ENGLAND

Millions of eager Londoners line the Thames waterfront and gather in Trafalgar Square, waiting for the city to explode in a dazzling display of sparks and color. At midnight, the tower around Big Ben pulses with fiery blasts timed for the 12 strokes of the hour. All eyes then turn to the London Eye as the famous wheel produces a swirling fireworks and light show timed to British rock music echoing through the city.

*www.visitlondon.com*

### PARIS, FRANCE

The City of Light becomes a city of fireworks on New Year's Eve. Hundreds of thousands line the Champs-Élysées, Champagne bottles in hand, for a view to the Eiffel Tower. At midnight, fireworks burst from the entire length of its iron structure, in one of this evening's most beautiful displays anywhere. Other gathering spots with great views include the steps of Sacré-Couer church and the Trocadéro.

*en.parisinfo.com*

### MADRID, SPAIN

Madrileños celebrate the new year by swallowing 12 grapes—1 for each stroke of the clock at midnight. Finishing them on time is considered to be a sign of good luck in the upcoming year. Tens of thousands gather in front of the clock in Puerta del Sol plaza for the annual ritual and line Gran Via to watch fireworks.

*www.spain.info*

### BEIRUT, LEBANON

Each New Year's is a promise that everything will be better in the capital of formerly war-torn Lebanon. Thousands gather to watch the light show on the city's 1933 art deco clock tower in Nejmeh Square, the heart of central Beirut. At midnight, couples kiss and fireworks burst, shining over a mix of floodlit church steeples and mosque minarets in this eclectic Levantine metropolis.

*www.lebanon-tourism.gov.lb*

### TOKYO, JAPAN

On New Year's Eve in Tokyo, streets and restaurants teem with people, many eating buckwheat noodles to ensure health and happiness in the New Year. Temples ring bells as a countdown to midnight, adding a dreamy quality to the celebration. Stay in town through January 2, one of only two days when the emperor opens the palace grounds to the public.

*www.gotokyo.org/en*

### CHRISTMAS ISLAND, SOUTH PACIFIC

Named after another holiday (and famed as the likely location of Amelia Earhart's missing airplane), Christmas Island, or Kiritimati (in the South Pacific republic of Kiribati), is among the first inhabited places in the world to celebrate the New Year. With only around 5,000 residents, New Year's Eve is an intimate affair, much of the island being a protected wildlife sanctuary.

*www.shire.gov.cx*

### SYDNEY, AUSTRALIA

Everyone comes to the waterfront in Sydney to celebrate New Year's Eve. The iconic Sydney Harbour Bridge and nearby buildings ignite at midnight with one of the world's most spectacular fireworks productions.

*www.sydneynewyearseve.com*

The Sydney Opera House, usually the focal point for visitors to the harbor, plays second fiddle to the New Year's fireworks display.

## ICE MUSIC
# Paul D. Miller, *aka DJ Spooky*
## The Antarctic Peninsula

**W**hosoever will be an enquirer into Nature let him resort to a conservatory of Snow or Ice.—Francis Bacon

The universe, according to most scientists, has been around for about 13.7 billion years. Although Antarctica has been in existence for only about 60 million of those years, it still is a place to measure the tempo of the world and the alterations occurring because of massive climate change. Match one rhythm to the other and see what beats you can mix.

OK, so here I am in the Antarctic Peninsula, creating a series of drafts for several compositions that I'll eventually turn into string quartet pieces, a gallery show, and a symphony out of the experience. I'm looking at how to collect impressions of the landscape, distill the material into something that I can use in the compositions (visually, sonically, and for writing as well), and arrive at a point where sound and art can create portraits of what's going on down here.

The next couple of steps are about how this all comes together. DJ culture is all about collage—sampling, splicing, dicing, etc., etc.; everything is part of the mix, and there are no boundaries between sound sources. There's a lot of room for mapping sampling techniques to the environment itself. The world is a very, very, very big record. We just have to learn how to play it.

My excursion to Antarctica was a journey into the realm of the hypothetical, a world where fictions clash with the realities of the everyday world. Music is a mirror we hold up to society to see what derives from tone, pitch, and sequence. Antarctica is a place at the edge of the map, but

we are aware of its deep reflections in how it regulates the tempo of the planet, the rhythm of the seasons. I just thought I'd give the idea a spin.

*Paul D. Miller, aka DJ Spooky, is a composer, multimedia artist, editor, and author. In 2012–2013, he was the first artist-in-residence at New York's Metropolitan Museum of Art. LEFT: Original artwork by DJ Spooky.*

"*My excursion to Antarctica was a journey into the realm of the hypothetical, a world where fictions clash with the realities of the everyday world.*"

Currently free of government and development, Antarctica and its Holt-edehl Bay remains the domain of ice floes, mountains, clouds, and sky.

# MARLBOROUGH SOUNDS

**Trek along the South Island's skyline ridges to hidden bays and tranquil coves in a coastal wonderland.**

The intricately etched, sea-drowned valleys of the South Island's Marlborough Sounds make up a fifth of New Zealand's coastline. From the heights of the Queen Charlotte Track, gaze across dappled emerald ferns that descend to turquoise waters sparkling under February summer sunlight, when temperatures range from 68°F to 78°F (20°–26°C) here in the country's brightest region.

Start the trail at Ship Cove at the head of Queen Charlotte Sound, one of New Zealand's most historic sites and beloved by Captain Cook. "So glowing were Cook's comments around this area, his favorite place, that for the next 50 years the English thought of New Zealand in terms of his description of Queen Charlotte," says Malcolm Campbell, a New Zealand naturalist and National Geographic expert.

Today, some 240 years later, the still rather isolated area holds the same allure, with its sparkling waters, remote inlets, stunning coastal trails, and rugged bush. Campbell adds, "My most memorable trip was walking by day and spending the evenings staying on a converted North Sea fishing vessel, eating fresh seafood from the area, and sampling the local wines in the evenings, swimming in the mornings, hiking each day, meeting, and sharing the good company of like-minded people that we met along the track."

**PLANNING Marlborough Sounds** www.newzealand.com/int/marlborough-sounds. The Marlborough Sounds Adventure Company *(www.marlboroughsounds.co.nz)* offers guided hiking, mountain biking, and sea kayaking trips in the Sounds.

## IN THE KNOW
*Steeped in the Maori: Te Tau Ihu*

The Maori call the northern end of the South Island Te Tau Ihu, "the prow" of the demigod Maui's canoe. With eight recognized *iwi*, or tribes, in the Nelson-Marlborough region, the area is steeped in Maori culture both ancient and modern. Visit *marae* (community gathering places) such as the one in Waikawa, outside Picton, where warriors will perform a *hongi*— the pressing of noses—before welcoming you into the carved meetinghouse for singing, dance presentations, and a shared meal. www.waikawamarae.org.nz

Trekkers along the edge-of-the-world Marlborough Sounds take in vistas both breathtaking and remote.

Adult and chick emperor penguins prep for a swim in Antarctica's Davis Sea.

THE ANTARCTIC

# ANTARCTICA

**Tuck into an on-deck BBQ and gaze at the penguins paddling by.**

It's been almost 100 years since the explorers of the Heroic Age—Amundsen, Scott, Shackleton—took on the challenge of reaching the South Pole, some of their team members dying in the process. But the vast, pristine "white continent" of Antarctica, one of the world's last great wildernesses, hasn't lost its power.

Antarctica's summer, from December to March, is the best time for visitors. During these months, encounter whales and penguins at play in the relative warmth of Earth's southernmost sunlight.

Sunniva Sorby, a member of the first all-female team to walk to the South Pole without dogs, extols the "shared sense of living" one experiences: "The Antarctic illuminates the isolation, the desolation, the reflection of who you are as a person."

Unlike those early expeditions, cruise ships now provide safe and easy land and water excursions. After a hike up snowy hills scattered with noisy penguin rookeries or a raft ride among electric blue icebergs to spot whales and seals, recharge your batteries with a warm, hearty barbecue back on deck. Reggae music and sizzling burgers might feel incongruous, but mulled wine feels suitably wintry. The only likely interruption? Having to rush to the railings to watch whales, sea lions, or penguins swim by.

**PLANNING  Antarctic Cruises** www.oneoceanexpeditions.com, www.quarkexpeditions.com, www.oceanwide-expeditions.com, www.nationalgeographicexpeditions.com. Most ships depart from Ushuaia at the southern tip of Argentina.

### GREAT STAYS
*Ice Camping*

When the raft drops you on the snow-covered banks with a shovel, sleeping bag, and bivy sack for the night, there may well be thoughts of, What have I got myself into? And that's *before* the digging starts of your "snow grave" that will serve as a bed for the night. There's no mattress, room service, or central heating, but camping overnight in the Antarctic snow is an unforgettable experience and a tiny hint of what Amundsen, Scott, and company went through here. Several companies feature camping options, including Oceanwide Expeditions (*www.oceanwide-expeditions.com*).

# CALENDAR OF EVENTS

## SPRING

- SOUTH BY SOUTHWEST FESTIVAL, AUSTIN, TEXAS: mid-March (pp. 20–21)
- HOLI FESTIVAL OF COLORS AND ELEPHANT FESTIVAL, JAIPUR, INDIA: after the first full moon in March (pp. 72–73)
- SAN JUAN CAPISTRANO SWALLOWS, CALIFORNIA: March 19 (p. 12)
- SPRING EQUINOX AT THE PYRAMID OF THE SUN, MEXICO CITY, MEXICO: March 20 (p. 34)
- SUMO WRESTLING GRAND TOURNAMENTS, OSAKA AND TOKYO, JAPAN: March and May (p. 76)
- HOLY WEEK: last week of Lent (Léon, Nicaragua, p. 31; Seville, Spain, p. 60)
- TIN PAN SOUTH SONGWRITERS FESTIVAL, NASHVILLE, TENNESSEE: early April (p. 15)
- TULIP FESTIVAL, ISTANBUL, TURKEY: late March through mid-April (pp. 62–63)
- MASTERS TOURNAMENT, AUGUSTA, GEORGIA: first full week in April (p. 25)
- KING'S DAY, AMSTERDAM, THE NETHERLANDS: April 27 (p. 42)
- VERMONT MAPLE FESTIVAL, ST. ALBANS, VERMONT: late April (p. 22)
- SAILING WEEK, ANTIGUA: end of April to early May (p. 30)
- NEW ORLEANS JAZZ AND HERITAGE FESTIVAL, NEW ORLEANS, LOUISIANA: last weekend of April through first weekend of May (p. 19)
- MAY DAYS, KIEV, UKRAINE: May 1–9 (pp. 74–75)
- GIRONA FLOWER FESTIVAL, GIRONA, SPAIN: May 7–15 (pp. 58–59)
- WORLD CHAMPIONSHIP BARBECUE COOKING CONTEST, MEMPHIS, TENNESSEE: mid-May (p. 18)
- ROMANY PILGRIMAGE, SAINTES-MARIES-DE-LA-MER, FRANCE: May 24–25 (pp. 52–53)
- INDIANAPOLIS 500, INDIANAPOLIS, INDIANA: last weekend of May (pp. 16–17)
- GRAND PRIX, MONACO: late May (p. 45)
- FLAG DAY AND NEW HERRING AUCTION, SCHEVENINGEN, THE NETHERLANDS: early June (p. 43)
- FEZ FESTIVAL OF WORLD SACRED MUSIC, FEZ, MOROCCO: early June (p. 66)
- BLOOMSDAY, DUBLIN, IRELAND: June 16 (p. 38)

### GENERAL SPRING DESTINATIONS AND ACTIVITIES

Craters of the Moon, Idaho (p. 13)
Theodore Roosevelt National Park, North Dakota (p. 14)
White-water rafting, West Virginia (p. 23)
Wine festivals, Virginia (p. 24)
Great Smoky Mountains, Tennessee/North Carolina (pp. 26–27)
Snuba, Puerto Rico (p. 28)
St. Lucia, the Caribbean (p. 29)
Cacao harvests, Ecuador (p. 35)
Guatemala Highlands, Central America (pp. 36–37)
Loch Lomond, Scotland (p. 39)
Wadden Sea National Park, Denmark (p. 44)
Paris, France (pp. 46–49)
Lake Como, Italy (pp. 54–57)
Bird-watching in the Danube Delta, Romania (p. 61)
St. Catherine's Monastery, Sinai Peninsula, Egypt (pp. 64–65)
Trekking in the Atlas Mountains, Morocco (p. 67)
Victoria Falls, Zambia/Zimbabwe (p. 70)
Shwedagon Pagoda, Yangon, Myanmar (p. 71)
Cherry blossom viewing, Japan (p. 77)

## SUMMER

- WHITE NIGHTS FESTIVAL, ST. PETERSBURG, RUSSIA: weeks before and after the summer solstice, June 20/21 (p. 129)
- GOLFING UNDER THE MIDNIGHT SUN, ICELAND: mid- to late June (p. 115)
- INTI RAYMI FESTIVAL OF THE SUN, SACSAYHUAMÁN, PERU: June 20/21 (pp. 112–113)
- QUEENSTOWN WINTER FESTIVAL, QUEENSTOWN, NEW ZEALAND: late June (pp. 160–161)
- NATIONAL CHERRY FESTIVAL, TRAVERSE CITY, MICHIGAN: late June through early July (p. 95)
- PALIO, SIENA, ITALY: July 2 and August 16 (p. 137)
- INDEPENDENCE DAY ON THE NATIONAL MALL, WASHINGTON, D.C.: July 4 (p. 103)
- CALGARY STAMPEDE, CALGARY, ALBERTA, CANADA: early to mid-July (p. 88)
- HEIVA I TAHITI, TAHITI, FRENCH POLYNESIA: early to mid-July (p. 155)
- GREAT NORTHERN ARTS FESTIVAL, INUVIK, NORTHWEST TERRITORIES, CANADA: mid-July (p. 81)
- NAADAM FESTIVAL, ULAANBAATAR, MONGOLIA: July 11–13 (p. 152)
- LA FIESTA DE LA TIRANA, LA TIRANA, CHILE: July 16 (p. 110)
- JUST FOR LAUGHS FESTIVAL, MONTREAL, QUEBEC, CANADA: mid- to late July (p. 99)
- CHINCOTEAGUE PONY SWIM, ASSATEAGUE CHANNEL, VIRGINIA: last Wednesday of July (pp. 106–107)
- NEWPORT FOLK AND JAZZ FESTIVALS, NEWPORT, RHODE ISLAND: late July and early August (p. 102)
- HONDA CELEBRATION OF LIGHT, VANCOUVER, BRITISH COLUMBIA, CANADA: late July through early August (p. 80)
- SALZBURG FESTIVAL, SALZBURG, AUSTRIA: late July through August (p. 136)
- EDINBURGH FRINGE FESTIVAL, EDINBURGH, SCOTLAND: August (pp. 118–121)
- MEDIEVAL WEEK, GOTLAND ISLAND, SWEDEN: early August (p. 125)
- PERSEID METEOR SHOWER: August 11–13 (pp. 100–101)
- IOWA STATE FAIR, DES MOINES, IOWA: mid-August (p. 98)
- TANGO WORLD CUP, BUENOS AIRES, ARGENTINA: mid- to late August (p. 114)
- TELLURIDE FILM FESTIVAL, TELLURIDE, COLORADO: Labor Day weekend (p. 94)

### GENERAL SUMMER DESTINATIONS AND ACTIVITIES

Bear viewing in Alaska (pp. 82–85)
San Juan Islands, Washington (pp. 89–91)
Pacific Crest Trail, California/Oregon/Washington (pp. 92–93)
Pawleys Island, South Carolina (p. 108)
Train ride through Copper Canyon, Mexico (p. 109)
Chapada Diamentina National Park, Brazil (p. 111)
Cornwall coast, England (p. 124)
Svalbard, Norway (pp. 126–127)
Cruise through the Baltic Sea (p. 128)
Parque Nacional Peneda-Gerês, Gerês, Portugal (p. 130)
Biking in the Pyrenees, France/Spain (p. 131)
Lavender fields, Provence, France (pp. 132–133)
Taking the waters at Switzerland's lakes and *badis* (pp. 134–135)
Santorini, Greece (page 140–141)
Opera in the Arena di Verona, Verona, Italy (p. 142)
Flood season in Okavango Delta, Botswana (p. 143)
Watching flamingos of Lake Nakuru, Kenya (pp. 144–145)
Seeing gorillas in the wild, Rwanda/Uganda/The Little Congo (p. 146)
Dune walking, Namibia (p. 147)
Cape Winelands, South Africa (pp. 148–151)
Beaches of Hong Kong, China (p. 153)
Climbing Mount Fuji, Japan (p. 154)
Great Barrier Reef, Australia (pp. 156–157)
Kakadu National Park, Australia (p. 158)
Skiing, Snowy Mountains, Australia (p. 159)

# INDEX

**Boldface** indicates illustrations.

# ILLUSTRATIONS CREDITS

Cover (clockwise from top left): Henry Georgi/Corbis, Smileus/Shutterstock; Johanna Huber/SIME; Design Pics/Corbis; 2-3, Michael Melford/NG Stock; 4, LOOK Die Bildagentur der Fotografen GmbH/Alamy; 6, Giovanni Simeone/SIME; 10-11, TAKASHI SATO/amanaimages/Corbis; 12, littleny/Shutterstock; 13, Dr. W. B. Karesh; 14, Don Johnston/All Canada Photos/Getty Images; 15, Will Van Overbeek/NG Stock; 16-7, William Manning/Corbis; 18, Randy Harris/Redux; 19, Amy Harris/Corbis; 20-21, ZUMA Wire Service/Alamy; 22, Robert F. Sisson/NG Stock; 23, Greg Von Doersten/Aurora/Getty Images; 24, Christy Massie/Courtesy of visit charlottesville.org; 25, Andrew Davis Tucker/Staff/the *Augusta Chronicle*/ZUMAPRESS. com/Alamy; 26-7, Visuals Unlimited, Inc./Adam Jones/Getty Images; 28, Vilainecrevette/Alamy; 29, Wildroze/iStockphoto; 30, Alison Langley/Aurora/Getty Images; 31, THALIA WATMOUGH/aliki image library/Alamy; 33, Hemis/Alamy; 34, Frans Lemmens/Hollandse Hoogte/Redux; 35, Owen Franken/Corbis; 36-7, holgs/iStockphoto.com; 38, AP Images/John Cogill; 39, Jim Richardson/NG Stock; 41, Stuart Monk/Alamy; 42, Paul van Riel/Hollandse Hoogte/Redux; 43, VALERIE KUYPERS/AFP/Getty Images; 44, Andy Rouse/naturepl.com; 45, O.DIGOIT/Alamy; 46, JTB MEDIA CREATION, Inc./Alamy; 47, CW Images/Alamy; 48, Bruno De Hogues/Getty Images; 49, PCN/Corbis; 51, *Bon Appetit*/Alamy; 52, Nigel Dickinson; 53, Luca da Ros/Grand Tour/Corbis; 54, Sandra Raccanello/SIME; 55, Massimo Ripani/SIME; 56, Craig Oesterling/NG My Shot; 57, Zoltan Nagy/SIME; 58-9, Owen Franken/Corbis; 60, Peter Turnley/Corbis; 61, imagebroker/Alamy; 62, Günter Gräfenhain/Huber/SIME; 63, Borderlands/Alamy; 64-5, Matt Moyer/NG Stock; 66, Bertrand Rieger/Hemis/Corbis; 67, Anders Ryman/Corbis; 69, Terry Eggers/Corbis; 70, Neil_Burton/iStockphoto; 71, Günter Gräfenhain/Huber/SIME; 72-3, KAMAL KISHORE/Reuters/Corbis; 74-5, kiyanochka/iStockphoto; 76, Orient/Huber/SIME; 77, JTB MEDIA CREATION, Inc./Alamy; 78-9, Richard Taylor/4Corners/SIME; 80,

Ugur OKUCU/Shutterstock; 81, Sasha Webb; 82, Mark Conlin/Getty Images; 83, Alaska Stock LLC/NG Stock; 84, Danita Delimont/Alamy; 85, Barrett Hedges/NG Stock; 87, WaterFrame/Alamy; 88, Steve Estvanik/Shutterstock.com; 89, Joel W. Rogers/Corbis; 90-91, Danita Delimont/Alamy; 92-3, Rich Reid/NG Stock; 94, David McNew/Getty Images; 95, AP Images/the *Record-Eagle,* Keith King; 97, BARBARA GINDL/epa/Corbis; 98, Marvin Dembinsky Photo Associates/Alamy; 99, Yves Marcoux/Getty Images; 100-101, Matt Currier Photography; 102, AJ Wilhelm/NG Stock; 103, Hemis/Alamy; 105, Buddy Mays/Alamy; 106-107, Medford Taylor/NG Stock; 108, Christian Heeb/laif/Redux; 109, Carolyn Brown/Photo Researchers/Getty Images; 110, Hemis/Alamy; 111, imagebroker/Alamy; 112-13, Keren Su/China Span/Alamy; 114, Ralph Lee Hopkins/NG Stock; 115, diddi@diddisig.is/Flickr/Getty Images; 117, Frans Lanting/NG Stock; 118, Marco Secchi/Alamy; 119, nagelstock.com/Alamy; 120, AdamEdwards/Shutterstock; 121, Jeff J Mitchell/Getty Images; 123, Gail Mooney/Corbis; 124, Pietro Canali/4Corners/SIME; 125, Albert Moldvay/NG Stock; 126-7, Ralph Lee Hopkins/NG Stock; 128, BOISVIEUX Christophe/hemis.fr/Getty Images; 129, Massimo Ripani/SIME; 130, Peter Essick/NG Stock; 131, Richard Manin/Hemis/Corbis; 132-3, Belenos/Huber/SIME; 134, Richard Taylor/4Corners/SIME; 135, mediacolor's/Alamy; 136, Massimo Borchi/SIME; 137, Grant Rooney/Alamy; 139, Jens Schwarz/laif/Redux; 140-41, David Noton Photography/Alamy; 142, Sabine Lubenow/Getty Images; 143, Richard Du Toit/Minden Pictures/NG Stock; 144-5, Chris Bolin/First Light/Getty Images; 146, Guenter Guni/iStockphoto; 147, Frans Lanting/NG Stock; 148, Monica Gumm/laif/Redux Pictures; 149, Justin Foulkes/4Corners/SIME; 150, Van Berge, Alexander/the food passionates/Corbis; 151, Michael Melford/NG Stock; 152, Bruno Morandi/Getty Images; 153, Walter Bibikow/Getty Images; 154, amana images inc./Alamy; 155, Rothenborg Kyle/Getty Images; 156-7, Fred Bavendam/Minden Pictures/NG Stock; 158, Peter Walton Photography/Getty Images; 159, Photograph by David Messent/Getty Images; 160, David Wall/Alamy; 161,

Doug Pearson/JAI/Corbis; 162-3, Giovanni Simeone/SIME; 164, Inga Spence/Alamy; 165, Jodi Cobb/NG Stock; 166-7, P Robin Moeller/iStockphoto.com; 168, Blaine Harrington III/Corbis; 169, Rolf Nussbaumer Photography/Alamy; 170-1, Paul Nicklen/NG Stock; 172, Allen Fredrickson/Icon SMI/Corbis; 173, Kevin R. Morris/Corbis; 174-5, H. Mark Weidman Photography/Alamy; 176, Doug Wilson/Alamy; 177, Pete Ryan/NG Stock; 179, Martin Thomas Photography/Alamy; 180, Chris Murray/Aurora/Getty Images; 181, Tyler Nordgren; 182-3, Michael Melford/NG Stock; 184-5, Bill O'Leary/the *Washington Post* via Getty Images; 186, Corbis; 187, Reinhard Dirscherl/Alamy; 188, AP Images/Marco Ugarte; 189, Dordo Brnobic/NG My Shot; 190, Sebastian Giacobone/Shutterstock; 191, Michael & Jennifer Lewis/NG Stock; 192, Dave Donaldson/Alamy; 193, Benoit Jacquelin/iStockphoto; 195, Cephas Picture Library/Alamy; 196, John Miller/Robert Harding World Imagery/Corbis; 197, Heiko Specht/laif/Redux; 198, Intrepix/Shutterstock.com; 199, CAMERA PRESS/Sergey Pyatakov/RIA Novosti/Redux; 200, Greg Dale/NG Stock; 201, Reinhard Schmid/Huber/SIME; 203, oktoberfestbrisbane.com.au; 204, imagebroker.net/SuperStock; 205, ARCO/C Bömke/age fotostock; 206, KIKETXO/Shutterstock; 207, Guido Cozzi/SIME; 208, Reinhard Schmid/Huber/SIME; 209, Yonatan Sindel/Flash90/Redux; 210-211, Dave Yoder; 212, NHPA/SuperStock; 213, Danita Delimont/Gallo Images/Getty Images; 215, Francois Lacasse/NHLI via Getty Images; 216, Huw Jones/4Corners/SIME; 217, Danita Delimont/Getty Images; 218, Alfred Cheng Jin/Reuters/Corbis; 219, imagebroker/Alamy; 220, Michael Yamashita/NG Stock; 221, PONGMANAT TASIRI/epa/Corbis; 223, Travelasia/Asia Images/Corbis; 224-5, Joseph J. Hobbs; 226, Dave Stamboulis/Alamy; 227, Michael Leach/Getty Images; 228-9, Roy Samuelsen/NG My Shot; 230, Alaska Photography/Flickr/Getty Images; 231, Rolf Hicker/All Canada Photos/Getty Images; 233, Joe McBride/Getty Images; 234, Chao Kusollerschariya/NG My Shot; 235, Diane Cook & Len Jenshel/Corbis; 236, Bill Hatcher/NG Stock; 237, Michael Rubin/iStockphoto; 238-9, Jeffrey Noble/Photo of Derrick

Suwaima Davis (Hopi/Choctaw), six-time World Hoop Dance Champion/Courtesy of Scottsdale Convention & Visitors Bureau; 240, Nik Wheeler/Corbis; 241, Evan Richman/the *Boston Globe* via Getty Images; 242, Patrick Batchelder/Alamy; 243, Irek/4Corners/SIME; 244, Michael S. Yamashita/NG Stock; 245, Cora/Bildagentur Schapowalow/SIME; 247, STR/AFP/Getty Images; 248, Used with permission from The Biltmore Company, Asheville, North Carolina; 249, Doug Perrine/Getty Images; 250-51, Shane Pinder/Alamy; 252-3, Günter Gräfenhain/Huber/SIME; 254, Orlando Barria/epa/Corbis; 255, Kenneth Garrett/NG Stock; 256-7, Medford Taylor/NG Stock; 258, Konrad Wothe/Minden Pictures/NG Stock; 259, Mike Theiss/NG Stock; 260, Raymond Choo/NG My Shot; 261, John Stanmeyer LLC/NG Stock; 262, Giordano Cipriani/SIME; 263, Catarina Belova/Shutterstock.com; 265, Bernd Römmelt/Huber/SIME; 266, Travelscape Images/Alamy; 267, O. Louis Mazzatenta/NG Stock; 268, Michael S. Lewis/NG Stock; 269, Yadid Levy/Photolibrary/Getty Images; 270, Yadid Levy/Anzenberger/Redux Pictures; 271, Eduardo Longoni/Corbis; 272-3, Horizons WWP/Alamy; 274-5, Frank Lukasseck/Corbis; 276, DEA/G. DAGLI ORT/Getty Images; 277, Press Association via AP Images; 278, Colin Dutton/SIME; 279, John Lamb/Getty Images; 280-81, Massimo Ripani/Grand Tour/Corbis; 282, Massimo Borchi/SIME; 283, Gregor Lengler/laif/Redux; 285, Anna Watson/Corbis; 286, Rune Rormyr/NG My Shot; 287, Stefan Volk/laif/Redux; 288, Emportes Jm/Getty Images; 289, Berthold Steinhilber/laif/Redux; 290-91, Guido Cozzi/SIME; 292, Martin Siepmann/imagebroker/Corbis; 293, Kajano/Shutterstock; 295, Lew Robertson/Getty Images; 296, Mandy Glinsbockel/Demotix/Corbis; 297, Guido Cozzi/SIME; 298, Allen Woodman/NG My Shot; 299, Eric Isselee/Shutterstock; 300, Imaginechina/Corbis; 301, Otto Stadler/Huber/SIME; 302, LOOK Die Bildagentur der Fotografen GmbH/Alamy; 303, Blaine Harrington III/Corbis; 305, HP Huber/Huber/SIME; 306-307, John Eastcott and Yva Momatiuk/NG Stock; 306, DJ Spooky; 308, Paul Abbitt rf/Alamy; 309, Tui De Roy/Minden Pictures/NG Stock.

# Four Seasons of Travel

## 400 OF THE WORLD'S BEST DESTINATIONS IN WINTER, SPRING, SUMMER, AND FALL

**Published by the National Geographic Society**

John M. Fahey, *Chairman of the Board and Chief Executive Officer*

Declan Moore, *Executive Vice President; President, Publishing and Travel*

Melina Gerosa Bellows, *Executive Vice President; Chief Creative Officer, Books, Kids, and Family*

Lynn Cutter, *Executive Vice President, Travel*

Keith Bellows, *Senior Vice President and Editor in Chief, National Geographic Travel Media*

**Prepared by the Book Division**

Hector Sierra, *Senior Vice President and General Manager*

Janet Goldstein, *Senior Vice President and Editorial Director*

Jonathan Halling, *Design Director, Books and Children's Publishing*

Marianne R. Koszorus, *Design Director, Books*

Barbara A. Noe, *Senior Editor, National Geographic Travel Books*

R. Gary Colbert, *Production Director*

Jennifer A. Thornton, *Director of Managing Editorial*

Susan S. Blair, *Director of Photography*

Meredith C. Wilcox, *Director, Administration and Rights Clearance*

**Staff for This Book**

Lawrence M. Porges, *Editor*

Carol Clurman, *Project Editor*

Elisa Gibson, *Art Director*

Nancy Marion, *Illustrations Editor*

Jennifer Pocock, Rhett Register, *Researchers*

Carl Mehler, *Director of Maps*

XNR Productions, *Map Research and Production*

Mark Baker, Larry Bleiberg, Karen Carmichael, Maryellen Duckett, Olivia Garnett, Adam Graham, Jeremy Gray, Graeme Green, Rachael Jackson, Tim Jepson, Justin Kavanagh, Margaret Loftus, Michael Luongo, Jenna Makowski, Barbara A. Noe, Christine O'Toole, Gabrielle Piccininni, Ed Readicker-Henderson, Emma Rowley, Jenna Schnuer, Kelsey Snell, Olivia Stren, Phil Trupp, Joe Yogerst, *Contributing Writers*

Marshall Kiker, *Associate Managing Editor*

Judith Klein, *Production Editor*

Mike Horenstein, *Production Manager*

Galen Young, *Rights Clearance Specialist*

Katie Olsen, *Production Design Assistant*

Sarah Alban, Danielle Fisher, Jane Plegge, Marlena Serviss, *Contributors*

**Production Services**

Phillip L. Schlosser, *Senior Vice President*

Chris Brown, *Vice President, NG Book Manufacturing*

George Bounelis, *Vice President, Production Services*

Nicole Elliott, *Manager*

Rachel Faulise, *Manager*

Robert L. Barr, *Manager*

CELEBRATING
**125**
YEARS

The National Geographic Society is one of the world's largest nonprofit scientific and educational organizations. Founded in 1888 to "increase and diffuse geographic knowledge," the Society works to inspire people to care about the planet. National Geographic reflects the world through its magazines, television programs, films, music and radio, books, DVDs, maps, exhibitions, live events, school publishing programs, interactive media and merchandise. *National Geographic* magazine, the Society's official journal, published in English and 33 local-language editions, is read by more than 60 million people each month. The National Geographic Channel reaches 435 million households in 37 languages in 173 countries. National Geographic Digital Media receives more than 19 million visitors a month. National Geographic has funded more than 10,000 scientific research, conservation and exploration projects and supports an education program promoting geography literacy. For more information, visit www .nationalgeographic.com.

For more information, please call 1-800-NGS LINE (647-5463) or write to the following address:

National Geographic Society
1145 17th Street N.W.
Washington, D.C. 20036-4688 U.S.A.

For information about special discounts for bulk purchases, please contact National Geographic Books Special Sales: ngspecsales@ngs.org

For rights or permissions inquiries, please contact National Geographic Books Subsidiary Rights: ngbookrights@ngs.org

Library of Congress Cataloging-in-Publication Data
National Geographic Society (U.S.)
 Four seasons of travel : 400 of the world's best destinations in winter, spring, summer, and fall / National Geographic Books ; foreword by Andrew Evans, National Geographic Traveler magazine contributing editor and "Digital Nomad".
    pages cm
  Includes index.
  ISBN 978-1-4262-1167-6 (hardcover : alk. paper)
  1.  Voyages and travels.  I. Title.
  G465.N365 2013
  910.4--dc23

                          2013010861

Printed in China

13/CCOS/1

The information in this book has been carefully checked and to the best of our knowledge is accurate. However, details are subject to change, and the National Geographic Society cannot be responsible for such changes, or for errors or omissions.